The
Ivy
House
Diary

**Rose-Mary Harrington
& Martin Banks**

ISBN: 1500190292
ISBN 13: 9781500190293
Library of Congress Control Number: 2014911114
CreateSpace Independent Publishing Platform
North Charleston, South Carolina

At a distance of nearly half a century some memories are understandably incomplete and where necessary we have used our imaginations to fill those gaps. We have also changed names and details to protect anonymity. However the essence of the memories are true as we both experienced them first hand at The New College of Speech and Drama.

ACKNOWLEDGMENTS

Special thanks to our families and friends for their invaluable support and encouragement in making this read possible.

To our editor extraordinaire Peggy Schwarz.

The photograph of the Rag queen is reproduced courtesy of The Watford Observer, March 3, 1967

The article and photograph of Jimmy Carrol is reproduced courtesy of The Newham Recorder, December 3, 1970

ALSO BY MARTIN BANKS: The Mysterious Loss of The Darlwyne. A Cornish Holiday Tragedy (ISNBN 978-0-9574742-1-5) Tamar Press, UK.

From: Rose-Mary
To: Martin, Sadie, Duncan and Noodle
Subject: New College
Date: July 20th, 2011 10:05 am

I am writing to ask you to be part of a literary venture that pays tribute to our years at New College. I propose collaboration in the form of a diary, written in the present tense that begins with our first year. Each of us will be assigned the same topic and a page limit (beginning with up to 3 pages and no more than 10 pages as we progress) for which we will have one month to complete. If you are agreeable to this quest, please respond by e-mail or snail mail. I am inviting you because I trust, admire and respect you for your honesty and integrity. My goal is to find a publisher for our collective experience or at least leave documentation of our unique education in theatre. I encourage your writing to be honest with no holds barred but if your memory falters you do have license to embellish a little. I have trepidation revisiting being 18 years old again but I really do believe we have a story to tell.

Love always.
Rose-Mary

From: Rose-Mary
To: Martin
Subject: Duncan's Whereabouts?
Date: July 20th, 2011 10:11 am
Hello Martin:

I don't have an e-mail address for Duncan. Any idea how I might reach him?

Rose-Mary

From: Martin
To: Edward Ball
Subject: New College Contact
Date: July 26th, 2011 1:30 pm

Hi Edward:

Hope you are well and enjoying your retirement. Can you help me? I'm desperately trying to contact Duncan Conway but have lost his address/e-mail. I'm trying to contact him on behalf of Rose-Mary Harrington in the States who wants to reconnect with him. I appear to have lost his home address. I think he is still in NW3. Grateful for any assistance.

With best wishes
Martin Banks

From: Edward Ball
To: Martin
Subject: Re: New College Contact
Date: July 26th, 2011 8:31 pm

Dear Martin,

How good to hear from you. Duncan's email address is dconway@aol.com

I am fairly new to retirement but adoring it.

Hope you are well.

All good wishes,
Edward.

PS: I assume you are on The New College Years mailing list but if not then do contact NewYears @aol.com

From: Martin
To: Rose-Mary
Subject: New College
Date: July 26th, 2011 3:37 pm
Sorry I did not reply sooner. I am astride the bucking horse of technology but have neither the Stetson nor the spurs!! Very interested to be part of it. I have Duncan's e-mail I will forward your message to him. Have you been following the New College Years website? I have an article about our time that I have yet to send them - mainly because it might open old wounds.

All the very best,
Love
Martin

From: Martin
To: Duncan
Subject: New College
Date: July 27th, 2011 2:27 pm
Hello Duncan:
I hope you are well and enjoying life.
Rose-Mary Harrington has asked me to forward the attachment to you.
I am well and living in the far west of Cornwall. Let me know how you are getting on.
With all best wishes
Martin

From: Martin
To: Rose-Mary
Subject: The Coil
Date: August 15th, 2011 4:15 pm
Dear Rose-Mary

Thinking of sending this to the Mr. Goggins who runs the New College website and e-magazine, do you think it is worth doing? I don't want to touch raw nerves. But it did happen. Look forward to your comments.

Wishing you all the best.

Love,

Martin

THE COIL- An Everyday Story of Country Folk.

1968-70 were the years in which student politics reached far beyond the conventional National Union of Students parameters and, for a time, almost took centre stage at New College of Speech and Drama.

Much of my spare time was spent at the experimental Arts Lab in Covent Garden, visiting other colleges, and even meeting radical French and German students; secrecy, however, was maintained at New College....Locally "revolution" was in the air with many Hampstead windows displaying the North Vietnamese flag as opposition to the American involvement in the war. We often received overnight stays from American draft dodgers on the run throughout Europe. Rapid and confrontational changes were seen in both society and the arts and even New College encountered its share. Following the government removal of censorship in 1968, the Phoenix Theatre at New College witnessed its first full frontal nude scene in a student production. May 1968 saw France shaken by the Paris student demonstrations while Hair rocked the West End with New College's own Geraldine Carol in a major role. And LSD did not mean pounds, shillings and pence at New College in the summer of '68. Then in October 1968 the massive anti-American Vietnam demonstration in Grosvenor Square took place and some of us were there.

Meanwhile, culturally, New College had launched a news and literary magazine entitled **The Ring** but, reasonable as this publication was, it did not appeal to the whole of the student and staff readership. There had been considerable growing discontent amongst some students (and even staff!) with aspects of the College academic and artistic life. And so following the example of The International Times publication in London, **The Coil** was launched from way below stairs in the student common room at New College. Like Malcolm McDowell and his revolutionaries in the final scene of the film **IF**, **The Coil** machine-gunned all aspects of New College life with its satirical and scatological literary bullets. Although many articles successfully discussed the philosophy of theatre and education and the current college curriculum, it was a sign of the times that the greater the shock and outrage to the establishment the more successful was deemed the copy! Freedom of speech was being upheld in the liberal college but things came to a breaking point with an edition that in 1969 attacked the whole college establishment. The curriculum, the teaching and support staff were publicly assessed by the editorial. Each member of staff had a piece devoted to them listing their perceived strengths and weaknesses. It still makes amazing reading some forty-two years later!!!

The liberal college was shaken to its core with libel actions threatened by some staff and several students faced dismissal threats. The New College of Speech and Drama Students' Union was totally dysfunctional and factionalized and even the staff became divided. Supposedly troublesome students were identified (some, of course, relished their notoriety) but others stood firm and confronted their accusers. Social and academic divides were evident amongst both staff and students and walk outs and lecture boycotts were not uncommon. Staff who enquired why students were not in their classes were often informed that if they wanted to see particular students they were waiting for them in the

Bull and Butcher pub! I was aware of at least two corridor confrontations between male staff members and students which were most indiscreet...

Other college and university radical student groups were contacted and plans for a major media sit-in were well under way when finally negotiations were successful between the antagonists and the impending confrontation was ultimately avoided. There are still muddying interpretations of what actually occurred but some staff at the time, with whom I am still in contact, were not happy with the manner of the College's reaction to some of the students' criticism. Surprisingly some of the most reactionary responses came from the seemingly most popular of staff and students. A compromise was finally reached but several students refused to attend the final diploma ceremony and a certain amount of ill-feeling definitely remained within the college community for several academic years. The demands for Brecht, Piscator, Meyerhold, Bond, Arden, Littlewood and film and television studies to be on the curriculum were not to be met but the Third Year Options the following academic year were certainly more positive and included: Experimental Theatre, Film Studies, and a Children's Theatre Company.

I left in 1970 with a Distinction in Children's Theatre. Completed an MA at the University of Warwick on Brecht and the British Theatre and within twenty years was lecturing at, and arranging European tours for the Brecht Centre and Berliner Ensemble in Berlin. A successful career in education and the arts has now been completed and I live in early retirement in Cornwall.

From: Rose-Mary
To: Martin
Subject: Re: The Coil
Date: August 19th, 2011 10:09 am

Dear Martin:

I apologize for the delay. My youngest son, Brendan graduated this week from the University of Oregon with a B.A. in History and we have been inundated with family and festivities.

Your "history" is well written and compelling. Regarding the inclusion of The Coil. I was especially drawn by the concrete examples and quotes. I wanted to know more about the staff altercations in the hallways. Were there fist fights? Punches? Or word whippings? However as a reader I believe I would be obsessed to rediscover the contents of the staff evaluations. In my opinion this would be obsolete in 2011 and lends itself to have the potential of being interpreted as mean spirited. I question how to now decipher youthful defiance and radicalism from authentic political conviction and resistance? I wanted more information regarding the underground-railroad which I was oblivious to, as I was non-partisan at the time and totally self-absorbed. My recollections are rosier and sentimental colored by the lifeline New College threw me. To quote Freud "If youth only knew, if age only could. "Peace.

Rose-Mary

From: Rose-Mary
TO: Martin
Subject: New College Diary
Date: September 2nd, 2011 1:47 pm
Dear Martin:

I hope that my recommendations regarding The Coil didn't offend, detract or diminish your article. I have to report that you are the only candidate willing to work on the proposed Ivy House volume. Sadie is hovering on the fence. I certainly don't want to bully her into contributing. Duncan and Noodle did not respond. I have run the scenario passed someone who is familiar with my work and they thought that we would make dynamic collaborators as our reactions and observations tend at times to be polar opposites. Please give me your opinion and intention and let me know how you would like to proceed?

Send a life boat to keep this undertaking alive.
Rose-Mary

From: Martin
To: Rose-Mary
Subject: New College Diary
Date: September 3rd, 2011 2:09 pm

No problem with your values, views on piece for Jeremy Goggins and the newsletter. I thought it might make different reading to the self-congratulatory and rather smug articles that seem to be filling the New College site. They retell the history without any objective analysis. And this is no disrespect to Jeremy Goggins for editing and creating the site. Well let's have a bash at the New College project you're proposing. You will have to run it by me in detail so I can fully absorb it, and then we can start. As William Holden says in the Wild Bunch "Let's go!" to which they reply, "Why not!"

All for now as I'm off to the Truro City Football Club for a Conference South game as they continue their climb towards football league status.

Love,
Martin

From: Rose-Mary
To: Martin
Subject: Re: New College Diary or the undecided
Date: September 4th, 2011 1:05 pm
Hi Martin:
My original idea was to write in Diary form as Adrian Mole or Andy Warhol. The trouble is having to come up with an entry daily. I believe we should tackle the first year only before we attempt the second. Let's start with our individual history of how we landed on the lawn at Ivy House.

Love
Rose-Mary

Rosemary: "Beginners Please."

"I should have strangled you at birth!" she shrieked. This spiteful spate from the woman who used to always brag that the almond tree in the garden, outside the lounge window bloomed the day I was born. The addition of the botanical wonder embellished my debut in the world. You see, I was born in February when almond trees are dormant. She had to say that, she was my mother. She had to portray my birth with an unbelievable exposition. Dramatization coursed through her veins. Without a scene how could she possibly have existed? My mother, Elsie Gwendolyn Mary Theresa had trained as an actress at the Royal Academy of Dramatic Art. She had been awarded a scholarship, which she was forever reminding me of. At the age of 12 she was declared a protégé on the violin. Gwen as she called herself, was the only child of scandalously separated, upper class Catholic parents. My grandfather lived in self-imposed marital exile on the Isle of Man, with the "other woman." My Grandmother departed before I was conceived.

I was born in 1949 in a basement flat adjoined to Stanmore Train Station. Flat 3 was underground like a bunker; making it perfectly safe during World War II. Gwen at that time was married to the love of her life, her first husband, Rick, a railway detective who received the flat as part of his compensation. In 1939 Rick was killed by a bomb after he jauntily ran upstairs to mail a letter during an air raid.

"I will just pop this in the post Gwen" were his last words. My mother discovered Rick's body a few feet away from the whimpering booking clerk whose fingers were blown off. Gwen was devastated and according to my older half-brother, Terry, she was never the same. Her second husband, Joe my father, could never compare to Rick. I came up with the moniker "Saint Rick" for Terry's father. I can still hear my mother's favorite declaration of frustration when things did not go her way: "Rick would never have treated me like this." In contrast to "Saint Rick", my father could never measure up.

According to my mother, "Joe was an Irish idiot." They met during her ten wayward widow years, when she indulged in booze, affairs and a passion for Americans.

Joe and Gwen were paired in a darts match at a local pub. Joe strapping, handsome, loquacious, and a romantic easily charmed his way into Gwen's heart with his carefree and happy-go-lucky attitude. Qualities which she later found exceedingly exasperating.

"Why doesn't he have any ambition? Why is he cack-handed?" She asked. Berating him for hanging the seascape bathroom wallpaper upside down with the fish blowing bubbles towards the ocean floor. Apart from his lack of attention to detail my father was a skilled glacier. He toiled for three years working at home crafting giant stained glass windows for a local church that had been destroyed in the Blitz. Just as the huge panels of the Last Supper were being hoisted over the high altar was it discovered that Jesus was standing knocked kneed and pigeon toed.

"He can't help himself," my mother insisted. "He's Irish."

Being Irish in England in the 1950's was not socially acceptable. Irishmen were slandered as navvies whose collective capabilities were to fix the pot holes in the roads. Restaurants bore signs "No Irish" such was the contempt felt by the mainlanders.

My mother borrowed money from Saint Rick's aunt Cherub. Her given name was Olga but her nickname was Cherub because of her good nature and philanthropy. Aunt Cherub was a childless widow, an octogenarian, a button of a woman with forget-me-not blue eyes, perfectly coiffed finger waved silver hair. She lived with her housekeeper, driver and maid in a villa on the Sussex coast. My mother always referred to her as "coming from good stock." Aunt Cherub willingly donated to my father's cause and gave him money to buy a second-hand, Bedford van to start his own glazing business.

On a rare Sunday jaunt when we could afford petrol, my father would load the family into the windowless box van and head up to Bishops Avenue on the North side of Hampstead. My younger brother, Tony would sit precariously perched in the front, between my father and mother on an upside down putty tin. As the favored child I sat astride my mother's lap. My father would drive slowly down Millionaire's Row. He was dazzled by the Daimlers, the Austin Healey's and his preference the Jaguars, parked gleaming in the driveways of the new money mansions. My mother would gossip about the home owners, Gracie Fields the singer and Billy Butlin the holiday camp magnate. On one excursion my brother, Tony and I were dropped off at the pond outside the pub, Jack Straw's Castle on Hampstead Heath. Tony had manufactured a paper boat out of newspaper. We were used to being left to our own devises whilst our parents imbibed. On the return inebriated journey my mother pointed out the Old Bull and Butcher pub. She started singing the song of the same name when her gaze fell on the stately, Tudor style house across the street.

"That's Anna Pavlova's house. Pavlova was a great Russian ballerina. She was known as the swan and in her garden she had a miniature ornamental lake where she kept her pet swans." From that brief view as we drove slowly by I knew that house was in some way going to have significance in my life. I had no idea how or why.

1 Ivy House

From: Rose-Mary
To: Martin
Subject: New College Diary
Date: September 10th, 2011 9:42 am
Dear Martin:

Have reached page 9 on the introduction. I believe that your writing will be of great contrast to mine.

I think we should keep our undertaking under our hats. The moment of truth. I am sending you my rough draft. I am reticent to allow you to read mine as there are aspects of my early life that I have never divulged. I probably have you hooked now. But I am trying to be as truthful as possible otherwise I believe the reader will detect invalidity. I am forever hesitant because this is the first time in my life I have revealed my "rich" home life. I feel vulnerable but I think I have to include the drama at home because that is what propelled me into theatre which became my salvation. I will begin my audition segment this week. (Still feeling insecure about sharing the content with you.)

Rose-Mary

Rosemary: "Ride A Cock Horse."

I loved living at Flat 3, Stanmore Station. From my bedroom I could hear the hiss of the brakes from the trains as they met the bumpers at the end of the Bakerloo Line. The noise of the shuntings, whistles of the guards and the footsteps of the passengers overhead were comforting during the times of slings and arrows that my parents were perfecting on each other. The hustle and bustle of the bowler hatted gentlemen on their way up to town to conduct business, the cacophony of the trains and station would have hailed my birth on February 20th, 1949 but it was a Sunday so the train service and serenade were minimal. The premature almond blossom signaled the perfect day for the perfect child to be born. My mother named me after a line from Hamlet: "Rosemary for remembrance, pray love remember." I don't think I stood a chance of not following in her theatrical footsteps.

My first stage appearance was reciting and dancing solo, the nursery rhyme 'Ride A Cock Horse To Banbury Cross.' I have been riding that cock horse ever since. The audience at Miss Millers Dance School, housed in a quonset hut were delighted by the petite, blond ringlets and the saucy, rosy-cheeked, confident three-year-old girl. Terry, my elder half-brother was thirteen, he carried me aloft his shoulders for all the world to congratulate me on my performance.

2 Rosemary Age 3

The adulation lasted until I was seven when I was not quite so delicate and endearing. In order to draw attention at my primary school I dedicated myself to fabrications. I had the kindergarten convinced that Hop-A-Long Cassidy and his sharp sidekick Lucky would gallop onto the campus, during playtime of course.

As a diversion from lying I was cast as an angel in the school Christmas Pageant, but my insatiable appetite for telling fibs and making up stories caught the attention of my stern-faced Irish grandmother. Grandma Harrington insisted that I be delivered to the Missionary sisters at St. Joseph's School who had their very own way of curing all sinners. Fibbing would earn you a rap with the ruler. A whopper that revealed you were to appear on the Huey Green Talent Show on television would not only reap a reprimand by the headmistress, Sister Perpetua, but also included audible praying for forgiveness and acts of contrition in her office for a week during recess.

St. Joseph's School, Wealdstone was located miles from Stanmore Station and I and my younger brother, Tony had to rely on public buses to get us to school. Money was scarce at home so we wore our uniforms seven days a week. Shoes leaked with huge holes in the soles. My father with Irish "ingenuity" would line the insides with cardboard to prevent the bottom of our feet from becoming encrusted with pebbles and gravel. Life was financially grim. Our one meal a day consisted of half a piece of toast and a boiled egg, if we were lucky. So I was not surprised in 1957 when my parents announced that we would not be receiving any Christmas presents. Miraculously on the morn, there was a used doll, a second hand pram and books for me and worn cars and comics for my brother, Tony. I suspect that those ruler, guilt wielding nuns together with my ostracized grandfather in the Isle of Man had intervened.

With all this monetary hardship, my mother somehow came up with enough cash to enroll me in Italia Conti Stage School in London. She insisted that I needed an outlet for my vivid imagination that was getting me into trouble. The first Saturday she escorted me up to town taking the Bakerloo line to Piccadilly Circus. Ascending the double escalators out of the tube, we skirted into Brewer Street, past the naughty nudes of the Windmill Theatre, round the back, into Archer Street opposite the stage door of the Windmill, where old men shuffled and one called leeringly out to me as I passed.

"Over here little girl." My mother responded by marching over to him, squarely glaring at him and bonking him soundly on the head with her umbrella. Then she strode me in through the crimson doors of Italia Conti where I was to study ballet, acting and modern jazz every Saturday thereafter, until I was fourteen. I would have gladly given up Christmas for what I received from the stage school. After that first visit I was expected to travel solo on the train. I would abstain from looking at the lewd feathered ladies on the marquee of the Windmill and ignore the enticements of "Would you like to come and see the show?" From the dirty old men queuing outside the theatre kiosk.

Italia Conti was my reformation. I gave up fibbing for good. My Saturday schedule consisted of ballet, modern jazz and the one art form I possessed any aptitude for, acting. Acting was taught by a white haired, wizened, frail Miss Conti. We began with Shakespeare's King John, the scene in which the young prince, Arthur, begs his jailor Hubert to spare his life.

"O save me, Hubert, save me! My eyes are out!

Even with the fierce looks of these bloody men."

I was able to transfer Arthur's pleadings with my pleadings of not to change from a public school to a parochial school. But like Shakespeare's Hubert my stringent Irish Grandma Harrington, an ex-school teacher, with her six foot frame, remnants of fiery red hair and knobby knit tweed suits, was never challenged in her decisions. At Italia Conti we gave final presentations at the end of the term. My mother must have squirmed during ballet and modern jazz as I had the knack of always being off beat and going the opposite direction of the other nubile dancers. One exceptional ballet student who became my friend was Marilyn Dern. I felt she was destined to become a swan, like Pavlova. She always allowed me to stand behind her so I might attempt to copy her agility and precision. I was helpless, hopeless and bloody useless by my own admission.

During acting class I was confident and able to indulge myself immensely with my penchant for over acting. At the end of the term recital for parents and friends I was performing the sleep-walking scene from Macbeth. The audience was amazed at my loud, expressive declarations only to break into snickers when during the repeated line by Lady Macbeth:

"To bed, to bed, to bed." My younger brother Tony brazenly shouted:

"Eight o'clock tonight." My mother put a damper on his smirk when she clocked him around the ear with her handbag.

I embraced acting and the bard with fervor, so much so that I wrote to Peter Hall the artistic director in Stratford-Upon-Avon and enquired if I might join the Royal Shakespeare Company. I was ten years old. He diplomatically replied that I was too young, but advised that I study and train and follow my passion. He hand scribed that he looked forward to seeing me at the Royal Shakespeare Company in the future. I made that my goal.

Italia Conti Stage School moved from Piccadilly Circus to Clapham North, a complex train journey with a long walk from the station. I was terrified of the dilapidated neighborhood and would bolt from the station to the confines of the stage school, in order to indulge myself in another Saturday of release and relief.

After taking and failing the eleven plus exam, I left the Missionary sisters and was placed in the custody of the Dominicans at a private all-girls school. My mother had finagled the fees in exchange for me performing my audition pieces whenever a bishop, monsignor or Catholic official visited the convent. I was the official drama queen of the school and began to accumulate medals in local drama festivals. That was until the 1961 Ruislip Drama Festival where I recited the Coleridge poem "Christabel" in a declamatory, over the top offering, competing against thirty-two other drama students.

The judge was Rita Scott, a slim, coquettish woman with a coif of perfectly tailored brunette shoulder length hair which enhanced her impeccable Cleopatra features. Her boat necked frock with piles of petticoats peaking at the hem, displayed her tiny waist. An orange French knotted scarf adorned her ivory neck. All eyes were on her. Rita's voice commanded attention, it was refined with a cultivated rasp. Her diction and enunciation could be heard a planet away. When she spoke there was silence in the auditorium. Everyone was listening as she ripped my rendering of "Christabel" to shreds. Rita was repelled by my interpretation and placed me very last. That was thirty-second out of thirty-two. I vowed to hate "that woman" for the rest of my life. I was twelve at the time. On the way back to the convent in my dad's van sitting on putty tins between two nuns, I sobbed. The sisters wept quietly, in particular Sister Aloysius who had coached me for the contest. The shame of being at the very bottom of the barrel was a terrible burden to bear. I felt I had let down my posh, expensive school and Catholicism to boot. Needless to say, Rita Scott was destined to go to hell and I would make sure of her damnation.

My standing amongst my peers at the convent was not tarnished and I went on to win medals at other festivals and from the London Academy of Dramatic Art. During one such drama examination the adjudicator made me promise that I would never give up acting because I had a gift. I had no intention of giving up acting as it was the only subject I was good at.

Acting took me out of the dramatic gin-soaked nights that my parents were indulging in since my mother had inherited a giant sum of money in 1960, when my ex-communicated grandfather had died on the Isle of Man. My mother sold his house out from under "the other woman." Gwen had a dark vengeful streak not far from the buxom blonde, bombshell persona she showed to the rest of the world. (Though I would never use the word bomb in her presence for it would spark an influx of emotion and tears.) Gwen possessed little in domestic skills. She preferred to discuss Shakespeare than to brew tea. She was educated and knowledgeable. She had been part of the Raj in India and attended boarding schools from the age of four. She knew how to capture attention. Her social skills were amazing. She could talk to anyone from a tradesman to a lord; everyone found her entrancing, funny and captivating. She owned this incredible voice that had been drummed into her at the Royal Academy of Dramatic Art. She was the ultimate broadcaster with perfect pitch and diction. She had been raised by nuns and possessed a moral compass made of steel. She had been propositioned several times during her stage and film career. She never faltered for fame and fortune.

"But for love that's a different matter," she divulged. Gwen was later bitter as she knew so many actresses who had slept their way to the top. Though she believed you could achieve anything if you set your mind to it.

"Never let anyone say you can't." was her credo to me. This coming from the woman who insisted I refrain from singing in church.

"Darling, you can't carry a tune. Mime the words. You want to be an actress don't you?" My mother was an enigma. She was loving, generous and kind one moment and cruel, selfish and mean the next. She was a contradiction in terms.

The result of my mother's inheritance was that she treated the family, including my cousins, to an epic holiday in Rimini, Italy. I was bathing in the Adriatic when I received my first kiss from the olive skinned, black haired Giuseppe, a twelve-year-old ardent Neapolitan. During that holiday I acquired a taste for coffee with whipped cream, but not for the opposite sex.

Upon our return from Italy we moved to a detached house in Bushey Heath. I was allocated my very own bedroom, a ten foot by eight foot box, which I referred to as the cell.

At fourteen I enrolled at Watford School of Music and Drama. I had a Saturday job at Fantos, a fabric and notions store in Watford High Street which meant the weekly pilgrimage to Italia Conti was no longer an option.

I came under the drama tutelage of Giles Gough a dashing fellow, in his thirties with an unruly head of brown hair and deep set amber eyes that affirmed his intensity. He was full of energy, charisma and encouragement. Giles disappeared as quickly as he had appeared, his attentions were redirected on his new favorite students at the drama department of a local college. His replacement was an attractive, fortyish, curvaceous, blonde, Glenda Howard who had graduated from the Guildhall School of Music and Drama. Glenda stood for no ego and no nonsense. I adored her. She believed I had talent but instinctively knew when I was slacking. She was a hard task-master, something I had not experienced before.

On the home front the turmoil continued. My parents had succumbed to imbibing a quart and half of gin a night. I knew the exact amount because either I or my younger brother, Tony was sent to buy the liquor at the off license. My mother appeared in a few movies, modeled as an outsize model for which the snobby girls at the convent teased and gossiped about. For a short time she worked for the Barbara Worth Talent Agency in which she used nepotism to have my brother and I cast as one of comedian, Arthur Haynes' children in his television show. At the taping, my mother reunited with her best friend from R.A.D.A. the comedienne Patricia Hayes. Patricia was portraying Arthur Haynes wife on the series. My mother hugged and embraced Patricia, they giggled as they reminisced about Charlie (Charles Laughton), as if it was yesterday that they had attended the hallow grounds of the Royal Academy of Dramatic Art.

3 Rosemary and Tony "Arthur Haynes Show" 1962

My mother realized that her career was exhausted so she put my petite, younger photogenic brother, Tony to work in the business. I was not a viable option as in her words

I was going through my "awkward stage." I was tall for my age and as my mother described me "big boned." Tony at 10-years-old was enrolled in the Gail French Stage School in Fulham. His career took off. He was small, blonde, blue eyed with a cheeky smile. He had a marvelous few years shooting commercials, films, print work and repeatedly auditioning for a role in the musical Oliver. He also had the inherited deficiency of the non-singing voice. Otherwise he was successful, that was until he hit puberty when he literally grew out of the parts he was auditioning for. At sixteen he ran away from home and worked as a stage manager at a theatre on the South Coast.

Tony was lucky to be cast out of the nightly Gwen and Joe show, as they were getting plastered every single evening. One moment they would be laughing and placing the lampshades on their heads and the next fighting and screaming. Eventually, my father would pass out on the couch. Then my mother would come looking for a fight with me, one that would involve a lashing with the dog leash for some minor infraction or look I had given her hours, days or weeks before.

My older brother, Terry immigrated to America in 1961, the year he turned twenty-one. He had seen the writing on the wall. That left moi to receive the brunt of my mother's frustration after she had verbally castrated my father. I would go out. I had a succession of beaus. In my mother's eyes none of my suitors were good enough. She had cruel nicknames for all my friends. I learned to voluntarily lock myself in my cell overnight to avoid the fray and wrath downstairs. In the morning, the lounge was a saloon, littered with empty glasses, mounds of cigarette butts, and the lingering smell of smoke which I abhorred.

My fabulous drama teacher, Glenda Howard was experiencing trouble with her ungrateful teenage daughter, who was my age. Glenda and I bonded, adopting each other and secretly wishing that our genetics could have made us related. I arrived extra early to my drama classes and we always had a cup of tea, digestive biscuits and a chat about her family's dysfunction. She was a divorcee. We discussed her romantic troubles. She was seeing two men, one daring, dashing and a bit of a rogue, the other stable and sensible but older. We contemplated her single parenting challenges of raising three unruly boys and one stroppy, ungrateful daughter. I was her pet and she was my mother mentor.

I never discussed my home life with Glenda or anyone. Perhaps, I felt somewhat responsible for the nightly goings on. I longed to discover the secret to making my parents happy and liking one another again. They must have been enamored of each other at one time.

The inheritance caused an enormous rift in the family. My mother was convinced that we were all "after her legacy" which was absolute rubbish. How could an educated, talented, social woman be so blind? She talked incessantly about "her money." She was possessed by pounds, shillings and pence.

My mother disliked Glenda Howard with a passion not only because she sensed my love and admiration, but they were competitors professionally. Once they auditioned for the same role in a film. Thank goodness my mother prevailed and took delight in telling all and sundry how she had won the part over her daughter's "so called" drama teacher.

4 Elsie Gwendolyn Mary Theresa

As the topsy-turvy world at home deteriorated I began to blossom from being "big boned" which made Gwen jealous and possessive. I began to pull away from her more and more.

Meanwhile back at school in order to gain acceptance by my peers at the convent. I invited girls from my class to see the Rolling Stones live at the Odeon Cinema in Watford. My enticement was that I would take them backstage to meet the pop group. I hijacked my mother's ocelot coat, wore her high heels and went overboard with makeup. During the concert I couldn't for the life of me comprehend why my classmates screamed and flung their arms to embrace the mouthy lead singer Mick Jagger. Following the performance, I escorted my friends to the stage door and in a commanding voice announced to the security guards.

"I am with the show." They parted to allow me and my gawking, giggling girlfriends backstage. From then on, whenever pop stars played Watford, I pulled the same trick for my newfound school chums. I was accepted and cosseted by my classmates. Despite the fact that my mother was rumored amongst my peers to model brassieres and corsets. How immodest was that in their Child of Mary eyes?

At the convent I was paired with Suzanne Gower, as my acting partner. Suzanne was a willowy classmate with wisps of blond hair kept off her rosy cheeks by bunches. She was clever, smart and an intuitive actress. We made a dynamic duo. We left our mark winning at festivals, especially when we performed "Children in Uniform" by Christa Winslow. Suzanne as the teacher, Fraulein von Bernburg and I her pupil, the besotted Manuela. Unbeknownst to either one of us was the play's hidden agenda of a lesbian relationship. Suzanne introduced me to the British Drama League and during the school holidays we would travel to London. I achingly couldn't wait for the sessions because it was here that I was introduced and fell in love with Brecht. We read The Good Woman of Szechuan. We discussed politics, prostitution and performance. I felt like a grownup for the very first time in my life. We undertook stage readings for days and I was captivated, listening to critiques, notes, and academics debating history and acting techniques. I began to tone down my own acting by being less over the top, less stilted, and more realistic. The British Drama League provided an environment where I thrived. I realized that my childhood ambition of joining the Royal Shakespeare Company was achievable through study and practical theatre experience. I had an insatiable appetite for all the British Drama League had to offer and counted down the days until the school holidays when Suzanne and I would return to embrace a stage full of ideas and opportunities.

From: Martin
To: Rose-Mary
Subject: Intros
Date: September 27th, 2011 9:23 pm
Hello Rose-Mary
Have been re-reading your intro and the following now strikes me. Because theatre and drama were inextricably woven throughout your early life what we get from you is a hugely impressive opening to what is essentially an autobiography with New College of Speech and Drama merely being a stepping stone on your life's journey. This I feel accounts for the detail and length of your absorbing introduction. There is, for you, no other way of presenting this. I merely trace the redirection of a youthful me at a time of social change with circumstance playing just as important a role as ambition. My family are never part of this new direction in my life. They played no further part in my career path.

Perhaps it is a good thing we have hit this particular barrier head on! This is perhaps where we would have benefited from the further input of others writing their versions as well. You have the kernel of an excellent autobiography if that is the path you wish to go down.

Look forward to your views.
Regards
Love
Martin

From: Rose-Mary
To: Martin
Subject: New College Diaries
Date: September 29th, 2011 9:42 am
Hi Martin:

I am cognizant that my introduction exceeds in description and needs to be cut back. I believe that when you read my audition piece there will not be a difference in our offerings. I am not interested in writing an autobiography. I think we should press on and I will try to be more concise as the calendar and events at Ivy House are snippets in my recall not as ingrained and sketched as the prelude. I have been waylaid in writing this week by a fist to the eye by one of my special needs students. She is non-verbal and becomes easily frustrated evidenced when she walloped me with a plastic toy. She is fourteen, non- ambulatory and totally unaware of the consequences of her actions. As a result, I am left with a permanent vision impediment and my questioning if I will continue to work with these teens.

Anyway the proposal was to write how we became entrenched in the theatre. So you get to re-live being eighteen. In order to set up the entwining recollections we first have to write a micro bio that sets up the following chapters which will be centered around the audition, the first day at New College then chronically thereafter.

I am off on vacation to Georgia and South Carolina so there is no urgency at the present time.

All the very best,
Rose-Mary

Rosemary: Limbo.

My mother insisted I leave the convent. She was not giving those nuns anymore of her money even though I had reduced tuition. I was enrolled in a business course at the local college of further education. I was miserable and hopeless at typing and even worse at shorthand. I took core courses in English, French and biology that took the sting out of the mind numbing secretarial curriculum. The college population was completely female, mostly "working class" teens who became deadly silent the first time I spoke in class. They teased me that they never expected a "toff" in their midst. Apart from their initial shock at my upper-crust accent they accepted me and took it upon themselves to educate me in street life, "proper fashion" and how to play hooky by faking small, but gruesome injuries without the teacher being suspicious. I never mentioned acting, or theatre as I thought they would think I was haughty. For one endless year I went through the motions of becoming a secretary.

To ease the pain of the doldrums of the dead ended all female secretarial classes, I went through a plethora of boyfriends. These young men helped fill the continuing void of male company. Danny was a drummer in the Sputniks a local band, I would attend all their rehearsals and gigs. There were weddings, retirements and an array of parties at which I danced with the other girl friends. I would be the drummer's sweetheart indefinitely, anything to escape the turmoil at home. The Sputniks entered a local music contest at Watford Town Hall. I placed myself front row and center in order to scream and shriek when the Sputniks took the stage. The Sputniks lost to a group from St. Albans called the Zombies who sang "Summertime" in perfect confident harmony. Backstage our crew were teary eyed trying to put on brave faces. On one side of the stage observing the misery was a striking young man with a Beatle haircut, ruddy complexion and a mischievous glint in his eye. He was wearing a fashionable camel sheep-skin coat. He nodded to me through the consoling chaos. As I help load the van with the equipment this mysterious stranger watched and when Danny wasn't looking he smiled at me. Then he was gone.

"Danny, who was that chap in the sheep-skin coat?" I asked.

"That's Pearce Sullivan. He's a reporter with the Evening Post. He was one of the judges. He's a bloody tone deaf bugger as far as I am concerned," Danny snarled. Danny had not detected that I had found that grin from Pearce Sullivan oddly endearing and disconcerting. I quickly finished orbiting with the Sputniks as they continued to plummet to mediocrity on earth. I had a new beau, Barry, who declared his undying love, taught me how to dance the stomp and to balance on a scooter. We attended church together and the coldest I have ever been was astride his scooter in a silk shirt, short skirt and helmet streaking through the streets of Mill Hill to Bushey Heath following midnight mass on Christmas Eve. Barry was followed by Graham who would leave flowers and chocolates on the doorstep. He drove an Astin Martin, much warmer than the pillion of the scooter. Then there was Henry, a straight laced banker who my mother fawned over.

"He has a secure job and good prospects," she smugly repeated. Henry was infatuated with cars. He took me to Brands Hatch, but I was not impressed by vehicles endlessly rotating around a circle. Following Henry came John with his amiable school boy charm. He had a grand plan to immigrate to Australia with me along. I wanted to escape the turmoil of home, but Australia? My mother always referred to that continent as a penal colony.

I met Chris Tyler late one night after a dance. He came upstairs on the local bus with the pop star Donovan. We started talking and I invited Chris to my birthday party the following week, which my mother referred to as my "coming out party." He showed up much to my mother's disgust because Chris sported a head of overly long curly hair that framed his hawkish nose and angular face.

"My god!" my mother exclaimed. Looking at the gold ring hanging from his lobe

"An earring?" Is he a gypsy?"

After they exchanged a long stare down Chris withdrew. On my mother's insistence, he was relegated to the gents' toilet for most of the festivities where he was happy to smoke marijuana. My mother dragged me aside and made me promise that I would never bring him home during daylight hours. Chris could court me at night when he would be a shadow to the neighbors.

Chris was a painter, he lived alone amidst gigantic collages by Edward Sterling at Bushey Studios. Chris eased the chaos I was subjected to at home by being kind, attentive, and encouraging. He expressed his love by introducing me to the Tate Gallery and insisting that I apply to the Film Artistes Association (F.A.A), the union one must join in order to work in film. One freezing Saturday with hard frost underfoot he accompanied me to Kensington where I would face the grueling panel interview of the F.A.A. I received their approval and a union card. The gallant Chris had hovered shivering outside, secreted in the pocket of his thin, threadbare hand-me-down cotton coat was a cobalt blue Indian bracelet which he gave me to celebrate my acceptance into what was known as a "closed shop." He took pleasure in indulging me and instinctively knew how much I loathed the secretarial school and sensed an underlying intensity at home in Bushey Heath. His ultimate surprise was that spring when he blindfolded me and led me into the floor to ceiling windowed studio, which he had conjured into a sea of daffodils. Daffs, in jars, paint pots, mugs, teapots, cups, glasses, the studio was awash in yellow, my favorite color. Hundreds of daffodils.

That fall, Chris due to economic reasons, relocated to Clapham to live with Edward Sterling and his young family. Chris served as the nanny, houseboy and carpenter in the renovation of the Sterlings rambling house. My telephone conversations were limited. My mother had installed a pay phone in the entrance foyer of our house.

"I am not going to pay for Romeo and Juliet to carry on their ill-fated romance." She announced.

His visits to the Bushey Studios became infrequent. He found another conquest, her name was Iris. Out of curiosity, I confronted him. I enquired if he was collecting flowers. I never heard from him or saw him again.

My heartbreak was repaired by Central Casting who frequently called with jobs in background work in commercials. One was for cigarettes. I didn't smoke but spent a week puffing like a pro. I was fifteen years old. I wasn't legally allowed to inhale or exhale.

I was called that summer to work as an extra on The Liquidators, a film starring Rod Taylor and Jill St. John. Jill became sick and in order to not delay shooting the director demanded a double. I was summoned, in front of the director, he pulled my dress uncomfortably tight whilst he studied my bum.

"Yes that's hers," the director declared.

"We will need to cut her hair and dye it red," he decreed. I was acutely embarrassed. I turned and loudly responded.

"I won't cut my hair, nor will I dye it red." I was ushered from his eminence whose mouth was agape. I was relegated to the very back booth of the interior scenes inside a casino restaurant, where Alan, a smarmy extra with greasy charcoal slicked down hair, wearing black tie and tails insisted on placing his hand on my knee under the table. I was saved by my Irish "uncle" Galen, my father's cousin who was a shop steward in Equity and worked as a double for Peter Lawford, and Robert Wagner and virtually any extremely debonair, handsome American/Canadian actor who shot films in England.

"Do you know Galen O' Grady?" I enquired.

"Everyone knows Galen. How does a pretty little thing like you know Galen?"

"He's my father's cousin. They came over on the boat together from Dublin." Alan, the knee offender withdrew his hand from being encased around my patella never to return again. "Uncle" Galen's name proved very helpful in keeping the wolves at bay.

5 Rosemary age 16 promotional shot for theatre agent. The Saluki belonged to the photographer and insisted in being in the picture.

From: Martin
To: Rose-Mary
Subject: New College Diary
Date: October 19th, 2011 8:51 am
Dear Rose-Mary

I have plotted the outline when I started at the funny farm, and can send this on to you. Hadn't thought of the introduction but will try to put something in perspective. This is, of course, us of now looking back to those times when we were seduced by Ivy House and all who sailed in her! I'll draft something up and let you have it-it's rather like having a tutor at the online Open University. Preparing for announcing at the local football match.

Pity they never ran that as an option at New College instead of those lunatic broadcasting classes in the garden shed with an old boy who seriously thought he was broadcasting from the Ritz in the 1930s. I forwarded the Jeremy Goggins New College Years to our mentors, Giles and Mary Gough and a got a lovely letter back. He's 81 now!!!! Giles of the Barnet In-Crowd-who'd have thought it.

Look forward to hearing from you

Take care

Love

Martin

From: Rose-Mary
To: Martin
Subject: New College Diary
Date: October 19th, 2011 1:23 pm
Dear Martin

I have begun writing the introduction with my heart. I think no more than five pages will suffice as the exposition as to how we landed at Ivy House. I will rewrite with my head and hope to complete by the end of November. Slow going, I know.

I have plays to submit, fellowship applications plus the tedium of work which is serving a dual purpose of income and research into the care of the mentally impaired. So what are your excuses? We will complete the task.

Love

Rose-Mary

From: Martin
To: Rose-Mary
Subject: Truro Football Club
Date: October 20th, 2011 3:23 am
Hi Rose-Mary
Go to Trurocityfc.co.uk. Page down to Match highlights, click short clip of Penzance wedding, then yours truly with the injured club captain doing commentary (the usual commentator was away) I thought my broadcasting days were over.
Cheers
Ken Wolstenholme Banks.

From: Rose-Mary
To: Martin
Subject: Over?
Date: October 27th, 2011 10:52 am
Hi Martin:
It isn't over until the fat lady sings. You could have imitated Pablo Ramirez (La Torre de Jalisco) at the England versus Brazil World Cup game in 2002 with his distinctive rendering of the word goal. "Goooooooooooo oaaaaaaaaaallllll."
Rose-Mary

Rosemary: Before My Time.

One sleepy, summer Sunday my brother Tony answered the pay 'phone in the foyer of our house.

"This is MGM Studios looking to speak with Rosemary Harrington," he laughingly said.

I flippantly grabbed the receiver from him.

"Sure it is. Very funny, Tony."

The female voice on the other end sounded exasperated.

"I know everyone I've telephoned has had the same reaction. I need you to report to MGM, Studio 11 on Monday at 5 a.m. wearing a dress from 1943."

"I'll be there." I hesitantly answered.

I wasn't even born until four years after World War II in 1949. My mother got wind of the situation and in true trooper fashion was able to scrounge an outfit together so that when I arrived at the pearly gates of MGM in Borehamwood before dawn on that Monday I looked as if I was ready to listen to Glenn Miller and dance at the Savoy. At 16 years old I was the youngest person on the film set by two decades.

The costume department refurbished me with a form fitting dress, very high heels and a tight knotted bun as a hairdo. The movie's title was The Dirty Dozen and if you blink you might miss the Fraulein in the aqua marine frock at the SS party in the mansion. That is before I am incinerated along with other "high ranking Germans" by arsonists Lee Marvin and Charles Bronson. The American actors were boisterous and cocksure, one of them seemed intoxicated, believe me I was an expert at diagnosing over indulgers of alcohol.

During the rehearsals and filming of the basement scenes before we, the Nazis, were doused in petrol and set afire, I would be observed off the set by an oversized actor who sat on the bleachers staring at me. My fellow "Germans" told me his name was Jevon Barnes, an American footballer. I had never seen an athlete as huge and intense as he was. I learned that American football is a game of gladiators who wear a uniform of skinny tight pants, shoulder pads and a helmet as they attempt with brute strength to take a cone shaped ball from the opposition. Americans are weird. I don't understand how they are so much bigger physically than we are. Jevon Barnes was a giant of a man. He couldn't take his eyes off me which although flattering was intimidating. If all American men are as huge and muscular as he and his fellow actors, I concluded that must have been the reason us Brits wanted the Americans to assist us in winning World War II. They certainly display an impressive overpowering confidence.

FROM: Martin
To: Rose-Mary
Subject: New College of Speech and Drama
Date: October 28th, 2011 6:22 am
Hi Rose-Mary
Will forward some outlines to you next week. Were you aware that I (along with Noodle) joined the funny farm in January 1968? I don't know what he was up to-something to do with Rita and private tuition, but I had been at university and disliked the course and my drama tutor knew Rita, proposed a transfer and I auditioned in November. I remember we were looked upon as aliens for a couple of weeks such were the close ranks of the inmates. Will this affect your structure..?
All the very best
Martin.

From: Rose-Mary
To: Martin
Subject: NCSD
Date: October 29th, 2011 3:30 pm
Hello Martin

I don't think the late enrollment will make a difference. Your drama origins and background are as relevant as your discontent with the university. Your sardonic wisdom always makes me smile. There isn't any hurry as yours truly has been pressed to return to work in order to make financial threads meet.

Oh the joy of capitalism! I substitute teach special needs kids so that when I have made enough money as a worker bee I can afford the luxury of writing. If only we could sell our house here in Oregon and relocate to Charleston, South Carolina, where sunshine and a cheaper cost of living abide. The real estate gods are toying with potential buyers who are discovering that securing a loan is an unfathomable riddle. Keep the words flowing. "Fill your paper with the breathing of your heart." Wordsworth

Love

Rose-Mary

Rosemary: Extra Cash.

I began to be called by Central Casting regularly to work as an extra or to be a hand artist for commercials. I was still enrolled and plodding along in the miserable secretarial course. On lengthy, boring Sundays my neighborhood friend Jill and I would take a jaunty bus ride to St Albans to hang out around the Cathedral. Or to be exact, The Cock public house and the recreation grounds around the lake. Jill had enormous breasts, which she was embarrassed about.

"Poor, plain Jill, with that bosom," observed my mother. Jill's mother was a mouse of a Welsh woman who picked off lint and threads from your clothes as she talked to you. She always wore high heels and when I was at Jill's playing monopoly or scrabble I saw her mother vacuuming in her high heels. I thought my mother was the only one who wore her stilettos to hoover. However, their choice of shoe wear was their only commonality.

What Jill and I were really doing near Hadrian's Roman wall was scouting for boys, who would either follow us or ask us to sit and talk with them. So it was on one of those reconnaissance Sundays that we came across a congenial Irish boy named Kieran. He invited us to listen to him and his friends play guitar in the park. The musicians were led by a boy, I mean a man, much older, who had the looks of a film star, he was the clichéd tall dark, sultry and extremely handsome. His name was Sean. He was aloof, which made him even more attractive. He was twenty-two, I was sixteen. Jill and I made weekly pilgrimages to St. Albans to sit at the feet of Sean as he strummed his guitar under a lavish oak. Sean eventually gave me a hint of a smile. My adulation paid off and we became a couple. Being so desperate to leave home I somehow became engaged to Sean. Only to discover that he wasn't Sean at all. He had not a drop of Irish blood which pleased my mother immensely.

"One Irish idiot in a family is enough," she announced. Sean's real name was Timothy "of Portuguese extraction" as my mother wheedled out of him. My mother nicknamed him "the bobby dazzler" with his tanned skin, thick dark hair and his swagger, he reminded her of Lawrence Harvey.

"What an improvement on that gypsy fellow," my mother would reiterate.

Timothy was more tortured than I realized. He had been hospitalized for a nervous breakdown when he was studying for his Physics and Chemistry A levels. He was agoraphobic, agyophobic, demo phobic. He was encumbered by more phobias than I could count on one hand, but I thought I could change and heal him. He was complex, anguished, self-absorbed and I loved him dearly. Our relationship ended badly. I realized that life with Sean/ Timothy would be as fake as his name, that I would be leaving my home of hell only to enter into another one, as his demons were increasing.

Breaking off my sham engagement gave me the courage to abandon my business career. I left the secretarial course and my working class mates. I declared that I was going to be an actress full time. The reality and retaliation was that my mother insisted I pay rent. Therefore in between my "acting" jobs I would work for a temp agency in offices. My theatrical agent sent me to audition for the Prime of Miss Jean Brodie.

"How tall are you?" The director asked. I had on ballet flats and attempted to bend my knees for he was looking for girls under 5' 1" and I was an Amazon at 5' 6".

"If you stand up you will tower over the other girls and look odd in front of Miss Jean Brodie." He explained. "But an outstanding reading of the script," he added.

When I was not waiting in line to audition or being an extra I would meet the challenges of different office venues, bosses and colleagues. If Central Casting called I would make my apologies and earn my living acting, dancing, dubbing or displaying my hands as a hand artist to the camera. I was still taking classes with my maternal surrogate drama teacher, Glenda Howard and winning the local drama festivals, much to the chagrin of her other not so favored students. One in particular, Sadie Jones who was angularly Josephine Bonaparte beautiful, with short cropped hair and runway model height. She possessed a unique high voice together with a great sense of comic timing. We were often head-to-head in competition. She was distant and reserved with me, Glenda Howard's star pupil.

6 Rose-Mary age 18 headshot for Spotlight

From: Martin
To: Rose-Mary
Subject: Introduction
Date: November 5th, 2011 9:32 am
Hi Rose-Mary:
Hope all is well with you. Please find attached introduction. Is this ok? Am I on the right track? I'm

ready to move on now to the first term at New College....
have made notes and so much happened it was a wonder
my head did not explode!!!

Am doing my Brecht show for the Penzance Lit
Festival next July and have another project about a
tourist disaster here in the 1960s which I am working on
with a friend who is still a professional actor. Busy times.
Trying to get the New College thing organized now.

Look forward to hearing from you. love
Martin

Martin: From East End to North End: The Play Begins…

I was born in 1948 to working class parents in the East
End of London. My parents had no artistic background or
ambitions albeit my mother was a pub pianist and my father
sang alongside her and played Puck in "A Midsummer Night's
Dream" whilst with the army in Burma during the Second
World War.

We lived in small flat in Plaistow near to Upton Park in
the London Borough of West Ham. My father was a bus driver
with London Transport and my mother worked as a canteen
assistant in British Home Stores. My sister who was seven
years older, married and moved away in 1959. I was the first in
the family to go to Grammar school and into higher education.
I was a pupil at Plaistow Grammar School (where Terence
Stamp also studied several years before) from 1959 to 1966.
I was very active in football and other sport. I loved English,
drama and history and as a result of good examination passes I
stayed on in the 6th form. This was against my mother's wishes

as she wanted me to leave and seek employment at sixteen. She was very much a remnant from the Victorian age!

Plaistow Grammar School was in a state of flux with a new generation of young, able and radical teachers joining what had been a very traditional staff room. I was very impressed and influenced by my teachers of History, English and Drama. I quickly discovered an amazing and imaginative other world: Chaucer, Shakespeare, Donne, Austen, Dickens, Owen and Sassoon (I was later to teach his great-great niece drama in the 1990s). In an exciting new personal dawn of history I discovered: the Crusades, the Medieval World, Civil Wars, World Wars, Imperialism and Poverty. I slowly began to form views of this new world that I discovered around me. A trendy young man with a German and Drama Degree from Bristol University took over the drama department and, via the drama society, introduced me to the works of Buchner and Brecht as well as the delights of Shakespeare and Sweeney Todd. We even performed "The Crucible" by Arthur Miller and I scurried around the stage as the manic Reverend Parris. Drama and theatre began to have an attraction and a meaning for this working class youth in East London during the mid-1960s.

Another important influence (but I did not perceive it at the time) was Joan Littlewood and the Theatre Workshop at nearby Stratford East (my best friend went on to become her lighting designer in the 1970s). As youths we used to hang around the theatre and sometimes she'd let us sit in on rehearsals. I spoke to some of the company and began to understand her philosophy and working methods and she also gave us encouragement to join the industry in order to radically change it from within. Politics had found me. My peers were all artistic and wild.

Malcolm had already started his career in theatre with a part in TV's School Comedy, "Please Sir" and had a decent part in Richard Attenborough's movie of "Oh What a Lovely War". Ray went to work with Joan as a lighting technician and then a designer. Doug started a band and began a life-long career as a professional musician. He came over to the New College of Speech and Drama and was my musical director on our third year directing option show. Wayne became a professional photographer and Tony a dancer.

I had been given a place at Lancaster University to study History and Politics but I was still uncertain of a career direction. At this time, 1966-7, the London Borough of Newham was acutely short of primary school teachers and there was a scheme for students with three A levels to act as unqualified teaching staff during the year before going on to higher education. At £12.00 per week and with a pension scheme this was too good an opportunity to turn down and so I entered the world of primary education and within two days of starting I was in charge of a class of thirty-five eight year-olds. It was simply a task of learning on the job and taking the daily advice and encouragement of the other teachers. It was challenging for an eighteen-year-old and I grew up pretty quickly in the primary school environment.

I attended an evening class at the local technical college to study A level British Constitution. At the same time I produced, wrote and acted in a show, "Provo 67", named after the anarchists of Amsterdam, which was staged at the Theatre Royal, East 15. Positive feedback from the audiences and my experience with the children in East London prompted a definite career shift towards primary education and drama. I opted for a B.E.D. Course at Avery Hill College in South London and began the course in drama and education in September 1967.

It was an unmitigated disaster....I felt trapped in a tweed jacketed world of fusty and frosty education and I was frustrated with the lack of hands-on, tangible drama within the timetable. The only upside in my life was our anarchic hall of residence, well away from the main campus, where sex, drugs and rock 'n 'roll became the staple elements of my personal curriculum. I did get involved with the Student Union Theatre Group's production of Brecht's "The Good Person of Setzuan", and gained a great deal by this initial contact with the great dramatist. I loved the clarity and power of this play and to this day it remains one of my favourite works of all time. I was a stranger at college lectures and following a long meeting with my drama tutor (a decent guy) he suggested a transfer to the New College of Speech and Drama in North West London where he thought I might flourish. He said that he knew a certain Rita Scott, who was Head of Department at the college, and he would contact her on my behalf. He organized the possibility of a transfer (but I had to put in a further 100% attendance and up my work rate to qualify) and by November I would be expected to renew my grant and attend an audition at Ivy House.

Little did I know it but my life was going to change forever...

7 Martin age 19

From: Rose-Mary
To: Martin
Subject: New College Diary
Date: November 11th, 2011 11:16 am
Hello Martin
Regular teacher training colleges were so uninspiring back in the 1960's. I owe a debt of gratitude to New College for giving me an educational foundation that I still draw from and use in academic settings.

Currently I am working full time, rising before dawn to be in the classroom at 7 am. I hope to take next week off so I can return to writing.

My play Illegal was named a semi-finalist for the Stanley Drama Award. This play deals with the Sheriff in Arizona who randomly jails Hispanics immigrants. Identifying a race as illegal is how the holocaust began. I hope this play gets picked up bringing attention to the migrant workers who certainly don't have a voice in Maricopa County.

I'd like to know about the tourist disaster project.

Love

Rose-Mary

Rosemary: Time Stands Still.

At home during the nightly gin soaked soirees my mother berated me for not having a plan. She repeatedly would ask,

"Do you want to end up like me? Nothing to fall back on. Married to an…" she hesitated and muttered under her breath, "Irish idiot". .

The malevolent term she used for my unsuspecting jocular father.

"Don't you know that to get on in theatre, film and television you have to sleep with the producer or the director or the camera man, even the clapper boy?" I had witnessed this first hand as an extra; many attractive young women who were known to wear their knickers on their head who would cozy up to the assistants and crew on the film. My mother had a hang up about show business immorality. She repeatedly asked me in her stupor,

"Are you ready to sleep your way to the top Rosemary?" She wore me down and I was sick of her interrogations. I reluctantly agreed to give up acting and acquire a regular job, settle down and find a suitable husband.

"One without all those silly phobias even though he was a dream boat," she advised. "Love and marriage that's what life is about." she insisted. *God* I thought to myself. *There must be more!*

I was hired locally for an import business that was run out of a residence about a mile from our house in Bushey Heath. I walked and dawdled to work, typed invoices and answered phones. There was an office uprising when a matronly employee of many years was requested to make tea for me by the owner of the business. My boss was a quiet, balding man with yellow teeth and overly large square black framed glasses. I thought I was going to die of tedium. There must be more to life than waiting around for some man to marry you and lead you to nirvana.

Jill and I had shortened our boy hunting expeditions, casting our net closer to home, scouring for males in Cassiobury Park in Watford. Acres and acres of greenery, forest and canals and an abundance of agile young men taking long walks no doubt on the same mission as Jill and I. On one excursion I had managed to procure a new boyfriend, Kevin Fox with freckles and a mass of unruly long red hair. He was studying math in order to enter university and he loved art as much as I did. He was the perfect candidate for he was detested by my mother. Not for his bohemian appearance, nor his unconventional dress from the army and navy store, he favored old military coats, and did I mention that unruly red hair. No, she absolutely hated him because he lived in a council house on a council estate. The more negative she was, the more I was determined to keep the relationship afloat. I would show her. If I was doomed to the desperate humdrum of life. I would create my own drama with the queen of theatre, Elsie Gwendolyn, of the Royal Academy of bloody Dramatic Art. Kevin was engrossed in obtaining his A levels so that he could apply to university. But as my mother reminded me daily,

"With a working class accent like that, what university would accept him? I don't care how clever he is. He will not be given a place because let's face it, he's from a council house."

There I was in a mundane job, an unbearable living situation, a boyfriend who would never measure up and an acting career that had been side tracked. What was my life coming to? The answer was a great big full stop, no incentive, no goal. "No field of daisies to sit in with my beloved." as D.H. Lawrence wrote. I was well and truly stuck.

I turned to Glenda Howard who sensed my desperation. Glenda procured an audition and interview for me at Brick Hall College, a local teacher's training institution, all female, secluded in the countryside. My mother actually went along with the plan and was appeased by the fact that I would become a teacher.

"Always have something under your belt. How sensible. These silly notions of going on the stage are unrealistic, look at me, I'm living proof, look where theatre landed me," she cautioned.

The audition and interview were arranged speedily by my savior, Glenda Howard. The questions at the interview were perfunctory. The audition was mind numbing. A stout woman wearing a tatty cream cardigan, dirndl brown skirt, thick brown stockings that looked like her legs were bandaged, ending at plump feet that slid into worn plain sensible brown leather shoes with straps. This matriarch had untidy gray hair swooped back in a stiff chignon. She displayed overgrown, dusty eyebrows that met in the middle of her forehead under which perched a pair of round framed National Health issue glasses that sat askew on her nose. This middle-aged woman was the head of the department of drama. There in her dingy, drab office lined with stained teacups and disheveled papers, she insisted that I read from Winnie-the-Pooh for forty-five tedious minutes. I tried to resuscitate the monotony of Tigger, Piglet and Christopher Robin, as I asked myself. *Is this really her idea of drama? Was I to succumb to three years of endless cold readings of children's fiction? God help me.*

If there is a God he didn't get my message until months later when I was immersed in studying for exams that would grant me entrance into the cloistered grounds of the all-female teacher's college. I had given in my notice as a secretary and enrolled at a S.W. Herts College of Further Education to prepare for the O' level tests that were required for admittance to college. I found inspiration in my new course load, and the fact that my classmates at S.W. Herts College of Further Education consisted of seventeen healthy, gusty, humorous males. I was fascinated by interacting with the opposite sex after eons of femininity.

Students were allowed to leave campus during free periods. I would gather with a group of friends in a café down an alley and over endless cups of coffee debate, art, movies, politics and religion and we would decide where to stage our weekly protests for ban the bomb in London and which pub to go to afterwards.

As the weather warmed we organized parties when unsuspecting parents were on holiday. We removed the household furniture so the rave could begin. Our biggest spree was at the home of Michael, an eccentric, bespectacled, cellist with a high pitched squeal of a laugh who resided in Bushey. He volunteered his parents rambling Victorian mansion for weeks. Drugs were rampant, beds tested by couplings, accompanied by an oblivious Michael playing Debussy on his cello in the library. I wasn't into the sex and drugs nor booze. I had enough of the latter to deal with at home. I was a passive bystander watching the goings on of the orgy but never participating, partly because my bloody Catholic conscience would not allow me.

One Saturday on an overcrowded bus to Watford, I was on my way to drama class and a conference and commiseration with Glenda Howard. I found myself hustled to the front of the double-decker, holding on for dear life. I looked down at the seat next to me and saw my drama rival Sadie Jones smiling up at me. Then she greeted me without the icy reserve that she usually gave me. The last time we had competed at the Watford Drama Festival, officiated by that reformed witch, Rita Scott I had won every single category, improvisation, poetry, mime, acting. No wonder Sadie bore a grudge. I could not fault her for not liking me. But today she was smiling up at me.

"How are you Rosemary? What are your plans for the coming year?"

"I've got accepted to Brick Hall Teacher's College." I enthusiastically bragged.

Sadie begins to beam from ear to ear when I retaliated with the same enquiry.

"And you? Where are you going?"

"I have been accepted to Drama School." Sadie gloated

"You have?" I replied with incredulity.

"Yes. Last year I applied to Central School of Speech and Drama, but I was denied because I failed the hearing test. So this year I submitted to New College of Speech and Drama and I was accepted. They only take one in a thousand or was it two thousand applicants," she purred.

"Congratulations," I managed to stumble.

Sadie continued eagerly.

"Do you know who is the head of New College?"

"No," I mumbled.

"Rita Scott."

With that Sadie stood up, all six foot of her and gave me her seat. She bent down and whispered in my ear.

"The deadline to apply to New College passed months ago. I thought you would want to know."

Then she was gone with the crowd of traveling prospective shoppers as they alighted to Watford Precinct from the bus. I sat stunned that Sadie had been offered a place at Drama School. A drama school headed by Rita Scott, no less. My fallen angel Rita Scott who had sung my praises at the last drama festival I competed in. The very same woman who had placed me last….thirty-second all those Catholic convent years ago. I was shell shocked.

At the very next stop I got off the bus, crossed the road to wait for another bus that would take me back home. I needed to write a letter to New College of Speech and Drama. I didn't know the address. I needed to write to Rita Scott herself asking, no begging for the opportunity to audition for a place. I would explain that I did not know that the deadline to apply had passed. Who said the nuns cured me of lying?

The reply to my application took months to arrive. Thank the gods that I was summoned to audition on December 19th, 1967. Now all there was left to do was inform my mother. To say that she took the news poorly would be an understatement.

She flew off the handle taking on the role of Queen Margaret in Richard III spitting and spewing.

"The folly of applying to Drama School. How could you? You have secured a place at Brick Hall Teacher's Training College. What on earth? You are an utter fool, a gutter snipe," she snarled.

"I can't stand Brick Hall. I don't want to go there," I responded.

My mother sensed she was losing ground as she sarcastically asked,

"What will your guardian angel, Glenda Howard think of this disastrous plan? When she pulled strings to get you admitted to Brick Hall?"

I couldn't help myself in my reply.

"She will be as pleased as punch, in fact she will be delighted, for at New College you train to be a specialist Speech, Drama and English teacher. If you would read the prospectus mummy, you would know that New College is bona fide and that they accept one in two thousand applicants. I have a long way to go before I am admitted."

My mother took a deep breath then proclaimed,

"If you insist on attending this so called New College, I will wash my hands of you. I've explained you need a job to fall back on. You need to be self-reliant in this world."

"I will be," I plead.

She would not listen and continued.

"If you are silly enough to study drama instead of being educated as a proper teacher I will not support you financially. I will not give you an iota to waste your time and education. You will live here, you will take the bus and train everyday back and forth."

"But I will get a grant," I interrupted.

"Not enough to live on, and you will not ask me for any of my money or anything else," she stated.

"I haven't got in yet," I sheepishly replied.

"Rosemary I will pray to God Almighty and Our Lady that you are denied."

With that she exited the lounge and shut the door in my face.

Glenda Howard was overjoyed that I was to audition. Glenda insisted we meet twice a week to rehearse and practice answering questions to prepare for the interview.

My mother sent me to Coventry. She hardly uttered a word except for her random chorus.

"I do hope you haven't jeopardized your place at Brick Hall by applying to that other place."

"I haven't," I tried to reassure her.

I still had a place at Brick Hall, that dreadful, all female bastion of Winnie-the-Pooh. I was actually praying to Almighty God and Our Lady that Brick Hall Ladies Teacher's College would never happen.

From: Martin
To: Rose-Mary
Subject: New College update
Date: November 20th, 2011 6:32 am
Hi Rose-Mary
Have just returned from a few days in London where a friend of mine has an exhibition. I also went to the National Newspaper Library in Colindale to research the 60s Cornish tragedy. Left London at 5 am this morning and am back early afternoon and am knackered driving. I've spoken to several people and the consensus is to write either a radio play or to write a documentary narrative of events. It was the Darlwyne disaster of the 1966 World Cup weekend when 31 souls were lost at sea off the Cornish coast in an unlicensed pleasure boat. Whole families were lost from all over the country and 27 came from the same hotel!! The court of inquiry was damning but the owner of the boat was only fined 500 pounds in 1967. I'm researching in detail so as to get the book published regionally as there's been no coverage of the disaster and its implication for the tourist trade. The children's possessions in the hotels were left as they lay for local charities to come in and take them. There's plenty to work on and that is what I'm doing at the moment.

Re: New College -I'm working on the first week and will send you some stuff once I'm satisfied with it. Things gradually come back through the mist of time.

Love

Martin

From: Rose-Mary
To: Martin
Subject: Darlwyne and New College diary
Date: November 24th, 2011 2:57 pm
Hi Martin:

What a tragedy the drowning of the holiday makers. I am not shocked at how despicable homo sapiens can be when material gain is the motive. I think that the story would be riveting dramatized on the radio.

I will begin my audition segment this week.

Love

Rose-Mary

Rosemary: The Audition.

"I should have strangled you at birth," my mother screamed.

I slammed the front door. The time for the audition was 6 pm. I had familiarized myself with the route. The 142 bus to Edgware and then the Northern Line train to Golders Green. At that time of night I would not be caught in the rush hour as the commuters would be returning home from London. However, the ticket taker at the station was our old upstairs neighbor, from Flat 3, Joan Doty with her round face, curly dark hair spiraling from under her official dark blue peaked railway cap. I was always captivated by her infectious smile.

After she punched my ticket for the train as I was walking towards the platform, she stepped out of her booth and yelled,

"Rosemary come and see me if you want a free pee. I have the key to the ladies lavatory and I can let you in."

I blushed with embarrassment and hoped that none of the other passengers had heard her offer.

The journey took an hour and a half. I walked the hill to Ivy House, 94 North End Road, just before Hampstead Heath across from the Old Bull and Butcher Pub. New College was perched on the hill, encased by a ten foot high wall.

The weather was blustery. I had swept my waist long hair into a cascading style that fell to my shoulders. The wind had blown it to bits. My new tall black high heeled boots pinched my toes and my knees rattled from the cold, for my mottled, rabbit fur coat stopped just above them. Underneath I wore a black turtleneck and a short red tartan miniskirt with black tights. I had recited my audition pieces all the way up the hill. I was extremely nervous as I entered the courtyard. A light was on in the foyer of the grand house. I opened the massive red oak door with its ringed handle and entered. I was greeted by a girl about my own age with long, stringy, brown hair, wearing jeans, a beige jumper and mustard coloured workman's boots.

"Hello I'm Rosy," she offered.

There was an awkward pause as she looked at a clipboard.

"And you are?"

"I'm sorry. I'm Rosemary Harrington here to audition."

She scoured down the clipboard of many names and made a tick.

"Yes, well they are busy right now. I'll give you a quick tour."

"Great," I replied smiling.

She did not return my smile. She was all business.

"You can leave your coat there," she said.

She pointed to an overly large hall table to the right of the front door. Immediately Rosy walked ten paces to a big plastic door with a porthole and indicated with her clipboard.

"This is the refectory."

"Great," I said again.

I stood on tiptoe to peer inside.

"You can bring sandwiches or buy what Winkie has."

"Winkie?" I queried

"Winkie is the cook, janitor and letch that lives here with his wife, Mrs. Winkie.

Mrs. Winkie is lovely. Winkie is a good cook, especially curry. He likes to leer," she divulged, nonchalantly.

Rosy looked disapprovingly at my high heeled boots and short skirt.

"He is harmless though," Rosy assured me.

She continued down the hall and we entered a space with a grand piano.

"This is the music and voice room."

She led me further down the corridor to a pair of double doors that opened into a spacious room with floor to ceiling windows at either end and glass doors that led onto a terrace overlooking the garden. Facing the windows was a wall of mirrors encased in an ornate gold frame.

"This is the rehearsal room. We practically live in here when we are putting on a show. It's a shame it's so dark outside. At the bottom of the garden is a huge pond.

There used to be swans but they have been replaced by a statue of Pavlova."

I stopped suddenly to ask,

"Rosy, do you mean Anna Pavlova, the ballerina?"

"Yes, this was her house didn't you know?"

I shook my head.

8 Historic Plaque Outside Ivy House.

"I thought everyone knew that," Rosy replied patronizingly. "We will go downstairs to the common room before we have to brave the cold."

She led me to the bowels of the mansion down narrow stairs. The basement was a labyrinth of low ceilings, chairs, aged settees, a public telephone box slung on a niche in the wall. She pointed to an office space where she informed me they produced the college rag and then onto a large open area where parties and dances were held. Here was a door to the outside.

"Brace yourself," Rosy said.

We walked up four uneven steps and pressed on into the teeth of the wind in the garden.

She pointed into the darkness,

"To the left is the new movement studio and ahead of us are the seminar rooms and Rita's room. Follow me on the path and we'll head up to the Phoenix theatre."

I followed her along the outside of the house, we came to a square building where the door was ajar.

"This is our black box theatre," Rosy proudly proclaimed. "This theatre has everything we need. We can change configurations of the stage and audience."

She pointed to the roof. "These are new 3" 150 Fresnels. We use them for spots to flood. It's more economical. The control console is in the booth we plug into a dimmer through a patch pane so we can assign more than one circuit to the dimmer."

Rosy was animated and on fire.

"What is your preference?" she eagerly enquired.

I had no idea what she was talking about. All I could offer was another mumbled

"Great."

Sensing my technical incompetence Rosy looked at her watch.

"Goodness time does fly. They should be ready for you upstairs."

Rosy must have seen the fear in my eyes

"Don't be nervous they won't bite," she offered.

Her assurance was too late my knees were shaking and I was apprehensive and losing my confidence. In my head I kept asking myself *What is a Fresnel? What is a dimmer? What is a Winkie?* Rosy marched me into the house up the marble staircase, swung open the double doors and announced,

"Rosemary Harrington."

The over lit room housed an over long table behind which sat the trio who would decide my fate. Front and centre Rita Scott, her once dark cascading hair cropped with curls encircling her handsome face. On her nose, a pair of trendy round spectacles. Rita looked over her glasses smiled, encouraged me to come forward. I hand her my audition pieces as I survey the other members of the tribunal. A red-cheeked man sporting a manicured comb-over, wearing a blue jumper, he didn't acknowledge me. At the other end of the table, a portly woman sitting upright, glaring. Her hairdo was a cropped pixie cut which suited her pretty but now scowling face. I begin my audition with a religious poem about Mary and Jesus which had served me well and garnered me the gold medal from the London Academy of Dramatic Art the previous year. The poem was to be followed by Rosalynde from 'As You Like It' when she is disguised as a boy and teases Orlando for not loving Rosalynde as much as he should. I am still unnerved by the tour.

I turn my back to the trio to compose myself. I turn around recite the poem with the exact emphasis, pause, interpretation and intonation as I had done many times before.

Out of the corner of my eye, I notice that only Rita is paying attention, she is smiling and glowing. The rosy-cheeked man has not moved. He appears disinterested as his hand covers his forehead and he stares intently at the table. The formidable woman on the right is poker faced and upright and by her expression she is unimpressed with my offering.

Why are those two not responding? I ask myself as I go on automatic recitation. Even the poet would appreciate this rendition. In the past when I've uttered

He stumbles with the cross.

A man too soon
Who scolded scholars
I did not know.

The audience would become very silent and moved. I am not connecting with Greta's cohorts. The last verse which depicts the crucifixion brings forth nothing of interest from the man and woman seated at either end of the table.

In the shadow
I face my son
Born alone.
Tell me the offence
I do not know.
I do not know.

The two pillars are stalwart. Rita on the other hand is exuberant and gushing.

"Jolly good, darling," she declares.

Maybe my next offering will awaken and cheer up the two grumps. So I hurriedly begin as Rosalynde.

"O, my dear Orlando, how it grieves me to see thee wear they heart in a scarf!"

Again I see the stone faces of the two and I am feeling grief and urgency that all is not going well in the Forest of Arden upstairs at New College. This extract should make you feel bright and bring a smile to your face, as she confides to Orlando, for Rosalynde is arranging her own marriage.

"I know into what straits of fortune she is driven; and it is not impossible to me, if it appear not inconvenient to you, to set her before your eyes tomorrow human as she is and without any danger."

The two panelists again seem disinterested. I am frantic. My inner voice questions.

Why is engaging the man and woman proving impossible? What more can I give Rosalynde that will grab their attention? The woman fidgets in her chair and crosses her arms in front of herself. The man is studying the table top. *What is going on?* I ask myself, attempting to remain in the character of Rosalynde

"Therefore, put you in your best array: bid your friends; for if you will be married to-morrow you shall, and to Rosalynde if you will."

The audition is over. I wait before their majesties for questions. There is a long silence.

They don't ask any questions. Don't they want to know about my choices? Sub text? Verse metre? Imagery? Alliterations? There remains an uncomfortable silence. The woman leans back in her chair and uncrosses her arms.

"I say absolutely not," she proclaims.

The man relieves his hand from his forehead, stops contemplating the table top, looks over at the woman.

"I'm inclined to agree with you Diane," he quietly responds.

Rita perks up like a startled ostrich. The woman continues adamantly.

"She's not serious. Yes, she can act. But she's going to use this opportunity to head off into a career in the theatre or film. Have you looked at her application? She's not coming here for the right reasons. She is going to use us as stepping stone to show business. She is not going to be a speech and drama teacher. We would be wasting our time. I am absolutely sure of that."

She looks directly at the man in the blue sweater. He half nods his head in agreement.

I stand frozen, shell shocked. Rita invites the man to speak. "Well Eamon?"

He hesitates and then replies in a quiet voice that has an Irish lilt.

"Yes I'm pretty sure she's talented, but she's not going into education."

My god! What am I hearing? I think to myself. Rita senses the fear and desperation in my eyes. She looks at me squarely and asks,

"Of course you want to be a teacher don't you Rosemary?"

Without hesitation I reply,

"Yes, I think I would embrace teaching what I love."

Rita winks as if to say "Good answer." The woman raps a pencil on the desk, looks me straight in the eye. She swivels in her chair to confront Rita.

"I am not going to be persuaded Rita," she says.

Rita invites Eamon to give his vote.

"I concur. A definite no for me too," he almost whispers.

I can't believe what I am hearing. I begin to pray.

Please God, please God, not Brick Hall, not Winnie-the-Pooh and all his friends.

There is another long pause. I can feel my heart beating. Rita stands up to speak, she looks at the two dissenters,

"Well I say she's in. I'm the head of this college and it is my prerogative. I know Rosemary, I have seen her perform. She is in whether you like it or not."

She came up to me put her arm on my shoulder and escorted me to the door. She called Rosy and instructed her to take me downstairs to meet with Kees the dean for the details. I was in shock. In a few seconds my life had changed.

I turned over in my mind what had just happened and Rita's intervention, her veto was an act of contrition. I would be in Saint Rita's debt forever.

I was still shaken and numb when I was introduced to Kees the principal. He shook my hand congratulating me. He led me into his tiny office adjacent to the staff room. He was a gentle bear of a man with an unfathomable accent that contained a hint of North America. I sat in front of his desk which contained a small mountain of paperwork.

His voice had a hushed quality so I leaned forward to hear what he was saying. He informed me my place was conditional. I would have to pass the necessary exams in order to be admitted. Then quite out of the blue he said decisively,

"We don't allow married students at New College. You won't get married?"

His statement struck me as extremely personal and odd. I had no idea where he might have deduced that I was the marrying kind. I simply replied,

"I don't have any intention of getting married."

"Good," he answered. Then he paused, "Of course it goes without saying you will not accept any theatre, television or film work when you are here."

"Of course," I respond.

He stood up shook my hand again.

"Then we look forward to seeing you in September."

From: Martin
To: Rose-Mary
Subject: Audition
Date: November 29th, 2011 3:37 pm
Hi Rose-Mary:

Lovely piece.......you are talented. What a lot of hypocritical tosh at your audition....the whole bloody place was geared up to theatre careers and teaching was an unfortunate by-product.

Love
Martin

Rosemary: Interim.

My joy at my deliverance from Brick Hall Teachers College was only overshadowed by the imminent tempest that I predicted I would encounter with my mother. Surprisingly when I told her of my acceptance to New College she congratulated me and announced,

"See you can do anything if you set your mind to it."

This mantra of hers I find perplexing. After all the consternation my application to drama school had stirred in our lives. Her statement was followed with,

"However I will not give you a penny of my money. You will have to live off your grant and work in the holidays."

I expected no less and was thankful that the cyclone had been diverted. She released me from Coventry. The battle between mother and daughter had found a truce.

Thus I was able to devote the time needed to study in order to pass the exams that would guarantee my admittance to New College.

In February I was elected Rag Queen of all the colleges in Watford, an unexpected honor. At the crowning ceremony I was informed that a press photographer from the London Times had requested to take pictures of me sitting in a vintage Morgan car. After the coronation I was ushered to the entrance of Watford Technical College where I posed on the front seat of the vehicle, with my head thrown back. I was attempting to imitate, the world famous model, Jean Shrimpton. Suddenly the driver of the car started the engine and began to pull away. He looked up at me and in an exaggerated commanding voice sharply instructed me to,

"Sit down!"

I slid along the back of the seat as he sped off into the darkness. I glanced behind and in front, I noticed that the Morgan was sandwiched between two non-descript vehicles filled with young men wearing dark glasses. The driver accelerated as we sped down a country lane finally pulling into ominous woodland. All three cars came to an abrupt stop and a dozen furtive young men wearing sunglasses sprinted over to the Morgan. I was overcome by fear. I placed my hands over my face, crying. I faintly muttered,

"Please don't hurt me."

One of the young men took my hands in his hand, removed his dark glasses and looked kindly into my eyes, he spoke gently,

"Do not be afraid we are not going to harm you. We have kidnapped you. We are holding you for ransom. We are all from Hatfield College. We are Watford Technical College's rival. We must hurry. We need to change cars, you have to come with us until Watford pays the ransom. And we have sent a couple of blokes to your house in Bushey Heath to inform your parents."

"Oh you haven't," I whisper.

"We thought your parents would be worried about you."

"Thank you," is all I can meekly utter.

Knowing full well that my parents' nocturnal custom was to be oblivious to the world after ten in the evening. I only hoped that they were snug in their snoring somniferous sonatas or to be more precise unconscious and undisturbed. I was still rattled from the fright of the kidnapping as I was escorted to another vehicle and driven to a secret location. On the way I was informed that I would be photographed with another kidnapped victim whose name was Hercules.

Hercules was a notorious white mouse that had made newspaper headlines when he was fed to a snake for supper and the following morning the snake was discovered resting eternally as Hercules triumphant stood or should I say scurried around his victim.

Once the Hatfield students explained their good intentions the caper sounded a bit of a lark and I forgave all my kidnappers for making my hair stand on end.

The Watford College Rag Committee was even more shaken than I was, for they had not yet received the ransom note. All they knew was that their Rag Queen had been driven off into the night. They made the sensible decision and called the police. The local police were concerned and they called MI5. Soon all the air waves on the radio were flooded with information and strategies for assisting the police with their enquiries in locating Rosemary Harrington, the Watford Rag Queen who had been abducted.

In Bushey Heath two nervous male students from Hatfied College hovered on the doorstep. They rang the doorbell to my house. No-one answered so they rang a second time and paused before they rang a third. Lights went on upstairs, the door was unlatched from the inside and my mother flung it open. She was standing naked in her see-through nylon nightie. She angrily demanded,

"What?"

Both young men were taken aback with what was before them. One, a Welshman began to stutter nervously,

"We're hhhhhhhhhhhhhhhhhhhhhhhhhhhhhhhhhh here.

To which my mother infuriated asked,

"You are here?"

The Welshman was losing his gumption as he tried to avert his eyes from the Botticelli before him.

"I'm........hhhhhhhhhh Here bbbbbbbbbbbbbbbbb because."

"Spit it out man for God's sake," she insisted.

The Welshman sucked in his breath,

"Bbbbbbbbbbb because we've kkkkkkkkkkkkkkkkkkkkkkkkkkk kkkkkkk your daughter."

"Kissed my daughter?" my mother asked incredulously.

The Welshman started to shake his head. Sucking in another breath.

"No, we've kkkkkkkkkkkidnapped your daughter," he concluded.

He was ready to keel over for lack of oxygen. With that my mother bellowed,

"Rubbish!"

She ferociously flung the door shut.

The two young men stood on the other side with frail and frightened faces. They retreated down the steps, through the front gate to hang out by the lamp post where they would soon after be picked up and interrogated by the police.

At the Hatfield College costume ball a few weeks later where I was an honored guest I overheard the same Welshman snickering and retelling that evenings exploits without a trace of a stutter. I can always rely on my mother to upstage an event.

I was introduced to Hercules the mouse and we both acquiesced to having our photograph taken together, both of us smiling. All the chaps drove me home in a convoy around 5 am after the ransom had been paid and MI5 together with the local police had been satisfied that the kidnapping had been no more than a college prank.

The following day the headlines in the national and local newspapers read "Beauty and the Beast" along with the photograph was the story of the double kidnapping. However there was a controversy over Hercules. Accusations were made that he was a fake, a double for the real Hercules who had passed away. This debate led to a telephone call from the reporter Pearce Sullivan who with all his charm tried to persuade me to give him the exclusive scoop on the authenticity of the mouse.

Pearce could sell sand in the desert, he is that charismatic. I'm not going to incriminate myself by divulging my decision. Though I should mention Pearce ran a front page story in the Evening Post denouncing the authenticity of the Hercules that I had encountered.

Pearce also insisted I pose for more photos in the local park which were featured in his exclusive.

9 Rose-Mary 1967 Rag Queen publicity shot.

Being elected Rag Queen was an ego booster. I visited retirement homes and at one was kissed by a centenarian wearing a cap, and tweed jacket with leather elbows. I was featured in the parade during Rag Week through the streets of Watford. The crowds waved as I sat atop my throne on a float. At the intersection of Woolworths and the Post Office in the High Street the throng of people was large and loud, they were cheering.

Out of the corner of my eye in the back row I spotted a woman waving, smiling, tears running down her face. She was my mother.

10 Watford Rag Queen 1967

In August via mail arrived a three page list of books I must purchase before the term began at New College of Speech and Drama. The recommendation for acquisition of these academic texts is Dillon's bookstore adjacent to University College London. I wander into the many chambered cavernous space clasping my three page shopping list looking aimless. A young man springs upon me. He resembles D'Artagnan of the Three Musketeers, a swashbuckler without the plumed hat. He sports long, lush brown hair parted to one side, a moustache and goatee beard that emphasizes his heart shaped face.

He is charming, confident, older.

"Can I be of assistance?" he asks.

He is smiling from ear to ear. I show him the list and he lets out a knowing,

"Ah!"

He helps me find my wares as we scurry along walls of books. He guides me from behind, whispering like a lover the directions to the whereabouts of the publications I seek. I am uncomfortable because I feel he is checking me out from the rear. What a shame that he can be both helpful and roguish, simultaneously. After handing him a large sum of money at the cash register he paws my hand a little too long with the change and a wanting smile. I thank this cavalier and lug my bulging booty homeward on the Bakerloo line.

From: Martin
To: Rose-Mary
Subject: Audition
DATE: December 10th, 2011 9:42 am
Hi Rose-Mary
Hope all is well. Have attached first draft of Audition-what do you think? Is it along the right lines? Am I sounding like a nineteen-year-old? Am grateful for any advice.

Trust things are going well with work and family.
All the very best
Look forward to hearing from you
Love
Martin x

Martin: The Audition.

For my forthcoming audition the New College of Speech and Drama has asked for the performance of a contrasting speech from Shakespeare and a modern play as well as the delivery of a poem to be followed by an improvisation set by them and then the final interview. I think my choices are pretty good and I have enjoyed the task of learning and rehearsing my favoured pieces.

The Shakespeare extract I've chosen is poor old Clarence's speech from "Richard III". I first studied this in a Spoken English class at school when Miss Burns made us read it one afternoon when I was fifteen. It had a great impact on me and the underwater imagery is just so vivid. I really like the fear apparent in the character's voice as he endures the premonition of his murder. I don't know that much Shakespeare but enjoyed reading Richard III and remember seeing Laurence Oliver's film at the cinema when I was a kid...and HE really frightened me! I think I should also be able to answer questions on the historical background.

And, as a distinct contrast, I feel that Mitchem's tough speech from "The Long and The Short and The Tall" by Willis Hall really does fit the bill...it's anti-war and brutal in its description of what can happen to soldiers in combat...I think I can act this one quite well and it certainly contrasts favourably with the aristocratic and tortured Clarence. I just love the Roger McGough poem, "Let Me Die a Young Man's Death" and I researched the Mersey Poets at Avery Hill College when we included them in a cabaret show. I also like Brian Patten and could have chosen several of his poems as well.

I decide on my "dramatic" look for this audition and so have gone for black jeans and "Beatle" boots, white shirt and black waistcoat. I wear this beneath my shorty black overcoat which is always worn with the collar up!! My hair as always is on the long side and I think I look a pretty damn good drama school student. I hope the New College staff at the audition agree with me.

So I have been sitting on the tube rehearsing my speeches as the underground carriage rattles me towards Golders Green. I don't know this part of London at all. Camden Town, Chalk Farm, Belsize Park, Hampstead…just unknown places on London's Northern line…and now here the train enters Golders Green Station. This is my stop for New College. Well that's it, up and off to face the audition and interview… Christ knows what I'll do if I fail this bloody audition. I'll have to find a job with London Transport and work on the buses with dad.

There's a bus terminus here with a huge BBC TV theatre next door and perhaps this drama school can get free tickets for the shows. I turn left outside the station and slowly walk up the hill following North End Road. It appears to be an expensive residential area and a long way from my social background in the decrepit old East End. I notice several North Vietnamese flags in the windows so it must be a fairly radical political area as well and this might mean an active and militant Students' Union in the College. It could well be that the New College of Speech and Drama is as exciting and political as so many of the colleges and universities in the country at the moment.

I hike up the hill and I arrive at this massive gabled house which is New College.

11 Back of Ivy House

It dominates the road and I see that the front entrance is through the car park. I notice a few purple and pink clad "intense" looking students strolling about but for now I have to locate the administrative office. I saunter through the front door only to be directly confronted by a huge staircase resembling the set of a Gothic Horror Film. A hand-painted sign to the college office is pointing up these stairs and so I climb the newly polished treads to discover the office and the resident Registrar, a pleasant middle-aged, well-dressed woman called Eileen Carfax. She welcomes me into the office and I formally announce my arrival at the New College of Speech and Drama....Martin Banks ready for a 2pm audition and interview.

She shows me to a chair outside of a large rehearsal room and tells me that I will shortly be called by the duty staff. After five minutes the door opens and a tall, middle-aged man with a strong central European accent invites me in. He tells me he is Kees Sjoberg, the College Principal, and he then introduces two women sitting behind a large table as Rita Scott and Peggy Lewis. They are both senior members of the staff and, alongside the Principal, they will audition me. I greet them all with a handshake and we exchange pleasantries. I am certainly nervous but confident I can impress them enough to offer me a place. After all they are looking for the potential in candidates and for those that will benefit from three years training at the College. I'm sure I can meet their requirements. Kees sits between the women and the one called Rita is smiling broadly whilst the other one, Peggy, is certainly more stern faced. Am I to get the good cop and bad cop routine? They ask me to begin the audition with the speech that I have chosen from the Shakespeare plays. I reach into my bag and hand them each a copy of the speech. I announce that the extract is from "Richard III, Act 1, Scene 4". I set the scene by telling them that I am playing George, the Duke of Clarence, who has been falsely imprisoned by his brother, Richard, the Duke of Gloucester. Clarence is telling a guard of a nightmare he has just had about drowning and this is to be a premonition of his own death when he is shortly to be stabbed and then drowned in a vat of wine by assassins following Richard's orders. I arrange the two chairs for Clarence's bed and sit down on them and prepare myself for the speech:

"Lord, Lord, methought, what pain it was to drown!

What dreadful noise of waters in mine ears!

What ugly sights of death within mine eyes!"

I rise from the bed acting the horror of Clarence's vision and I am aware of my audience following every move that I make:

"Methought I saw a thousand fearful wrecks;

Ten thousand men that fishes gnawed upon;
Wedges of gold, great anchors, heaps of pearl,
Inestimable stones, unvalued jewels,
All scattered in the bottom of the sea."

I'm really doing well, the words flow and I'm successfully conveying the character of poor Clarence as he retells his nightmare. I imagine I'm performing on stage at Stratford East portraying Clarence as part of Joan Littlewood's Shakespeare season. I turn to directly address my critical audience of three:

"Some lay in dead men's skulls; and, in those holes Where eyes did once inhabit, there were crept, As 'twere in scorn of eyes, reflecting gems…"

I power through the speech and let them feel every word, get close to them, stare at them, I become the poor miserable, cowardly wretch that Clarence is, I let them enter his very soul:

"Which wooed the slimy bottom of the deep,
And mocked the dead bones that lay scattered by."

I feel everything is in order. I pause at the end of the speech. I stare at them. I let them feel the horror of his nightmare and the dreadful vision that is Clarence's premonition of his own death. It all seems pretty powerful to me, and so I keep the character in motion at the end of the speech and then pull away signifying the extract is finished. Well I think that seems to have struck home and the critical trio are busy writing notes on the papers in front of them. Rita Scott looks at me, smiles and then asks why I chose that speech for the audition. I tell her that "Richard III" is one of my favourite Shakespearian plays and I think this speech conveys the dream imagery and the sense of the supernatural that permeates the play. I mention the concept of hubris that affects the major characters and notice Peggy raises a smile at this point in the interview. So I have come this far and all seems well. I waffle on about having studied medieval history in the sixth form at school and being, therefore, interested in how Shakespeare rewrites the country's recent civil war history for his Tudor political masters. I outline the debate of Richard the demon as opposed the Richard the decent monarch albeit history still seems to blame him for the death of the princes in the Tower. This all seems to satisfy them and I finish by talking about the sea imagery reflecting the great age of Elizabethan exploration and Shakespeare's interest in all things nautical. I feel pleased with my progress so far.

Kees now asks me to move onto my second contrasting speech. I tell them it is Sgt. Mitchem's speech from Act 2 of Willis Hall's "The Long and the Short and the Tall". This is a contemporary, tough and brutal play concerning the morality of war set in Malaya just before the Fall of Singapore in 1942. Mitchem's speech is a harrowing insight into how extreme nationalism can make soldiers believe themselves to be "heroes" before they usually meet a gruesome and unheroic death. Mitchem is a tough soldier and speaks as he finds things in a raw and violent world. I have slightly edited the speech and begin immediately. I aim to hit them hard with it, I won't pull any punches, I will convey the cynicism and toughness, and the actor cannot hide with this speech. I tear into the rough soldier's diatribe about the local women loving to see their men in uniform and how the men are so stupid to fall for this hollow glory and how all roads will lead to the finality of the battlefield. It's going well, I've certainly got into this character and his words are literally being spat out as he describes his brutal world view to his fellow soldier. The images are strong and vivid and I'm accurately conveying them to my audience. I'm coarse, I'm brutal; I cynically describe the soldier's small taste of glory before his lonely and pitiful death on the battlefield. I sneer through this next section as the character's tough cynicism shakes the text to the core. It really is going well, I begin to reel them in, and let them enjoy the earthy humour and then: POW! I allow it to explode like a hand grenade right in their faces and the young soldier is just a disintegrating pile of blood and guts that the wind blows across on a lonely, foreign hillside. I physically quake as the character howls his god forsaken truth to those that will hear. I glare at my audience: my character is a burning statue of anger and fury. Mitchem is not a thinker but he simply states the brutal facts of war as he sees them. That's it; keep this strong physical stance as an image on which I will finish the speech. Silence...a long silence. They just look at me and I wonder who is going to speak first. Peggy looks over her glasses at me and then proceeds, very slowly, to ask me what other modern writers I like. This is a green light for the Stratford East material and I reel off the following: Brecht; Behan; Pinter; Naughton; Bond; Beckett; Osborne and Wesker. I tell them I'm also very impressed with Chilton and Littlewood's "Oh What a Lovely War". Rita then asks me do I like any other musicals? This is certainly a shot across my bows and I struggle...again E.15 to my rescue as I mention Lionel Bart's "Fings Ain't What They Used to Be" and "Oliver". I also like the older London musical, Noel Gay's "Me and My Girl", which made the Lambeth Walk Dance famous before the Second World War. I don't know the musical but I bluff as I have read from the notes to the sheet music my mother possesses for the Lambeth Walk. As a child I had witnessed many family parties where the Lambeth Walk was danced and so I have an attachment, if not an affection, for it. This satisfies them and they return to their copious note taking. I wonder whether I am worth so much written comment.

Rita then asks me for the poem I have prepared. I tell them it is Roger McGough's "Let Me Die a Youngman's Death". I hand them the copy and get ready to start. I really like this poem as it is a poem about now, the1960s, and it is full of grace, irreverence and humour…So here I go and I fire away on all theatrical cylinders. I include lots of movement, I apply plenty of pace in the poem and I move around the room showing them I'm not afraid to experiment with the physical delivery of a modern poem. I jauntily move towards them offering my various terms for a suitable death to compensate for my somewhat raffish life as an irreverent child of the revolution. I'm thoroughly enjoying the delivery and revel in the poetry of my time. It seems to be going exceptionally well and they're all clearly listening and there's even a smile from Rita. I feel everything has worked, I have remembered the words, I have provided decent variation of pace, and I have included physical movement and vocal emphasis in the right places. My audience still seems to be attentive and I feel so full of confidence that I'll finish with a bit of a flourish and show them how to finish a modern poem in a truly theatrical manner. I quite simply speak the final line and then launch into a cartwheel across the floor until I arrive at the door as if I'm off to continue hawking my poetry through the streets of swinging London.

I finish with a broad grin and I am totally satisfied with the presentation. They're all smiling, even Peggy Lewis who is still writing something in her notebook. I feel ready for whatever they might ask. Kees enquires how I came to find the poem and I tell him about the cabaret show I devised at my previous college and how I used McGough and the other Mersey poets. Peggy asks why I didn't speak the poem in a Liverpool accent and I reply that I feel the work is Modern British in its concept and not just a regional piece.(Not a brilliant answer but I think it'll get me off the regional accent hook.) I ramble on that the poems go well with contemporary music in a cabaret-style programme. This seems to satisfy them.

Now for the improvisation and Rita smiles that welcoming smile again and asks me to present an improvisation on the subject of: "Sales". I have no time to prepare but I launch straight into the improvisation. I stand solidly in front of them and commence:

"Well ladies and gentleman, here in this Department Store you have a most rare purchasing opportunity. You are able to buy a precious drama student (I move between the roles of the seller and the student). He looks the part (statue) can move freely (march and then skip across room) can sing (first verse of 'Only the Lonely') recite Shakespeare (opening lines of speech) become inanimate (tuning in as a television set). He comes cheap at the price and is most capable of developing into a valued addition to the college and the exciting world of drama and education."

They grin broadly at this and I feel the piece has worked.

Then I sit in front of them and they ask me questions about my application. Why had I wanted to leave Avery Hill? What were my experiences as a primary teaching assistant? Could I speak about my theatre experience and my career ambitions? How might the New College of Speech and Drama assist me with my career goals? I speak fluently and keep to the subject. I stress my career aim of becoming a drama teacher.

I say that I am aware of the amount of written work that I have to catch up with and I have already timetabled the first six weekends of the term for this work if I am able to join the course.

Then they all look at each other and nod in agreement and Kees tells me they are willing to offer me a place starting in January. They feel my teaching and drama experience and previous college study will only benefit my future education at New College. I rise, shake their hands and thank them for the place and then Rita and Peggy leave and Kees takes me to the office where the clerical staff complete administrative details. Kees suggests when they have finished that I take a stroll around the campus to see what might be happening.

This I do and I wander down into the large gardens as a winter dusk is falling. There are several students about and I can see a couple of lectures taking place in the prefabricated classrooms. Kees has identified the theatre and suggests I look in. I make my way there and quietly slip into the back of the stalls and I watch what seems to be a rehearsal of a pantomime. It's fairly chaotic with plenty of shouting and movement but they do seem to be enjoying themselves and, of course, there are plenty of pretty girls. I quietly leave and make my way down the hill to the station.

There is a tube train waiting and I begin my journey back across London. My thoughts are all concerned with my future as a student at the New College of Speech and Drama. The New Year will not come soon enough.

From: Rose-Mary
To: Martin
Subject: Audition
Date: December 12th, 2011 1:27 pm
Hello Martin:

I am impressed. I believe this format will work. I like the fact that our styles are so different. You are the yin to my yang.

Love,

Rose-Mary

Rosemary: First Day.

Entering the courtyard of Ivy House on a cool September morning. I espy a girl with a mane of red curly hair and a dinner plate sized hole in her hand knitted brown jumper who is sitting looking bored on a low wall that fronted the refectory.

"Where should I go?" I enquired.

She points to the theatre and teasingly laughs.

"Hurry up or you'll be late."

I am thirty minutes early but already there are forty first-year students sitting apprehensively in the auditorium.

The assembly starts right on time. Kees introduces each member of staff individually, they enter from the wings as if taking an encore after a play, they bow, wave, smile, or just take their seats on stage. The cast of characters is colourful and confusing. But I remember that the pixie haircut woman is Diane Winter, Professor of Literature and an Oxford Scholar. Eamon is Irish, his surname is O'Braden and he is a

12 Phoenix Theatre.

Professor of Psychology. He still holds his glance downwards and stares uncomfortably at something on the floor. The last staff member to waltz on stage is Beatrice Franky, the costume instructor along with her dog Feste who is given a formal introduction to the amusement of all. Kees comes to the lectern and begins with a rousing speech that turns into a political rally as he refers to the Pope as the largest arms dealer in the world. I think to myself that they never mentioned that in Catechism classes. Kees reminds us that we were selected from thousands of applicants and that if we the chosen few do not meet the requisite academic standards and artistic criteria we will be shown the door. There is a hush in the auditorium, as we collectively realize that our tenure is tenuous. We are expendable. The pressure is on.

"It is not who you are at eighteen, it is what you become afterwards that matters."

Kees concludes and steps away from the stand.

To end the proceedings there is a question period. In the front row sit two strikingly attractive girls. They trip over themselves plying the staff with queries. One girl has long strawberry blond hair, she is confident and intense. Every time she raises her hand she flicks her hair back. She speaks with a Liverpool accent as does her brunette haired companion. They seem in competition with one another, to see who can ask the most innocuous questions and be the centre of attention.

"What time is lunch?" The blond beauty asks.

Her eager accomplice raises her hand and inquires,

"How much homework are we to expect?"

Not to be outdone her Liverpool colleague follows up with,

"What electives do we have?"

More than once they are answered by the same spokesman on stage. The man is familiar to me but I can't place him, he sports facial hair, along with a cascading side parted brown mane, and wears a cheeky smile. Then I recall that he is the very same cavalier salesman who had assisted me at Dillon's bookstore. His voice is as smooth as silk and he seems to be chatting up the two lovelies in the front row. His name is Frank Leer and his specialty is English Literature but I have a sense his real interest is nubile young women. I will keep well away from this charming wolf. The two in the front row are obviously friends and a force to be reckoned with. The rest of us sit, stupefied by their boldness.

Next we are instructed to assemble in groups at specific locations within Ivy House. I wait anxiously to hear my name. I am directed to the refectory, along with fifteen other newbie's. One of whom is Sadie who does not acknowledge me and averts her eyes at my every attempt to engage her. I guess she is well and truly peeved and fed up with me interloping on her territory. I don't really blame her but I want to offer an olive branch, but she refuses to look at me. To add to the mix of those gathered amongst the tables and chairs in the refectory are the two self-assured, cocky and as Americans say "cool" girls from Liverpool.

Rosy my audition tour guide still sporting her mustard coloured boots strides through the porthole doors, gives us a briefing and schedules. Our day will begin promptly at 9am and end at 6pm there is a half hour allotted for lunch. She informs us that when we are in production we will be rehearsing to 9pm or 10pm. Rosy hands out supply lists, book lists and locker numbers. Rosy is wrapping up the session when Kees bursts through the porthole door. He looks worried, he addresses us in his distinguished Canadian German accent,

"I need your help. I am supposed to give a pep talk before you leave for the day, but Feste, Beatrice Franky's dog has gone missing. I suggest we all adjourn to Hampstead Heath and form a search party so we can find Feste. Beatrice is beside herself. By the way the designation for your group is C. Group C follow me."

And so we did, leaving our schedules, and lists on the tables.

We march to Hampstead Heath a distance of about two hundred yards. We form a search party cordon, walking through the bracken and trees calling out to Twelfth Night's clown "Feste." A tall skinny student with short brown hair named Clive begins reciting Malvolio's lines from the play.

"Not yet old enough for a man nor young enough for a boy; as a squash is before 'tis a peascod, or a codling when tis almost apple."

In between we the newly named Group C give a loud communal shout out "Feste." The two audacious girls from Liverpool, Kay and Lynn pick daisies and make chains as they feign looking for the missing canine. Kay places one atop Clive's head as he recites,

"Nothing that can be can come between me and the full prospects of my hopes." Clive is staring intently into Kay's eyes, it is obvious he is smitten. The group refrain of "Feste" weakens as we are out on the hunt for two hours or more. Kees calls us together in the middle of a grove of trees. He genuinely thanks us for our assistance. He assures us that he is confident that the missing Feste will turn up. We are dismissed for the day to return the next to start in earnest. I am very reserved and held back taking in the nonsense and enjoying every minute. We saunter back to Ivy House unable to resist the group urge to call "Feste" as we pass the Fox and Hounds and the Old Bull and Butcher Pubs which are situated across the street from New College. We collect our belongings in the refectory. I am headed home when a short, rotund girl with long dark, cascading wavy hair announces,

"I'm off to the pub. Anyone care to fucking join me? By the way I'm Michelle, my friends call me Micki." With that she marches out of the hall through the humongous oak door as all of us follow like the children of Hamlin.

We enter the Old Bull and Butcher only to find that the occupants are fellow New College Students. Micki orders a beer and raises her glass,

"Here's to fucking Feste!"
To which Clive quips,
"I hope not."
We all laugh.

Rosemary: First Week.

I begin to familiarize myself with the schedule, staff and campus. Voice class is first in the morning. We sing scales, resonate and attempt to control the diaphragm.

Group C stands like soldiers in front of the grand piano as the formidable Peggy Lewis plays scales. She wears a cabbage rose print dress, her dark page boy hair that flips up at the ends. She is a matronly aristocrat with a commanding voice. When she plays a note she expects you to reproduce that note precisely and immediately. She is relentless in seeking perfection from our collective "vocal apparatus." She doesn't smile or laugh but amazes us when she rotates her elbows, she is double jointed and if you defer in replicating the note she has played, she flips up her arms and her elbows disengage.

This causes quite a stir the first time she manipulates her joints. As Kate Barnes later commented,

"Her elbows are freaky."

This coming from a girl that never utters unkind words. Kate is a petite blond, with high cheek bones and pouty lips. She is the natural leader of Group C. She reminds me of Portia "fair and.....of wondrous virtue." As I am shy by nature Kate invites me to sit with her at lunch and encourages me to converse.

The morning continues with Elizabeth Lee a silver haired, slight woman who speaks softly. She seems unflappable, even when the Liverpool birds Kay and Lynn attempt to draw all the attention. Elizabeth steers the class to theatrical representation. She encourages debate and interaction. In our first encounter she takes Kate's handbag and empties the contents and tasks each of us to describe the lifestyle of the person who owns the lipstick, the Tampax, the diary, chewing gum, address book and condoms.

We explain how we came to these conclusions. Our assignment is to bring in an image of two people who represent the 1960's. Elizabeth informs us that during the first term we will deduce why the Greeks wore himations, the colour codes of the Roman togas and the significance of codpieces to the Elizabethans. With the mention of codpiece Clive our lanky, resident Renaissance man quotes from Much Ado About Nothing,

"Cupid is called king of codpieces."

Then covering his groin with hands crossed in front of him he feigns pain and announces,

"Don't stab my vitals."

To which we all laugh including Elizabeth. She seems the only human amongst our professors.

Rita Scott is our phonology instructor. Rita insists,

"Phonology, darlings is based on the sciences, anatomy and physiology, physics and phonetics."

We are supposed to distinguish sounds by a linguistic shorthand, this is very complex and I am flailing in my dictation. When we are not practicing rib reserve breathing we are exercising the labio-dental sounds by endlessly repeating to our reflections in the mirrors of the voice studio.

"Forty fast and furious furies flew the fortified frontier while the first fort was defended by fifty ferocious faithful Kaffirs."

I am schooled in producing a series of oral ingressive clicks so that if I ever encounter a member of a certain South African tribe I will be able to converse. Rita is also our teaching mentor. She informs us that we will prepare and present a group lesson in her studio to a class of junior school children. This is to prepare us for our teaching practice which happens in the spring semester. Rita solicits ideas for a lesson plan subject and we all agree our topic is to be animals, which have universal appeal to children.

Music is taught by a jolly, equine faced fellow with spiraling hair that sprouts all over his head to the nape of his neck. His name is Paul Cavel. He is positive, upbeat and funny. I am terrified of music as my history of rhythmic incompetence is a family joke. Consequently during the first lesson with simple percussion instruments I become unhinged. Paul requests that I stay behind after the class is dismissed. He questions why I am so intimidated by a tambourine. I tell him that I have an affliction of not being able to keep time with the music. Paul's response is to laugh and put his arm around my shoulder.

"I have never met anyone who couldn't keep the beat. I don't believe it. But if you are so distraught over a silly tambourine you don't have to come to class."

"I don't?" I question with disbelief.

"But if you do decide to give it another shot, I think you will be surprised at how easy keeping the beat is. I leave the decision up to you."

Right there and then I knew I would go back and conquer my fear.

One of our academic tutors is Frank Leer whose name is appropriate for he looks at any female form lasciviously. I think he would make a pass at any attractive woman He is only a few years older than his charges and is aware of his charm and suavity which he uses on the two Liverpool girls. There is Kay with her strikingly handsome face, sprinkled with freckles and her long lustrous sun kissed blond hair. Lynn her cohort, with short cropped dark hair, small upturned nose, their Liverpudlian accents as smooth as melted toffee. Together they highjack Frank Leer's history of drama seminars by overtly flirting with him. Their behavior is disconcerting as in a few short weeks before the Christmas break we will be challenged with written examinations. Time is of the essence. We have not yet begun to explore or discuss the history of drama. None of us can afford to receive a low academic grade which could result in dismissal. I am beginning to resent Kay and Lynn for their time wasting antics. Especially since I am acutely aware that I am scholastically below standard with regard to my peers. I need all the help I can get.

For poetry we have Palash Singh an Indian mystic. He is disinterested in the antics of Kay and Lynn and refuses to give them the attention they crave. Palash reads poems as if he has composed them. The lilt of his voice when he reads Donne, Shelly or Keats is mesmerizing and helps with the deconstruction and understanding of the verse. Palash is in contrast to John Smithfield, a tall solid ordinary man with glasses, side parted hair plastered to his overly large head by Brylcream. John's intent is to hone our English skills but his teaching is hampered by his monotonous, nasal monotone voice.

Psychology is the subject offered by Eamon O' Braden. He speaks so softly and fails to make eye contact with his students, still preferring to address the floor, the wall, and the window with lectures on Gestalt, Freud and Jung.

Kees is the education lecturer, the class is conducted in the costume shop in the basement. We sit on hampers, surrounded by breastplates, plumed hats, crinolines and bustles. Kees talks endlessly about the aims of education and theories of practitioners but deep in the womb of the dimly lit wardrobe, Group C collectively begins to nod off.

First year lectures are held upstairs with Groups A, B, C, D present. Diane Winter is the senior professor for Drama and Literature. She is reputedly a powerhouse of knowledge; a force to be reckoned with. She stands stiffly at the lectern. She demands punctuality, she is precise and punctilious. Diane Winter is the only senior lecturer who painstakingly takes attendance. There are sixty of us packed into the room. God help you if she pauses after calling your name, as she did mine on the first day. Looking straight at me Diane Winter demanded,

"Rosemary Harrington I remember you. You are here? Are you any relation to Pooh?"

To which there is a resounding giggle within the confines of the upstairs lecture room.

"Pooh Harrington?" she insists. "She is a second year student here."

"No", I whisper.

But Diane Winter was already calling the next name. She begins with the Greeks. She rattles off the names of Aeschylus,

Sophocles and Euripides as I limp along attempting to spell the Athenian dramatists. I am out of my depth. Her assignment for the week is to compare the Greek playwrights' treatment of the Orestia. I am very intimidated and overwhelmed.

At lunch the robust Micki shouts across the table,

"I hope we are expected to read more than Greeks in comparative literature. I studied the fucking Greeks in the sixth form."

There is a hush throughout the room. She continues.

"I thought we were going to be fucking challenged here at drama school."

There is silence throughout the refectory and all eyes focus towards our table. All eyes are on Micki. Micki stands up, defiant looks at everyone and asks,

"What the fuck are you all looking at?"

Kate tugs at Micki's arm to sit down, which Micki does. Kate scolds her playfully,

"Now Micki is that anyway to introduce yourself?"

Micki laughs. Profanity and swearing are obviously passé at New College. Everyone is so refined.

Afternoons are spent in the theatre with Richard Wilkins who is in charge of stage management. He is good looking with a lean cheerful face and a head of dark unruly hair. Richard is slightly disheveled and wears the same brown corduroy trousers day after day. I learn through gossip that he has six young children, so no wonder his appearance is un-kempt and dark circles under his eyes suggest he is sleep deprived. He demonstrates safety and how to avoid electrocution when threading a red and green wire through a three pronged plug. Simultaneously he trips over a cord or walks into a ladder, or a flat wobbles precariously behind him. He is very patient and shows great enthusiasm for technical theatrics and it is his unintentional accidents and endearing clumsiness that keep us riveted. I now know how to cut styrofoam with a knife that has been heated over a Bunsen burner.

Dance class is in the afternoon and our instructor is the newly hired Tricia Curtis. A china doll of a woman, herself a recent graduate of dance education. She is petite, perfectly proportioned with high cheek bones and blue eyes the size of saucers. She is newlywed but this does not deter Frank Leer from putting her on his radar. He is forever in her company. Tricia is strict and extremely competent in coaxing the more reserved males of Group C, clad in jockstraps and tights to participate eagerly in the stages of Laban movement. Tricia shows us how to massage each other and how to relax by lying on the floor and visualizing.

Dance is followed by acting where we are once again guided by the expertise of Peggy Lewis. We are instructed to improvise inanimate objects. Kate, Danny and Micki are the first to strut their stuff. Danny is tall with brown hair he sports long sideburns that are his only show of rebellion. He speaks with a soothing soft voice which is a noticeable foil to Micki's deep lower register and Kate's sweet intonation. The three are marvelous as a disgruntled cup, saucer and teapot. They are able to play off one another and are totally in synch. I am amazed at how they accommodate each other and their spontaneity and unselfishness in their ad-libbing. I am in an improvisation cluster that is not nearly as accomplished, we are seeds that germinate into flowers, we are dull and lackluster. Next week we are to bring in a memorized Shakespearean extract, which will be critiqued.

In between classes and lectures I've been on the periphery of the socialization of Group C. I lunch with Kate, Micki and Fran, a jolly hockey sticks girl, who sports blond curly hair. She is very self-reliant and gives the impression that she is able to tackle any situation. I don't interact much as they are such strong, interesting, independent personalities. I listen a great deal which is fine by me.

Sadie is still ignoring me with a vengeance. She sometimes drops by the lunch table with her room-mate. Sadie lives in a bed-sit locally in Golders Green with a boisterous, heavy weight of a girl named Judy. This Judy calls everything "darling". She and Sadie gush about their "darling digs, their darling landlord, and how they intend to be darling flat mates for the next three years." Thankfully "Darling Judy" is assigned to Group B which according to her has an abundance of "the most darling, talented fabulous people."

At home the white flag is hoisted high when my mother notices the text books that blanket my bed and floor. Out of the blue she offers the dining room as a more appropriate place to study. She genuinely enquires about the college, curriculum and the staff. I confide to her about my concerns regarding Diane Winter and how I feel she despises me. My mother listens and declares,

"You are going to have to win her over."

"But how?"

"You are going to have to study like you never have before. You are going to have to write the best essays, you are going to have to make her a believer and more importantly you are going to make her your ally."

"What?" I reply.

"Work diligently, show her that you are serious." Then there was a long pause before my mother resumed, "You have shown me. Now you will show Diane whatever her name is."

I agree but in my heart I am an agnostic. Diane Winter is hell bent in my mind on never giving me any acknowledgment except her icy glare as she takes attendance.

Because of my mother's over-night conversion I decide to perform the fairies speech from a Midsummer's Night Dream for the demanding Peggy Lewis's next acting class. This extract beginning "Thorough bush, thorough briar." had been performed by my mother in a production at RADA. However on a whim I decide to give the speech a comic twist by delivering the text in a Cockney accent. I am very confident in my choice and can't wait to perform before my peers and Peggy. I am last to be called up for the soliloquy in acting class. Everyone else has been passionate and intense. I act the fairy with great East End gusto. Group C is in fits of laughter at the cheek and bravado of the up until then "shy girl" in the class. Peggy however stands arms crossed in front of her bosom, stone faced. She is not laughing, she is not smiling. She is frowning. She is fuming. When I am finished her critique is simple and direct,

"I am sending you to Rita to improve that terrible sibilant "s."

Peggy is not amused unlike my comrades who congratulate me on my nerve before the almighty Peggy. I know I will now pay for my folly. The week has come to a close.

I am a little worse for wear. I am estranged from Diane and I have aggravated Peggy. I have my work cut out for me.

Rosemary: Doctor Barnados.

By October I have settled into the routine. I can usually cadge a lift from my father or brother to Edgware train station. My father will pull out two pounds from his back pocket,

"Don't tell your mother."

I am becoming reclusive as I don't get home until after seven in the evening. I grab tea and head into the dining room to study before retiring to my cell. My parents continue to imbibe but are content to leave me alone and concentrate their misplaced anger towards one another in whispered threats before they pass out for the night.

Sadie has been discarded by "darling" Judy. Sadie now accompanies me on my homeward bound journey a couple of nights a week. She has temporarily returned to living with her parents in Bushey. Sadie and I have begun to converse. I think she will grant me an act of contrition as she now insists I call her Sad which she prefers to Sadie.

I have been recruited by Kate and Micki to participate in the volunteer Doctor Barnados Show which is an annual event that takes place in the theatre for orphans and displaced children. The show precedes a Christmas party for the children, the intention is to spread some Christmas cheer to those less fortunate. Kate also enlists Nora a demure but noticeably pretty member of Group C with blue-grey eyes and a perfectly shaped oval face framed by wispy lengths of long honey blonde straight hair. Micki recruits Valerie a technical savvy first-year from Group B who will stage manage for us. Valerie has an honest face, dimpled cheeks and wise brown eyes. But it is her straight, hip length long light brown hair that is her real beauty. She conducts herself with certitude and I admire her prudent confident style. We are to prepare a belly dancing routine to the music of Ravel's Bolero with Micki as the choreographer. We practice an hour every night for three weeks. I amaze myself that I am in time with Kate and Nora as we sway and swivel our hips. I relay the details of our routine to Sad on the train one night on the way home and she signs up to perform a solo act but is yet undecided as to what to do. She keeps telling me,

"I am confident that I will come up with something."

The show takes place on a freezing December Saturday. We are shaking and shivering backstage clad in erotic flimsy billowing pastel pink pants, bare midriffs, skimpy brassieres covered in golden coins and ankle and wrist cuffs adorned with bells.

Nora and I pull our strawberry blond hair high into pony tails. We look like mythical genies without magic lamps. We tinkle our bells wherever we go. Our only modest attire is a yashmak that covers half our faces. The auditorium is filled with children and young teens, all who are anything but shy. As we jingle from the wings centre stage. A single wolf whistle is heard as the music begins, by the final chorus the boys are standing up waving their arms, there is a cacophony of whistles. Finally the belly dance is over but the boys stand up and chant:

"More, more, more."

Sad is to follow and she has not confided to us what she is about to present. We skedaddle to the wings as Sad stands center stage. She is wearing a black leotard, black tights and white elbow length gloves. She is Aphrodite, majestic and composed waiting for her music cue. The hooligans are quieted down and are intrigued by Sad's stillness.

Sad waits for her music cue. The instantly recognizable drum rendition of the Stripper by Sandy Nelson begins. Sad methodically removes one glove at a time and then for two minutes five seconds reenacts a striptease through mime. The audience is going wild.

They have forsaken whistling for hooting and by the end of the music are yelling:

"Take it off." "Take it off."

The crescendo comes and the stage goes to black out. Sad, I and the other dancers sprint out of the door of the green room at the back of the theatre, only to hear the refrain of "Take it off," continuing.

We bolt into Ivy House to change out of costumes to assist with the party that is to follow. I am stopped in the hall by a young woman wearing a conservative navy pencil skirt, navy shoes and a sensible white blouse. She has shoulder length blond hair and a tapered nose. She speaks to me authoritatively,

"Do you know the whereabouts of Kip?"

Kip is a third year student with a voice of velvet. He has curly black hair, unshaven stubble on his chin, he is tall, an Adonis of a man, beloved by all the females of the college. He is the producer of the Dr. Barnado's Show.

"Kip is in the lighting booth," I respond.

Without a thank you she struts off towards the demanding overture coming from the theatre.

"Who was that?" I enquire of our stage manager, Valerie.

"Oh that is Heather Raymond she left last year. She's with the Royal Shakespeare Company now," Valerie responds.

"She is?" I ask.

I am impressed. Valerie shrugs and continues,

"Heather and I were in the National Youth Theatre."

I am star struck. For I have never relinquished my aspirations of being a member of the Royal Shakespeare Company.

"She's in the Royal Shakespeare Company," I repeat.

Valerie seems nonplussed.

"Oh, she is talented but she knows how to play the game, if you know what I mean."

I nod in agreement but I am unsure of what Valerie is implying. So we continue up the stairs two at a time to change in the loo, discarding our costumes before we serve tea sandwiches and cake to our audience of ruffians at the after party.

Rosemary: First Term.

The date for the model lesson draws near. Arrangements are made to import real animals into the curriculum. I am assigned the introduction along with Nora my lithesome, belly dancing partner and Pat a bashful, soft spoken member of Group C. Pat hides behind her long dark locks parted in the middle like lank curtains. Her hair style belies her lack of confidence and hesitation which I find bewildering. Pat is fretful and nervous, not about the song we are to sing but her fear of facing a horde of school children. We are to be accompanied by Danny on the guitar. We will sing a rousing verse of the Peter, Paul and Mary folk song "We're all going to the zoo today." Which in my mind is ironic since we are bringing the zoo to the unsuspecting children who are on loan as test subjects to us novice teachers. Following our sing-a-long, Clive recites The Rum Tum Tugger poem by T.S. Elliot. Subsequently there is a lively discussion with the school children about their pets and there is evidence that some of them are disgruntled because their dad or mum won't let them have a dog or cat. Or as one innocent put it,

"My parents don't want a wee-wee machine."

One apple-cheeked boy asks,

"How do you know if you have a stupid dog?" He does not receive a reply, then beaming offers, "Buries tail, wags bones."

There is communal groan.

Sad and Gerald are up next to divert the children's attention by having them participate in a lively game of animal charades. Sad and Gerald are both accomplished in acting. They captivate their young audience. Sad is an immediate presence on any stage with her height and Gerald tall, muscular with thick blond hair and deep set blue eyes has all the little girls swooning.

It is up to sensible Duncan a stocky fellow with rounded spectacles, tight chestnut curls secured to his skull and a telling Birmingham accent to subdue the school children with a short offering from C.W. Anderson's Favourite Horse Stories. As he is concluding he asks the children to close their eyes and listen.

Micki, Kate and Fran have been given the task of renting a horse and hiding the equine until the right moment. Jolly hockey sticks Fran is courageously perched astride her 18 hands shire. Fran is clad in full riding regalia, jodhpurs, hat, boots and a riding crop. She steers her steed across the staff parking lot towards Rita's studio in the garden. The children have their eyes closed and their ears open listening intently.

Unfortunately no-one in Group C has thought to ask Mrs. Winkie to remove her washing line that now hangs invisibly like a garrote between the studio and Ivy House.

Consequently Fran almost decapitates herself as she rides the horse stately down the garden path. The children not only hear the clip clop of hooves but Fran's agonizing scream as her neck crashes into the strung guillotine. Rita remains calm and collected, rises serenely from her seat instructing the children to open their eyes,

"Darlings, shall we see what this magnificent steed likes to eat?"

She leads the children outside to feed carrots to the horse as Fran dismounts and tries to stop sputtering and spewing.

We return to Rita's voice studio for the piece de resistance. Kay and Lynn the lively, lithe Liverpool lassies lead a discussion about zoos and the children's favourite animals. The monkey is voted number one. This is the expected outcome as Kay and Lynn are joined by Joann, a late member to Group C, a square faced girl with silky dark hair that hangs to one side. Joann is always trying to cover up her voluptuous breasts, which she is acutely embarrassed about, she does this by tugging on her cardigan which draws attention to her self-imposed affliction. The trio have arranged for the visitation of a pint-sized capuchin monkey along with his trainer.

The guests arrive on cue with the capuchin sitting on the keeper's shoulder. The keeper and the primate wear matching red vests. The pink-faced monkey sports a tiny yellow fez on his head. The monkey is named Carl. Joann gives a factual summary of habitat and body distinctions of the capuchin. She points her index finger to the light fur around the monkey's neck. He responds by hissing and attempting to bite off her digit.

Joann is unnerved. She shakily continues imparting information regarding the use of capuchins as street entertainment. This employment gained them the name as the "organ grinder monkey." The keeper commands Carl to perform a somersault, to catch a ball and to play the cymbals. After each trick he gives Carl a black Monukka grape. Carl grabs the fruit greedily, pops it in his mouth, then vehemently spit's the skin and pips at the audience, much to their delight.

Next up is Sandra. She is a small girl with a small square face, short no-nonsense hairdo and black rimmed glasses. She gives the impression of being super intelligent. Sandra consolidates our group lesson plan by asking each child to bring a story or poem about a monkey to school in the next week. She concludes with a heartfelt reading of The Owl and the Pussy Cat by Edward Lear.

The children are chatting and laughing as they leave. A couple of boys are imitating apes swinging their arms low and gibbering as they scamper up the garden path.

We in Group C are relieved that our first "real" lesson is over.

Rosemary: Pantomime
Elizabeth Leigh is the director for our initial venture into theatre performance.

At our first rehearsal she brings in a green leather bound book of Russian Fairy Tales.

Elizabeth informs us that we will be adapting one as a pantomime which will go on tour to schools in London. Before we begin reading the compendium, I am aware that Elizabeth is glancing at me, she is smiling kindly. I am wearing my waist long hair in two braids. Unexpectedly she announces.

"Wait a minute, we will definitely require a princess and I would be remiss if I didn't insist that Rosemary play that part with her luxurious Rapunzel like long hair." She pauses and looks at Gerald. "And of course Gerald will make the perfect prince." Poor Gerald turns red with embarrassment. He is athletic, with sandy hair and Mediterranean blue eyes. I don't think he knows how attractive he is. Elizabeth Leigh continues, "All the other parts will be divided equally. Now we have to unearth a viable outline to turn into a script that will fit our needs. I will require a stage manager?"

Kate raises her hand.

"A props master?"

Micki raises her hand.

"You will all be assigned technical and backstage duties that come with a touring production. Now let's get down to reading."

We select a story Ivanushka the Little Fool which we promptly rename Ivan the Ninny. By the time we have re-arranged the elements of the plot and improvised characters the original story is unrecognizable. Our Ivan the Ninny is as his name suggests - in the beginning is a less than clever prince, who is tormented by his two cruel but comic brothers to be played by Clive and Danny. The simple story line involves Ivan being expelled by his conniving brothers by way of a sea journey where he is to retrieve twenty-five thousand rubles, a pretty princess to marry and a copper ring.

The narrative involves a boat. Micki is in charge of creating a sail that is collapsible and compact enough to be transported. I have to change clothes between scenes and in most schools we are allocated an empty classroom. I am shy and not used to stripping off in front of others; another hang-up from my convent education. I solve the problem by wearing a white lace body suit, which gives me a false sense of security, as I notice Clive always happens to be around when I am hurriedly changing. He is such a letch. Gerald on the other hand is a real gallant and is always looking for something that will act as a screen for me to disrobe behind. Elizabeth Leigh has insisted that Gerald kiss me at the end of the show, which he and I share mutual trepidation about.

The pantomime is well received. The children enjoy the simple story line of Ivan's quest and upon his return to his kingdom his clemency to his two scheming brothers. We have emerged as a traveling company, complete with a hamper of gorgeous, garish costumes, odd buckets for bailing out the boat, fake swords and the six foot sail.

Our final show is scheduled on Monday in the East End of London, in Bethnal Green. However this particular Monday the whole of Great Britain is blanketed by a snowstorm. All transportation is delayed. But as the saying goes "the show must go on."

Sad and I are charged with being stage hands. We arrive at Ivy House an hour late, shivering with cold. Micki and Kate are waiting forlornly in the vestibule, surrounded by the hamper of costumes, buckets, swords and the six foot sail.

Usually we travel as a group, but since the blizzard, Group C students that have already called into New College have been instructed to go straight to the junior school in Bethnal Green and that the curtain has been postponed for four hours. There isn't an alternative. We must hand carry the props, hamper and six foot sail and travel by train. The four of us trudge down North End Road. Micki and Kate with the six foot sail, followed by Sad and I with the hamper. We all have swords protruding from our pockets and belts. The buckets swing in our arms like handbags. Micki is wearing black sequined peep toe shoes and half way down the hill, en route to the train station she stops, takes off her shoes and proclaims,

"Fuck this!"

She is now wading through the icy grey slush in bare feet. The passengers on the platform at Golders Green Station glare at us because it is rush hour we have to squash onto the train, standing with our six foot sail, the hamper, and an assortment of bulging props, much to the annoyance of the commuters headed towards the city.

We arrive at Bethnal Green to be met at the station by Elizabeth Leigh who heartily congratulates the four of us on our stamina in conveying the set, props and costumes. She treats us all to a strong hot cup of tea at a workman's café tucked under a railway bridge. The locals give up their seats and laugh at Micki struggling with the sail.

"Brought your bed, did you?" one workman facetiously asks.

"No, I brought my bloody boat," Micki retorts.

All the old codgers chuckle.

"And where you sailing to France?" The same workman taunts.

"I wish. Might get some decent weather over there," Micki replies.

"Yes, but them frogs aren't half ugly," he offers.

"Well if I ever have the chance to kiss a bloody frog, I will let you know."

Everyone guffaws. But the workman is determined to have the last word.

"Yes he might turn into a prince." Then he pauses, "No a frogs a frog. Bloody ugly like me."

To which the crowd unanimously replies, "Yer." With that Micki laughs raises her chipped tea cup,

"Touché," she toasts.

The warmth of the tea is beginning to de-thaw us. I wonder what my mother would think of me having a cuppa with the riff raff. I wouldn't mention this foray into the underworld.

We arrive at the school, a red brick, three storied Victorian with small paned windows, fronted by gigantic iron gates and a tarmac playground. We meet up with the others from Group C and begin the show. The audience of children are excited. At one point during a scene I break the fourth wall and ask the children,

"What shall I do?"

Out of the corner of my eye I see four boys in the back row no more than nine years old giving me what looks like the inverted victory sign, which means fuck off. *Maybe it was the peace sign.* I tell myself. At the conclusion of Ivan the Ninny I again ask the audience to make a decision concerning the fate of the two devious brothers of my sweet prince. At all the other schools there has been a resounding

"Forgive them. Let them go."

But not here in Bethnal Green, home of the murderous gangster Kray brothers. Here they are undivided shrieking:

"Kill them! Kill them!"

My pleadings go unanswered as I implore them:

"Ivan's brothers are very, very sorry. They promise never to be mean again."

To which Clive and Danny nod their heads in agreement and improvise,

"We promise we will never ever be nasty or horrible."

I continue,

"Did you hear that children? They are changed. Let us forgive them."

The auditorium is swelling with the voices in concert pitch:

"Kill them, kill them."

Gerald has been observing from the wings, he leaps on stage with his glistening sword drawn. There is an instant hush. He brandishes the sword and boldly announces:

"I will not kill my brothers. They are repentant for their misdeeds. I will banish them for three years to Ivy House."

A voice from the auditorium shouts out:

"Is that the clink?"

"Yes," Gerald affirms and then continues administering a sentence to his wayward siblings. "From this day forth you will be exiled to Ivy House far away, beyond the heath."

At that Clive and Danny make a hasty retreat. Gerald takes my hand. The princess in me is developing a crush on my pantomime suitor. He kisses me before the final song, it is a romantic kiss. This only confirms my ardor for him. We have become great friends.

We are in a foursome that includes Gerald, Sad, Duncan and I. We like to spend time together. We discuss assignments, homework and laugh at our mistakes. More importantly we support one another. Gerald squeezes my hand again as we sing to the music of "I'm getting married in the morning." With the words "We'll have some parties. Eat lots of Smarties. We'll be at the church on time." I look out at the sea of disappointed maleficent sprites who had demanded an execution. I see the four boys in the back, now accompanied by their schoolmates in the same row, they are all in synchronization as they flash me the v sign.

We strike the set and pack up in record time to avoid meeting the rapscallions on the playground. We are not fast enough and as we make a dash for those massive iron gates, we are pelted with snowballs. Micki slams the iron gates shut, she retaliates by giving our attackers the v sign as they scamper to pitch more snow grenades over the red brick school wall.

Rosemary: Before the Christmas Holidays.

Once a week in the evening I am scheduled to go to Rita's voice studio. This is the sentence imposed by Peggy Lewis for my sibilant "s" but I suspect it is a punitive measure for my impudence in her acting class. I am joined by another guinea pig, Doug Cooper from Group A. Doug resembles a mad professor. He has Einstein hair that sprouts in bunches from his head, bushy eyebrows above large puppy dog brown eyes. We have both been diagnosed with the dreaded sibilant 's' sound that needs immediate attention and correction by Rita.

Her remedy is a round of vocal warm ups and tedious tongue exercises in front of the wall of mirrors in her studio. Doug and I wag our tongues, thrust them upwards and downwards, sideways and backwards. Our tongues are becoming acrobats. When Rita's back is turned Doug pokes his tongue out and makes faces. I try to stifle giggles.

I don't think my sigmatism is improving and neither does Rita. By the end of the term she gives me an ultimatum,

"Darling, you will need to have your jaw and teeth realigned if we are to obliterate that elongated 's'."

Rita is deadly serious. So am I. I have no intention of procuring any such medical procedure. Rita can read my reluctance in my polite reply.

"I will need to consider my options."

She is very matter of fact when she responds.

"Well darling, if you decide not to follow my advice, there is nothing more I can do for you."

With that we part ways and I suspect I am not as favored as I once was.

Rosemary: Christmas Party.

The hallways of Ivy House are papered with flyers announcing a Christmas Party to be held in the common room, the next Saturday. With such short notice the only Group C participants are Clive and Duncan. All the others are going home for the weekend or meeting up with boyfriends, not one mentioned studying as an excuse for not attending. I don't fancy traveling alone on the tube back to Edgware, waiting for the perpetually overdue late night 142 bus to take me home.

I invite my cousin Andrea who is down from Leeds University. Andrea is a petite brunette with dark curls that frame her angelic face, her large luminous brown eyes, her soft voice combined with an infectious smile is appealing to all. She is studying theology I don't why because she has always been a confirmed atheist since leaving an all-girls Catholic grammar school. Whenever we go out, she is the centre of male attention, all eyes are on Andrea the goddess. We take hours to get ready, wearing mini dresses, thigh high suede boots and dark eye make-up. When my father drops us off at Edgware train station we are greeted by rambunctious teenage boys who take delight in a chorus of wolf whistles as we purchase train tickets.

Before we enter the common room taking the stairs to the basement the walls are vibrating with The Beatles "Love Me Do" blasting from a record player in the corner.

Andrea is an immediate hit with the attending men, who trip all over themselves to dance with her. I espy Duncan standing awkwardly in the corner. I ask him to dance with me and we shuffle onto the dance floor attempting to be cool as we gyrate to "All You Need Is Love." Clive is moving next to us, he is wearing a voluminous black cape. He is dancing with Mary from Group B. Mary is a dainty, pretty girl with golden curls that reach past her waist. At the conclusion of the record, he leads Mary to the couch where he precedes to lie on top of her in full view of the partygoers with his cape spread across his back like a vampire bat. Andrea is in deep conversation with a student she somehow knows. She walks over to me

"Who is that?" I ask.

"That is my two-timing ex-boyfriend Simon."

"How did he come to be here?"

"He's a friend of that tall chap with a Beatle cut."

Andrea looks across the room at James Wilson, from Group B. He is a mirror image of Paul McCartney.

"Simon and that guy are childhood friends. Simon is a two-timing prick. A child himself," Andrea murmurs.

James must have noticed Andrea pointing at him and he asks me to dance to the Beatles 'Hello Goodbye'. Halfway through the song I noticed Andrea locked in a passionate embrace with Simon. The record changes to a baritone belting out 'If I Were A Rich Man.' Dancers on the floor erupt with a group "no!" looking for the culprit who had put Topol's recording on the player. Duncan secretly smiles in the corner by the record player. The Fiddler On The Roof music is replaced with 'Love Is All Around' by the Troggs. I find myself slow dancing with James Wilson. I peek over his shoulder to see Andrea grabbing her coat, she catches my eye and mouths,

"I'm leaving." She turns and disappears with Simon.

James's grip around my waist gets tighter. I look up at him and to my utter surprise I find his lips on mine. I am taken aback. When the record is over, I awkwardly look at my watch uttering,

"I've got to go, if I am to catch the last train."

"I will walk you to the station. You never know who is lurking in the bushes on North End Road."

I try to dissuade him.

"No that's not necessary."

"My pleasure," James insists.

We stride down the hill, before we see the lights of the Hippodrome he reaches for my hand and pulls me to him and gives me a French kiss. I am perplexed and taken aback by his forwardness and passion. He has always seemed so reserved, if not solitary during lectures and lunch. He smiles and with schoolboy charm asks,

"I was wondering if you would like to come back to my place? Since your cousin has jilted you for Simon."

"I can't," I reply.

"Why not?" he persists. "We could have fun making love."

"I don't know you, James."

"What is there to know? This is the age of free love." Then he sings the first line of the Stones 'Let's Spend The Night Together.' Look all the girls at New College are into women's lib and shagging. What's your position on the free love movement?"

We are at the turnstile at the station, as I walk through I turn to him and quietly say,

"Seems to me the only position in the free love movement is horizontal. Thanks for walking me to the station."

James is standing forlorn. His bottom lip pursed over his top. As if he can't fathom what took place.

Christmas term exams are looming. I'm glad I don't have any relationship distractions. Kevin, my council house suitor is immersed in math equations at Bath University. We barely communicate. My mother has not removed the pay phone from the hall and I find I do not have the money nor inclination to spend time calling Kevin, as we both fabricate how much we miss each other. When I am not buried in books on theatre history, plays, costumes, phonetics, education, psychology, poetry and literature; I am popping up to town at the end of the day accompanied by Sad with the hope to secure cut price theatre tickets at the Royal Shakespeare Company in Aldwych. There is nothing more splendid sitting high in the balcony on a frigid winter's night snug in the gods. We are able to catch Helen Mirren in the National Health. I am impressed when she accidentally falls on her buttocks during a pivotal scene. Helen immediately rights herself and continues on without a hitch. She improvises dialogue about the hospital floor being wet and slippery. I wonder if I could be as quick on my feet, literally.

Every six weeks I attend the opening night at the local repertory theatre at Watford Regal Theatre. I am escorted by Mark Perry a director of the Regal Theatre's Youth Theatre. Mark is a midget of a man who compensates his small stature with an over-sized ego. We met the night I was crowned Rag Queen and he has been pursuing me since. He is a Lothario and is blatantly consistent in wanting to have sex with me. I am definitely not into reciprocating his far flung fantasy. The result of my non-interest only adds fuel to his fervent fire. He likes to show me off to his peers. He has a Napoleonic complex and having the Rag Queen on his arm strokes his already inflated self-image. For my part I feel sorry for this little man who is forever trying to measure up. He is an insightful director; he is funny and apart for his notorious sexual appetite I believe him to be a pussy cat under the giant façade.

When I attend the theatre with Mark I am guaranteed a ride and a free ticket plus he introduces me to the cast and crew. Last month after The Caretaker he steers me to a somber, swarthy, attractive man, sitting at the far edge of the bar smoking a cigarette.

Mark has his lines down pat,

"This is Rosemary, Watford's Rag Queen."

To which I roll my eyes.

"She is a first year drama student."

The dark haired stranger, takes a drag on his cigarette.

"A drama student? Where?" he asks.

"New College," I respond.

"What did you think of the play?" he asks.

I pause momentarily before replying, "I didn't understand the sub-text, but my mind didn't wander."

I notice Mark has a look of terror on his face. The man smiles,

"Well, that's a good thing."

He takes another drag on his cigarette,

"How old are you?"

"Eighteen," I reply.

Now he pauses for a few seconds.

"I think you will understand when you are older."

Mark looks agitated. He leads me away as the man returns his attention to smoking.

Out earshot Mark explodes.

"What were you thinking?"

"What do you mean?" I respond innocently

"Telling him you didn't understand the play."

"I didn't say that. He asked for my opinion. What does it matter?"

"Because he wrote it," Mark declares. "That is Harold Pinter."

"So what did you want me to do? I was being honest. By the way he's quite a dish."

Mark looks at me with mock gravitas.

"Bit old for you."

"I thought he was about your age, Mark." I chuckle.

"Very funny."

There is at least ten years between him and the luscious Harold Pinter.

"I need a drink." he declares.

He barges his way to the bar. He buys me a bitter lemon. Standing at the bar holding court is the newly appointed theatre critic for the Evening Post, Pearce Sullivan. Mark breaks into Pearce's inner circle and shepherding me in front of Pearce makes his usual introduction:

"Pearce meet Rosemary the local…"

Pearce interrupts.

"Rag Queen," Pearce continues mischievously. "Rosemary and I go way back, to when she was a groupie. Don't we?" he teases.

Then he winks and smiles at me. I know Pearce is a cad, but there is something inexplicable between us. Pearce's date for the evening appears and drapes herself all over his shoulder. He inevitably is seen with brassy young women.

"This is Denise," he offers.

Denise smiles like a well fed cat. Mark is annoyed and guides me from the bar.

"What is going on between you and Pearce Sullivan?"

Now I am annoyed.

"I have no idea what you mean," I lie.

I still have the glass in my hand. I weave my way through the crowd back to the bar.

Pearce is talking animatedly to the rosy-cheeked middle-aged bar woman. As I hand her my glass. Pearce sidles towards me

"Mum this is Rosemary."

His mother answers knowingly.

"The Rag Queen."

I laugh.

"It's not a very glamorous title is it?"

"Pearce told me all about you."

I see Pearce blush. Mark has fought his way through the crowd, he has hold of my arm.

"We're leaving," he insists.

I smile at Pearce's mom and she returns my smile as I mouth "Goodbye."

I am whisked away by Mark. Sitting in Mark's car outside my house in Bushey Heath, he asks again.

"What is going on with Pearce Sullivan?"

"There is absolutely nothing going on."

"Besides when would I have the time? I have a boyfriend, he's at Bath University," I try to convince Mark.

"Well you should know Pearce is bad news, especially with women. That hard scrubber, Denise he was with tonight applied to the youth theatre. I gave her an audition. She was an absolute disaster. Then I received a letter from her begging for another chance, at the bottom in a postscript she had handwritten "I fuck like a traction engine.""

"She should have a great career ahead of her then," I joke.

Mark laughs and then leans over and attempts to fondle my breasts. I remove his groping hands.

"Really Mark I don't know why you keep trying? I am never going to sleep with you."

He shrugs and whispers,

"You can't blame a bloke for trying."

I reach for the door handle.

"Trying is what you are."

I emphasize the word trying and with that I exit his mini.

Rosemary: Christmas 1967.

The grueling end of term exams are over. I am concluding writing a collection of essays from the Greeks to the Middle Ages that are to be scored and marked by Diane Winter. I am learning to organize research on the dining room table and writing is becoming less intimidating. My mother has a desk in the corner of the dining room where she handles her accounts. I misspell the words 'deus ex machina' and open the top drawer of the desk searching for an eraser. As I rummage I come across an open cheque book. I pause. I remove the cheque book. I can't be reading the name correctly for the bearer is in the name of Elsie Annie Shawcross, my deceased grandmother. I look at the date of the last cheque in the register, November 3rd 1967. I replace the check book and shut the drawer with shock. My grandmother died before I was born. I ask myself *Can a dead person have a bank account?* At dinner that night I simply enquire.

"Mummy why do you have cheques that have Elsie Annie Shawcross as the bearer on them?"

"Where did you see a cheque like that?" she asks accusingly.

"In the drawer of your desk."

"What were you doing in my desk?"

"I was looking for an eraser"

"Did you find one?"

"No," I reply.

Then my mother continues firmly.

"Well if you must know. I'm the executrix of my mother's will. Now are you satisfied?"

"Yes," I mumble sheepishly.

"Keep out of my things." She blinks and quickly changes the subject, "Now tell me about the tour of the pantomime. I was on a professional tour after I left RADA. I was in the Bluebird with Patricia Hayes. I have wonderful memories."

I offer up a bland account of Ivan the Ninny. I am questioning if my mother is capable of looking me in the eye and lying to me. She is of course an actress.

The exam results are posted on the bulletin board outside the refectory. All the first years turn up to see their fate. I have passed miraculously. A reprieve from expulsion. I leave the comfortable confines of Ivy House to take a Christmas job with the Post Office in Watford. Many of my friends and acquaintances have returned from university and are assigned temporary work at the sorting office. I am employed in the letters which are hand sorted and put in pigeon hole boxes according to the areas of London. I catch an early morning bus and am familiar with some of the travelers including my old friend Jill, who is now a cashier at Barclays Bank. Jill is the perfect person to help me solve the mystery of the cheques. Jill informs me.

"Dead people cannot have checking accounts."

When I return home from the post office after sorting piles of Christmas cards on their way to S.W. London. I decide to confront my mother during the nightly soiree in the lounge. I burst into the room as my parents are sipping from their gin filled glasses listening to the record of Frank Sinatra singing 'Strangers in the Night.'

"Rosemary, what is the meaning of this?" my mother slurs.

"Dead people cannot have checking accounts," I blurt out.

My father toddles over and lifts the gramophone needle. There is silence amongst the gold couches, red carpet, blue glass and Doulton ladies staring, imprisoned within the china cabinet. My mother pauses, inhales deeply and then without warning begins a small tirade.

"What are you thinking? Coming in here? Disturbing your father and I?

Shouldn't you be studying? Or something?"

I do not move. I will not be bullied or lied to again. I calmly repeat.

"Dead people can't have checking accounts."

I am determined to get to the root of this matter. I stand erect, steadfast looking at my father on the gold armchair and my mother on the gold sofa. I sense the confrontation is over. Again there is a long silence before my father half whispers,

"You should tell her Gwen."

My mother shrugs her shoulders.

"Alright, you are of course correct dead people can't have checking accounts."

"Well what does this mean?" I ask.

"This means that your grandmother, my mother Elsie Annie is alive."

"Alive, like not dead?" I hear myself question.

"Alive and well, living in Hastings. She is soon to be relocated to the retirement home here in Bushey Heath the one just around the corner."

"Where has she been?"

There is another long pause, my mother clears her throat.

"My mother, Elsie Annie has been in an asylum for forty years."

I am amazed and repeat.

"Forty years in a mental hospital?"

Another pause before my mother answers "Yes."

"Why didn't you tell me?"

"Because I didn't think she would ever be released."

"Why?" I ask.

My mother hesitates.

"Because she was very ill, psychologically, she was a drug addict, she was possessed by religious mania."Then as if all the air from her body was being sucked out of her, my mother sighs and then inhales before she continues. "Because, Rosemary, your grandmother tried to kill me, she tried to stab me with a knife. She was insane you see," tears flood her cheeks. "Elsie Annie was beautiful, but she was addicted to cocaine and heroin. You don't go all over talking about your mad mother. There's a stigma surrounding insanity. She has had many rounds of electrical shock treatment. I visit her every couple of months. Recently she has shown remarkable progress. She is going to be discharged. She is going to live around the corner. You are going to meet her. She is a meek old lady now."

"When were you going to tell me?"

"I was waiting for the right time." Another pause before she quotes King Lear "Time shall unfold what plaiting cunning hides." She sips her drink. "Is there anything else you want to know?"

I am dumbfounded. I'm trying to take in all this information.

"I don't think so."

I excuse myself fly upstairs to my cell, close the door, lie on the twin bed and wonder about being enlightened on the mystery of the cheque book and trying to understand my mothers' reason for withholding the information about my grandmother.

A few days later, I am introduced to a square, stocky short woman with her white hair wound in a snug bun. Elsie Annie is aloof but she is a keen observer of the reality of the shenanigans at our house in Bushey Heath. I visit her occasionally at the old peoples home. I catch her with her silk white hair not yet pinned severely to her head. Her silver hair falls to her coccyx. She has a favorite chair in the day room.

When I ask her about her new residence she replies with a Mancunian accent.

"It's fine. Except for this obnoxious older man who stares at me with beady eyes."

"Maybe he fancies you," I tease.

"Like you fancy Pearce Sullivan"

I am bowled over by her statement.

"You know how I know?" she says.

"The way you light up whenever his newspaper column is mentioned or you talk about him."

"I don't even know him."

"That doesn't mean you don't fancy him."

"Yes it does," I protest and close the conversation down.

Elsie Annie begins to integrate into our family. She arrives to spend Christmas day with us. My mother has agonized over the festivities. During Christmas dinner my mother enquires of my grandmother.

"Are you enjoying Christmas mummy?"

To which my grandmother completely deadpan replies.

"I don't know why you are celebrating Christmas Gwennie?"

"What are you talking about mummy?" my mother casually asks as she cuts into the chicken on her plate.

"Because your father was a Jew. You are Jewish."

All eating and talking at the dining table ceases. All eyes are on my mother, who has turned very pale. My brother Tony, begins to snicker in his serviette. My father looks perplexed. We watch as my mother face transforms from bone white to beet red. She is fuming.

"You are a Jewess, Gwennie," My grandmother insists and then resumes eating.

Seething my mother asks,

"Are you off your rocker mummy?"

My grandmother pauses with knife and fork in hand and declares,

"No, but for decades I was thought to be."

Nonchalantly my grandmother cuts through a slice of gammon on her plate. My father sensing a Vesuvian eruption grabs a bottle of champagne from the sideboard.

"I bought this to celebrate our relatives." He unscrews the cork a little and then releases it to the ceiling. "Here's to our family," he exclaims as he quickly fills our champagne glasses. He raises his glass saying, "To whatever denomination we might be."

My father smiles at my mother. I see a look of devotion. He has been able to divert an emotional outburst. "I love you Gwen." He clinks his glass with hers. "I love you all. Cheers."

At last Christmas holidays are over. My mother is obsessed with delving into her Jewish genealogy. So far she has traced her ancestry indirectly to Lord Hartley Shawcross, the Attorney General who represented Great Britain in the Nuremberg trials.

Rosemary: January 1968

Group C has a new recruit. A tall slim Norwegian male with a coif of hair that stands in a wave above his forehead like a refined Teddy Boy. His name is Martin, he speaks English very precisely. He is an ethereal Norse god, he glides from class to class.

He is older but refuses to disclose his actual age. He does not reveal much about himself. I notice sometimes that he is looking at me as if he can read my history.

Gerald, my pantomime prince asks me to accompany him to the pictures to see the Margot Fonteyn and Rudi Nureyev production of Swan Lake at Golders Green Cinema. At the showing he leans forward with his hands cupping his face, he is spellbound by the ballet. Afterwards at the entrance to the station he gives me a perfunctory kiss on the cheek. I'm not quite sure what is transpiring between us, our relationship seems to be in reverse as we are becoming more platonic.

From: Martin
To: Rose-Mary
Subject: First Day
Date: January 3rd, 2012 9:42 am
Please find attached first draft for the first day. I could develop it further with more description but

it's been a memory test to get this far. What do you think of it? Are we traveling on similar trains? I'm off to London for a week on Monday and will get back to the desk on the 3rd February. I've a few old friends to visit and so it should make a break. I haven't been back for a year...I'm more Cornish than the Cornish. One of my old friends I'm meeting is a tv producer and I want to discuss my Cornish holiday disaster. I'll give you details shortly.

Hope all is well with you
Look forward to hearing from you
Best wishes
Martin.

Martin: First Day at New College of Speech and Drama.

Well here I am, Monday 8th January, 1968, which is my first day at the New College of Speech and Drama. I move into my lodgings at Mrs Huckle's large apartment on Sunday afternoon with a suitcase full of clothes and books to get me through the first week. I travel to Golders Green from Upton Park on the tube and I feel ready to face my new life at New College. My room is spartan to say the least with just a paraffin heater to keep the cold at bay. It is snowing heavily across London and Golders Green is certainly " deep and crisp and even." My room has a large bed, a desk, and the aforementioned paraffin heater. I share the kitchen and bathroom with my landlady, Mrs Huckle, who is a rotund lady of indeterminate years, and who is seldom seen outside of her large room further down the brown painted dingy corridor. Last night was so cold that I decided to go to the Golders Green cinema to sit in the warmth and watch Sidney Poitier star in "To Sir with Love." The film was set in an East London I did not recognize but the cinema was warm and so I was content to engage with the sentimentalities of the film.

I have to be at the College for 8.30am and so I get up today at 7.00am, breakfast quickly on toast, tea and jam and don my winter clothes (which hardly differ from my spring or summer clothes). Roll neck pullover, Levi jeans, Levi jean jacket, leather boots and short, black overcoat is to be my attire for today. Books and writing paper in a canvas shoulder bag of dubious military origin and here I go.

The metal stairway from Mrs Huckle's flat is covered in ice and is quite lethal and so I descend with caution not wishing to end up in the local casualty ward of Hampstead hospital as opposed to the hallowed halls of learning at New College. The walk up hill towards Ivy House is slow and slippery and I'm self-conscious of not wanting to destroy my newcomer's mysterious image by falling flat on my face like Stan Laurel! There are obviously a few students about as they also slowly struggle up North End Road towards the College. I feel somewhat isolated but accept this is part of the "game" as I join the course a term late and obviously friendships and partnerships have already been established amongst the first year students. I do feel, however, this will give me a certain outsider's objectivity as I move amongst my new peers. I have to report to the office where I went for my audition before Christmas and so that is where I go. I register and am told to wait outside and someone will come to collect me.

There is a tall, willowy chap sitting there and we get into conversation and it seems he is also joining the course today. He is a Norwegian called Martin Lordahl and he now lives in West London. He appears very amiable and I think we'll get along quite well. The man that I recognize from my audition as the Principal approaches and asks us both to walk with him to his office. Once there he sits us down and describes how the College operates, how it is a small community of three separate years and how the college functions on continual assessment and external written and practical examinations. We are again warmly welcomed and he says that if either of us has any problems settling in to contact him immediately. He informs us that we are to be in separate groups which populate the timetable in the first year. Martin is allocated "C" and I'm in "D" group. Mr. Sjoberg says that if we wait outside someone will come to take us to our groups. He shakes our hands, wishes us well and shows us where to wait outside of his office.

Before long a large, beaming male student appears and in a strong west country accent asks for me. I acknowledge him and he says his name is Rick and that I should follow him as he is taking me to my seminar group. I say goodbye to Martin Lordahl and follow my new friend Rick deeper into the bowels of the Ivy House. We finally reach a door and Rick tells me this is where my group is having a vocal studies lecture and I should follow him in. There are about a dozen students sitting on the floor and standing in front of them is a small, dark haired young woman who introduces herself as Sylvia Gonzalez, the voice tutor. She welcomes me to the class and suggests I sit next to Rick and to follow the session as best I can. The group have apparently finished their vocal warm-up and are now concentrating on vocal improvisations. I am in a group consisting of Rick and a girl called Maisie and our current subject is "The Shipwreck." We vocally probe the nautical world of shanties, creaking timbers and flapping sails, not to mention the roaring winds and crashing surf on rocks that quite overwhelm the terrible cries of the shipwrecked sailors. We're pleased with our effort and we receive praise from both the rest of the group and the tutor. I'm thinking that this is not a bad start to my New College career when our next subject arrives: "The Busy High Street." Immediately my imagination takes me back to the busy Green Street of my childhood on a Saturday afternoon on the way to Upton Park to watch West Ham play football. Between us we quickly develop a lively vocal portrayal of the street scene and this again meets with approval as we present it to the group and Sylvia Gonzalez. I find the final part of the session-the relaxation- a bit bewildering but gather it is based on the Alexander technique. I soon learn it as it is regularly practiced by the Voice and Speech Department. I must remember to bring a large textbook to my next Voice session so as to rest my head on it when I relax in the prone Alexander position.

It is now lunch time and Rick kindly takes me under his wing and we go down to the canteen together. The small place is heaving with student life and we join the ragged queue which leads to the counter where the cook and college caretaker, "Winkie" and his wife, Mrs. "Winkie," are serving the hungry student throng. After choosing particularly greasy plates of egg and chips, Rick and I find room on a table where Rob and Gordon sit. Rob is small and wiry and comes from Wiltshire whereas Gordon is tall and he is wrapped in a New College scarf. He has a "Norman" haircut and his manner is gruff yet friendly. He is a fellow Londoner from across the Thames in South London and quickly tells me he wishes to be a famous actor and in his spare time is intently studying the Stanislavski Method of Acting. They ask me about my past and how I ended up at New College this January and I vaguely outline my convoluted journey since Sixth Form which resulted in my being washed up on the thespian shores of this famous academy.

As a group we have one lecture in the afternoon and it is called Theatrical History and Representation; it is apparently an academic study of the development of the theatre.

After this morning's lecture I find it strange to see a room organized along traditional lines with desks and chairs and a board in the front for the lecturer. The lecturer is a Mrs Elizabeth Lee, a slight energetic figure, who is loaded down with papers and books. She speaks briefly to me saying that she will talk to me after the lecture and that I should make notes as she lectures on today's subject. I understand that last term the group studied Classical Theatre via Greek and Roman texts. This term they are moving on to Medieval Theatre and I immediately feel at home as I studied Medieval History at school only a couple of years ago. She refers to the textbook, "The Seven Ages of Theatre" by Richard Southern and talks about the social history behind the Miracle and Morality plays of the Middle Ages. I'm content as none of this comes as a surprise and I can easily answer the questions she asks. I've certainly landed on my feet with this subject; the group must think they have a medieval scholar amongst them. By the time I've bored them with the Black Death, the Crusades, Monasticism and the Wars of the Roses, the lecture comes to a satisfactory end. Elizabeth thinks I will quickly catch up on the first term's work and gives me last term's notes to copy as soon as possible. These are kindly donated by fellow student, Maisie Tueart. The day is ending and the students mill about in the reception area (except for the second year cohort that is apparently away on teaching practice). I slowly descend the main staircase with my bag full of pages of notes to be copied. I finally feel that I look like a drama student. I've more or less settled in: I have made some acquaintances; I know that I belong to Seminar Group D; I have a fair understanding of the geography of the place and I have not been cast adrift by today's lectures.

Now the long walk back down the steep hill towards Golder's Green and Mrs Huckle's abode as the snow begins to fall once more…I look forward to an evening of note copying and a night of dreams lit up by the shining, youthful stars of Group D of Year One from the New College of Speech and Drama.

13 Martin at New College of Speech and Drama 1968

Rosemary: New Students.

We are scheduled to be present at New College for a few months before we are dispatched to elementary schools for a month of teaching practice. Until then classes continue. Diane Winters is bent on trying to prove that Jesus and Mary were part of a coven. Rita is still stimulating our speech organs and training our primary articulator, the tongue. Elizabeth Leigh is leading us through the medieval mysteries, moralities and interludes. Her nemesis, Frank Leer is into the chemise cagoule and sexual preferences of the Middle Ages. John Smithfield is correcting our sentence structure. Noel Niven is readying us for radio. Peggy has us on her morning resonating chain gang. Richard Wilkins has moved on to lighting. Group C arrives for his first seminar in electrical engineering in the Phoenix Theatre. Group D are concluding, they are stringing lights. We wait patiently on the entrance steps to the auditorium. At the back standing underneath a newly hung spotlight is a young man I do not recognize. He is tall, his fair hair in a bowl cut, he wears a jacket and jeans. He resembles the illustration of Sir Galahad by Walter Crane when the knight is introduced to the round table. Group D are gathered around him, he is floodlit, he is quite gorgeous. Micki sidles up to me and whispers,

"He is delicious, who is he?"

She jolts me from my fantasy with Sir Galahad.

"I don't know," I casually reply.

Richard Wilkins appears downstage and calls us to assemble as he explains the intricacies of connecting a Fresnel to the dimmer system in the lighting booth. I am not paying attention. All I can think of is the Arthurian Legend that I have witnessed. I want to know who that marvelous male specimen is.

We have expanded our lunch time participants and now sit at a large table in the centre of the refectory. We are often joined by Maisie, Jenny and Miriam from Group D. Of course Micki takes the initiative.

"Who was that bloke in the theatre?" she asks Maisie.

But it is Miriam, a petite dark cropped hair student who sports a pink cravat, she is always ready to gossip and she supplies the answer.

"That's Martin, he's new."

"He's fucking fab," Micki offers.

"He is. Isn't he?" Miriam eagerly replies as Micki offers her some Oxo crisps.

"Do you think we could swap our new Martin for your new Martin?" Micki asks.

"You have a new student with the same name?"

"Yes, haven't you heard it's the year of the Martins. Except yours is more desirable than ours. Don't get me wrong our Martin is a Nordic vision....but he is older and doesn't seem interested. Does your Martin like young , nubile, females?"

Miriam nonchalantly replies, "I don't know. He's nice."

Micki continues, "He's probably got a fucking girlfriend."

"Probably," Miriam sighs.

"Or he lives in a grotty, frigid bedsit with stained carpets."

Micki gives Miriam the rest of her Oxo crisps

"Find out for us will you?"

With that lunch is over and we hurry to change for movement with Tricia Curtis. I am intrigued by the mystery of the other Martin.

From: Rose-Mary
To: Martin
Subject: First Day
Date: January 4th, 2012 3:36 pm
Dearest Martin:

Happy New Year. I haven't expressed my appreciation for your part in this process. We have two totally different perspectives. Your first week is captivating. "The best mirror is an old friend." Ours is a two way mirror. Keep writing.

Rose-Mary

From: Martin
To: Rose-Mary
Subject: New College Update
Date: January 20th, 2012 6:32 am
Hi Rose-Mary

I have been pre-occupied with researching the 60s Cornish tragedy.

Re: New College I've been working on the first week which I am sending. I have decided to combine first footie match with later visit to Hendon College with rag fiasco. This way the piece should be more entertaining and carry the spirit of the time. I still participate in football through the Truro City FC who have entered administration and so I'm involved with the campaign to save the club. As you can see I am very busy with other projects.

Will keep you updated.
Love
Martin.

Martin: The First Week: Voice, Philosophy and Movement.

I venture to my first Voice and Speech session with the Head of Department, Mrs. Rita Scott. The seminar is to take place in the Voice Room, which is a large classroom in the prefabricated buildings located in the gardens of Ivy House. I have already had a brief meeting with Rita where she outlined the work I had missed and the new subjects that we should soon be covering. It's all rather scientific and I must say I don't feel that confident in joining this part of the course. I amble down into the snow covered gardens and I discover there is already a line of students queuing outside of the Voice Room and I get the distinct impression that Mrs. Scott likes her lectures to start on time. I acknowledge various students and join the end of the line where Maisie Tueart and Miriam Ziegler are standing. They are very friendly and Maisie offers me her Voice and Speech notes from last term to copy which is very kind of her. Mrs. Scott appears at the top of the path and glides effortlessly down to the room with two male students in her wake carrying piles of papers and books. I recognize them as Rick Coulder and the Scot, Ken Dotson. Rita certainly knows how to make a grand entrance.

"Morning, Darlings!" she cries as she stoops to unlock the classroom door and quickly enters. We all follow glad to shelter from the cold January morning. The chairs are arranged around the edges of the room and we sit ourselves down as Mrs. Scott fusses over papers and books which the boys have put on her desk at the front of the class. She opens her register folder and quickly calls the names of Group D and everyone is present and correct.

"Well, darlings, before we start I'd just like to give a huge welcome to our new student, Martin Banks, who has joined us after transferring from Avery Hill College. He is bound to feel a bit lost and so I want you all to be absolute darlings and to look out for him and help him all you can. I'm sure he is going to be a wonderful addition to both the group and the college. We expect great things of him."

I'm taken by surprise by her plaudit and I blush like a red traffic light. I grin weakly at the beaming tutor and students. Rita then tells us that we are to work on the resonator scale this morning and we all have to turn to her own textbook, "The Study of Voice and Speech". She then instructs us to turn to the chapter on Tonal Quality. We are told we are going to address the Figure of Eight Tone Scale but first of all we have to undertake a physical and vocal warm-up. We all stand and face Rita and she tells us to closely follow her movements. During the next ten minutes we roll our heads and loosen our shoulders and I must say everyone follows her lead with intense concentration. Rita now feels that we are physically ready and so we prepare vocally and we begin by making random animal sounds. We bleat like sheep and then cluck like chickens and crow like farmyard cocks. On top of this we then drone like bees and hum on "n" making it sound like a summer swarm of flying insects. The room is shaking and rattling to the sounds coming from the lecturer and students and I must admit I'm rather enjoying the experience and try my hardest to help vocally recreate the animal and insect world. Rita is happy with our input and we now move on to the Figure of Eight Speech Exercise. We move from Hard through Hay into Heed and then return through Hay to Hard and move on to Hawk to reach Hoot and return via Hawk to finish at Hard. We whisper the sequence and then vocalize it and Rita seems pleased with our efforts as we work through the Figure of Eight. Rita leads from the front like a conductor with an orchestra and we are the mere musical instruments directed by her hands. Then we quickly divide into sub-groups of three to work on some Speech Practice for presentation. I'm with Maisie and Rick as we rehearse the following:

When the night wind howls in the chimney cowls,
And the bat in the moonlight flies,

And inky clouds, like funeral shrouds, sail over the midnight skies-

When the footpads quail at the night-bird's wail,

The black dogs bay at the moon,

Then is the spectres' holiday-then is the ghosts' high-noon!
(W.S. Gilbert)

I'm thinking we could send the shivers down the bravest soul's backbone when we give our performance presentation. Rick and I are certainly disciples of Vincent Price and Lon Chaney Junior and Maisie is without doubt giving the banshee a run for her money! Rita is pleased:

"Darlings that was a very good effort and you certainly went a long way in creating the tonal quality for the piece. Perhaps you booming boys might have eased back a bit as you were drowning dear Maisie at points but nonetheless a valuable effort."

Well although I'm a booming boy I still get some credit and I feel that overall this seminar has been a success.

We leave the Voice Room and traipse up the garden towards the main house. I glance at my timetable and see that the next seminar is Philosophy with Frank Leer and it is somewhat strangely located in the main Rehearsal room in Ivy House. Oh well, mine is not to reason why and I follow the group up through the gardens and into the main entrance hall which is very congested as large groups of students attempt to make their respective ways to the next subject on their timetables. I follow closely behind Miriam and Maisie, who are turning out to be my guardian angels during my first week in the College. There is then a mad dash to both the coffee machines and the toilets before the group shuffle on down the corridor to the main rehearsal room.

This is a large space with a huge window and balcony overlooking the garden and on the opposite side is one massive wall mirror. The chairs are arranged in a semi-circle around a single chair on which sits Frank Leer. He is in his late twenties and has longish hair and a beard; he is wearing a brown corduroy suit with hush puppy shoes and has a blue folder resting across his lap. He says a quick hello to me as a greeting and grins and so I feel at once comfortable in his presence. I sit in the second row of the chairs and await my first taste of "Philosophy" at New College. He mumbles through the register and the number of "Frank" replies indicate to me that this is going to be a pretty informal session. He looks up and then says to Lesley Dayne, a pretty, pleasant and jolly girl,

"Les, what do I mean by the expression 'Art for Art's Sake?'"

Lesley seems slightly embarrassed and mumbles something about the importance of art in a society. He replies that does she think that art is part of the society or does it stand outside? She does not reply and he opens the question to the group. Ken Dotson believes that the artist stands outside of society in order to create his art...

"Or her art," as Miriam Ziegler reminds him.

Anita Pendleton, a tall, attractive and willowy girl dressed in a long flowing dress, interjects forcefully:

"That's stupid! How can anyone stand outside of society?"

Pam Reason, a matronly older student in her mid-twenties, comments:

"Well over the centuries artists have always criticized their society and have often stood outside it."

I'm beginning to enjoy this class as one by one the other students in the group add their differing opinions and Frank Leer allows the discussion to roll along gathering pace and energy as opposing views fly about the room. There are obviously plenty of different ideas about art in this particular seminar group. I'm feeling comfortable now in this session and decide to speak:

"Surely any given society, like ours in the 1960s, is made up of differing social groups based on age, gender, class and ethnic background. These must be an influence on the way people produce, appreciate and consume art."

Ken Dotson, the dour Scotsman, reasons:

"The class divisions are breaking down in modern Britain."

Anita fires back at full volume:

"Like fuck they are…you should see the council estate my mum lives on, the people there are most clearly working class"

I like Anita as she doesn't seem to take any bullshit. There is a certain amount of consternation in the group as voices are raised but Frank Leer seems to be enjoying the cut and thrust of the debate and so the session continues.

"Give me an example of how the classes are different?" Frank asks the group.

I throw a social incendiary bomb into the arena:

"Education, work and sex!"

"Exactly!" choruses Anita as she folds her arms and crosses her legs.

Frank grins broadly and then proposes:

"Well let's look at sex amongst the different classes."

"Oh My God no!" laughs Julie Davener and theatrically pulls her jacket over her head.

I feel that perhaps the group has been down this particular path in their Philosophical discussions long before I arrived on the scene. There is a great deal of coughing, mumbling and murmuring as the group teeter on the edge of the great yawning social abyss of sex and society. I'm quite prepared to let the discussion unfold but I am also aware that we are getting quite close to the end of the hour's seminar time.

"There's no difference at all," says Ken Dotson slowly and coldly.

"Yes there fucking is!" retorts a now visually animated Anita.

"Evidence then, please," requests Frank Leer, leaning forward in his chair.

"Well to begin with," replies Anita, "the working class turn the light off when they are about to do it"

"Hear, hear!"

I loudly endorse her and the group explodes in cat-calls, laughter and varying levels of disagreement, disapproval and support. I've certainly helped stir up this particular hornets' nest. Frank, grinning broadly, looks at his watch and says that the session is now finished but hopes we all think about what has been discussed as we will be looking at Art and Society in more detail next week. The group quickly rises and make themselves ready for the dash to the canteen with all thoughts of the working class and sexual conduct dashed by the mouth-watering prospect of Winkie's latest lunch-time culinary spectacular.

I sit with Christopher Donaldson and Rob Dameron for lunch in a very overcrowded and animated student refectory.

Christopher has shoulder length dirty blonde hair and a goatee beard and he is wearing a "Wild West" style tasseled jacket with red flared trousers and cowboy boots. To him everything is either "Cool" or "Far Out" and he tells me he is eagerly awaiting the release of the second Country Joe and The Fish album. There is nothing in the least bit drama-school about Christopher and I have my suspicions that his daily breakfast cereal might be of the rolled weed variety. Anyway he is friendly in his own laid back style and he seems happy to let the New College world pass him by come what may. Rob is a small bundle of nervous energy from Wiltshire and he is totally mystified as to why he has chosen a career in Speech and Drama; he tells me he would like to become an Engineer and he is even unsure as to how he has finally ended up at New College. Again he is very friendly and he offers me the opportunity to copy up any of his notes in order for me to catch up on the work I have missed. He then becomes somewhat depressed and I ask him what is troubling him and he reminds me soulfully that after lunch we are scheduled for our two hour afternoon movement session. Rob has neither the build nor appetite for dance and he informs me it is the worst two hours of his college week. He glumly reminds me that we have to take a University of London Diploma Examination in Movement in our second year and he already feels sick at the thought of such a practical examination.

Nonetheless he rises from the table and reminds Christopher and myself that we have to get changed in the male changing room upstairs and then find our way down into the gardens where the dance studio is located. Rob leads the way like a prisoner going to his execution and Christopher and I shuffle along behind him. We collect our dance gear from the student lockers and proceed up the main staircase to the changing rooms. These are cramped as we all stumble about changing into our dance outfits. Now I can't believe it as I see them all pulling on and wearing black bloody ballet tights! We are all wearing black T shirts but I'm wearing my black gymnastic trousers which the male students used for movement at my previous college of Avery Hill. As I stand here in front of the changing room mirror I must admit that I look a pretty reasonable specimen compared to the rest of them. They hop about insect-like half in and half out of their black tights and I really do question my eyesight. And when we move through the college towards the main entrance I feel like I'm walking with a bunch of misshapen spiders as the boys flash their black tight covered legs for the stunned world to admire.

The black male spidery trail reaches the dance studio down in the gardens. It is a large room with a wooden sprung floor and mirrors and barres along two walls. The girls, clad in leotards and tights, are already there as the spiders' express train steams in. The tutor, Tricia Curtis, is standing at the front of the class putting a record onto the turntable of the record player. She is in her early twenties, small with jet black hair and tons of black eye makeup and is very pretty in a Victorian doll–like way. She asks us all to find space in the studio and I find myself at the back alongside Rick Coulder and Rob Dameron. I know that I am grinning like a lunatic as I just can't get over the sight of the "boys in tights." The warm up exercises begin and I follow the exercises she gives us and I have to half close my eyes so that I can't see the spiders' chorus shambling about with their tights sagging at the crotches. When she feels we are warmed up (poor Rob is steaming like a pressure cooker) she commences to teach us the simple step-ball-change dance step. I'm fortunate because I've already covered this in my movement sessions at Avery Hill and I fairly sail through the exercises. The same can't be said of the male spiders that manage to crash and stumble and slide across the floor in desperate attempts to step-ball-change or ball-step-change or step-change-ball. Rick and Ken manage to crash into everyone on the floor with their tights at half-mast. I feel the spidery dancers have done particularly well in managing to keep out of time with the music throughout the duration of the exercise and dear old ballerina Anna Pavlova, who lived and danced at Ivy House many years ago, must be spinning in her grave!

We now move onto the main part of the session which is all about planning and executing a piece of choreography to a show song. Tricia has chosen "All the Sad Young Men" from the musical "The Nervous Set" and I'm pretty pleased as I know the song well as it is on one of my Davy Graham LPs. We spend much time discussing the music and the movement shapes it gives us for the choreography and I must say I find this really stimulating and interesting. We develop slow, swirling gestures developing from the passage of time denoted in the song and the image of the blue smoke swirling in the bars where the young men in the song drink their cares away. There are some very good dancers amongst the girls in the group and the standard of the movement is very high.

The boys do well as helpless drunks draped across the city bars and all marvelously excel as they slide drunkenly and dramatically to the floor. This is after all the only movement that they basically achieve for the whole of the afternoon's session…

So here I stand at the end of my first dance session at New College with two things on my mind. One: how on earth are some of us (boys) going to pass a practical examination in movement in a year's time and, Two: are the boys black spidery tight clad legs enough to turn any passing homosexuals heterosexual?

The class leaves the dance studio and as I walk through the hall towards the main staircase I'm stopped by two male students who I don't recognize as being from my year. The large one with long black hair and a Zapata moustache introduces himself as Kip Saunders, a third year, and the other is Jack Chapson, a second year student, who has just arrived from a local school where he is currently placed on teaching practice.

"Are you Martin Banks who has just joined the course?" asks Kip.

"Yes, that's me," I reply.

"Well Jack and I run the College football team and we wondered whether you play?"

"Sure I do. I'm a goalkeeper and played for West Ham Schools Eleven and for my school first team as well as Sunday morning club teams."

"Fuck me!" says Kip.

"This is brilliant. Can you come training on Wednesday afternoon in the elective slot? Our session is football training and we play on the Heath."

"Yeh," Jack adds.

"We've got a team in the London University Colleges' League and, to be perfectly honest, we're desperate for a goalkeeper."

"No problem," I reply.

"See you Wednesday."

They both shake my hand and then they quickly disappear out of the front door. I am standing at the foot of the staircase as the humanity that is the New College student population swarms around me on their way home at the end of the day. And here I am nearly half way through my first week and off to football training with the college team… I hope to God they don't wear those bloody black tights as well!

Martin: The First Week Football Practice.

It's Wednesday afternoon elective classes and as no member of staff has bothered me with any other information I've taken it upon myself to join NCSD Rovers' football practice on the Heath. Jack Chapson and Kip Saunders gave me details earlier in the week and I'm off upstairs to the male changing rooms. I enter and immediately find a guy I recognize as Mike from the third year and tutor Frank Leer both getting changed into football kit. They greet me and Frank tells me that they are really keen to make a success of the team as it is now in the University League and struggling at the lower end of the division and getting regular thrashings from some of the more Neanderthal Polytechnic Colleges. Frank is impressed with my football background and says I should expect to play on Saturday when they have an away fixture at Hendon College. Apparently they are taking turns as goalie (a bit like school-boy football) in the team and the news has already spread that I'm a keeper and with that position filled the team should surge up the league like a well – oiled soccer machine. I'm pleased to note that the team still possesses the drama school fertile imagination. Frank leaves the room and Mike waits for me and says that I might as well go in my boots as the training area is just across the road on a piece of Heath scrubland (and England are the World Champions!). I do as I'm told and we both clatter down the staircase in our studded boots and crunch our way across the graveled car park and then dodge the traffic and totter across the road to Hampstead Heath.

A group of about seven students and Frank Leer are kicking a ball about with much enthusiasm but little apparent skill. The Rovers are obviously a physical side far removed from the fluid skills of a pure soccer playing outfit. Just like when I was a seven-year-old in West Ham Park I take my place between the two piles of clothes that make up the goal posts. The bar will feature in our collective imaginations stretching above my head (Gordon Banks, the great England goalkeeper, eat your heart out!). Kip Saunders, the player-manager, chooses two teams of three and four, both of which will shoot against me as I defend my muddy clothed goal posts. The practice match ensues with much over-lapping and inter-locking, late tackles and balletic dives, wild gesticulations and foul language. It is not long before I spring into action to clutch a drive from the tenacious Frank Leer.

"Fucking hell," comments our player-manager. "He caught the fucking thing!"

From this comment I gauge the goalkeeper-sharing that the team has undertaken so far this season has without doubt contributed to their lowly league position. I kick the ball out and watch helplessly as it is chased by a pair of black Labrador dogs that have suddenly appeared from the bushes. They seem to enjoy playing muzzle passing with the ball until a loping

Christopher Donaldson weaves his way between them and, like a George Best incarnate, dribbles the ball back to the main arena leaving the baffled and vanquished doggie defenders floundering in his wake. He is certainly skillful but plays in a rather slow motion fashion which indicates he has shared a team joint in his sporting preparation for the Rovers' training session. Nonetheless the enthusiasm is there for all to see and for the next hour or so we play as though we are in a Cup Final at Wembley Stadium and victory is to be our just reward.

Suddenly Kip blows his whistle and the steaming, mud spattered players know they have done their very best for the Rovers in this important training session now finished as a damp winter's dusk covers the Heath. The goal posts are quickly dismantled as everyone collects their coats and we stand around awaiting our player-manager's words of encouragement. A beaming and animated Kip enthuses:

"Fucking great, just fucking great! We'll be alright with Martin in goal and Chris at centre forward on Saturday. We've got the two Sixth Formers from King Alfred School across the road playing so we should have a full team. Fucking great! Just fucking great!"

With that he turns on his heels and leads his team across the road and back into the grounds of New College and I am happy to be part of the team. As we enter the College and climb the main staircase to the changing rooms I am aware of the damp, dripping, muddy snail's trail that we leave behind us but as nobody seems to care I stay quiet on the subject. I am, however, given some advice by the player-manager in the changing room:

"Just one thing –don't let Rita Scott know that you're playing football as she's really against it as she doesn't want any of her pretty baby-arsed drama boys injured if they're scheduled to be prancing about in one of her Rita de la Mille New College fucking epics!"

I assure our boss that, of course, I wouldn't let Rita know of my sporting ambition but his comment does make me think that is there a distinct aura of counter culture emanating from our third year leader.

All I have to do for now is to remember to rendezvous on Saturday at midday with the rest of the Rovers at Golders Green Station as we make our way to do or die in the soccer inferno that is Hendon College of Technology's Sports Ground.

Martin: The First Week: Comic Acting Class.

It is now Thursday morning and I'm timetabled for a practical session on Acting with Peggy Lewis. I've been told by the other students in the group that we're to be looking at the art of comedy which will follow on from their experiences in the pantomime at the end of last term. Now I realize I wasn't here then but I have done a fair amount of comedy work quite recently, notably the Cabaret Revue at Avery Hill and the Provo 67 Revue at the Theatre Royal, Stratford East. I also have a great love of acclaimed comedians like Tony Hancock, Kenneth Williams, Norman Wisdom, the Marx Brothers, the Goons and, of course, Laurel and Hardy.

The session is due to take place in the large rehearsal room overlooking the gardens. I walk down the corridor to the room with Lesley Dayne and Jilly Bradcaster, two friendly and attractive girls, who tell me about their experiences in the pantomime project last term and from what they describe I'm glad that I was somewhere else. The rest of the group are already there and sit in a semi-circle of chairs facing the window. I find a chair between Miriam Ziegler and Sally Shrewsbury just as Peggy Lewis sweeps into the room and to say it is a dramatic entrance is an understatement. She places her cape across the back of her chair and with her glasses poised perilously on the end of her nose she quickly takes the register in a manner that would put most Company Sergeant Majors to shame. There is an uneasy atmosphere in the room which I can't quite decipher so as I'm the new boy I decide to adopt a low profile.

As Peggy introduces the lecture, I can't help but remember my experience of her at my audition where she started out most stern faced but had at least smiled by the end. Perhaps the same will happen again in this practical session and I will therefore bide my time before honing my comedic skills. Peggy quickly divides the group into pairs and we begin with some standard concentration style exercises which, of course, have to contain the bloody mirror image exercise. I despair as I face Sally and we silently copy our movements and facial expressions. If I've done that exercise once I've done it a thousand times since I left Plaistow Grammar School. One of these days I'd love to stand in front of a mirror and just see someone else there; so please come back Dorian Gray all is forgiven! I'm brought back to the subject of the lecture when Peggy tells us that we all will be required to present an individual comedy improvisation to the group using the room as our set. I think that this will be fine if you're in the first group but pretty awful if you're one of the last. Peggy says that she'll work through the group alphabetically which drops me in it from the start, but I am sympathetic as Miriam Ziegler mutters:

"Great, last to go again ...shit!"

I get the impression, perhaps wrongly, that Peggy is getting some pleasure from putting the new boy through his paces first. I look at the group and there is certainly no show of enthusiasm (or life) from this particular audience. They have obviously been on a most torturous path with Peggy in the past as their expectation levels seem pretty low. Oh well what do I know, I'm new and I might just well put my proverbial foot straight in it. Peggy calls my name and says it would be nice to see what I have to offer the group as I'm new to the College. She's sure it will be delightful...I feel there's an element of mockery in her voice but I smile weakly and then walk into the specified performance space. I see an upright piano, possibly left over from last term's pantomime rehearsals, and decide I'll use this with a gag that I've seen played at my local youth theatre. I get Rick Coulder and Ken Dotson to assist as we move the upright piano to centre stage. I then place a chair facing the keyboard but just too far away to reach the keys. I leave the stage and then say I'm ready. I wait a few moments for the audience to look at the piano and pianist's chair. I hope that they are falling into the trap of thinking that the "crew" has placed it too far from the piano and I haven't noticed. Ah well, so I let the gag begin...

I enter grandly in the operatic style, beaming to my audience and taking expansive bows. I blow kisses to the balcony and obsequiously bow to the Royal Box in this grand theatre. I walk to the piano and, with the most expressive gestures befitting the grandest of artistes, place my music on the stand of the piano. I turn several pages until I've reached the page I require. I step back and admire the sheet of music and then return to stand by the chair. I bow once more, lift my jacket tails and then I settle on the chair. The famous pianist is ready for the concert to begin and is seated in front of his piano.

I stretch my arms and shake my hands still beaming at my audience. I crack and wiggle my fingers and raise my arms ready to deliver the opening chords of the great piano concerto. My hands descend but miss the keyboard by about a foot and I look despairingly at the audience. I stretch my whole body forward and reach my arms towards the keyboard that I cannot reach. I look confused, I scratch my head and I stand and look at both the piano and chair and then quite suddenly it dawns on me that the gap is too wide between the piano and the chair. I grin foolishly to my audience and I gesture to them the extreme width between the chair and the piano. There are smiles from my audience as this clown of a performer realizes his mistake and I show them that I just need to bridge the space between chair and piano.

After specifically measuring the gap I then proceed to close it by struggling in a slapstick manner with the heavy piano which, after great personal toil and torment, I finally manage to move towards the chair. My task accomplished I bow to my audience, lift my coat tails and sit in the chair ready to start the concert.

So that's it…guffaws from Rick Coulder and Gordon Holmes and a pretty good response from the group and even Peggy manages a weak smile. She talks about me being indebted to the Music Hall for this routine and I simply tell her that I picked it up in practical sessions with a youth theatre and I recollect our drama tutor mentioned the importance of the Music Hall tradition for modern British comedy. The rest of the group thinks I convey the humor of the piece and Pam Reason says the clowning is superb. Well that's over with and now I can join the audience for the rest of the presentations without forgetting poor Miriam, last but not least to tread the stage.

Well we're two thirds of the way through the session and there's a range of work which on the whole is pretty impressive. Peggy informs us that for the final exercise she wants us to work in groups of three and to present to the rest of the class a dramatization of a joke. There are groans and comments of displeasure as Peggy proceeds to divide the groups into threes and I am placed with Miriam Ziegler and Sally Shrewsbury. We are given ten minutes to decide upon a joke and to dramatize it and then present it to the rest of the group whilst in the hope we can retain the characters and the humor of the original.

We look at each other and grin weakly as no-one wishes to proceed with the joke telling. I'm not sure about their sense of humour but I decide to throw the old hillbilly joke at them for consideration. I tell them that it has three characters, lends itself to some characterization and has a punch line that stands alone on-stage. They listen intently as I tell them the joke and they both wince and laugh at the punch line. I did pick this one up in a pub in West Ham over Christmas and, although not in the possible best taste, it is neither racist nor sexist. I think as they have got nothing else to offer they're glad to join in and present the American hillbilly joke.

The room is humming with activity as the whole class runs through countless jokes attempting to select the best one for each group's presentation. Our casting is straightforward: Sally is the Mother and Miriam and I are the two children. The scene is swiftly set and we get the opportunity for several rehearsals and I feel that we have at least fulfilled the object of the exercise. I'm quite impressed how quickly the two girls have entered the spirit of the joke and I'm sure we'll get a decent reaction from the class as a whole, if not from Peggy Lewis, the tutor.

We sit as part of the audience whilst several groups present their jokes to us and Peggy discusses the finished product and its comedic components. The results are pretty good but some do not successfully transfer from the spoken word to the stage. The discussions prove interesting and I can see the logic behind the exercise. A joke that is told relies on the spoken word and the listener's imagination. In the theatre we have to make that joke three-dimensional, develop situation, characters and dialogue and to stand it up in front of an audience.

Suddenly it is our turn and we move to the performance area in front of the class and the stern faced Peggy perched on the edge of her chair with her glasses balanced on the tip of her nose. I contemplate that if this is how she responds to a class on comedy, God knows what she expresses when she's exploring tragedy! We have to introduce the joke and set the scene before the performance commences. I stand between Miriam and Sally and begin the introduction:

"Imagine we are in the rural Southern States of America at the time of the American Civil War and our location is an isolated farm in the backwoods. Sally will play the farmer's wife and Miriam and I are the children. The farmer's wife is baking bread in the kitchen on a hot summer's day."

Sally has placed a board across two standing chairs and mimes bread-making whilst she sings "Dixie" in a particularly screeching and tuneless voice. She conveys the southern heat by wiping her brow. Suddenly Miriam and I as the farm children come rushing onstage:

Miriam: "Ma! Ma!"

Sally: "Lisa ma dahlin child. What is it that ails you?"

Martin: "Ma! Ma!"

Sally: "Bless ma soul. You too Jacob, what is the matter?"

Miriam: "Why it's pa ma…!"

Martin: "Yeh ma it's pa ma!"

Sally: "Lordy! Lordy! What do you mean ma children?"

Miriam: "He's in the barn ma!"

Sally: "In the barn?"

Miriam: "Yeh ma he's in the barn!"

Martin: "And he's hung himself ma!"

Sally: "Bless my soul! Lordy! Lordy! Well did ya cut him down?"

Miriam and Martin together: "No ma, he ain't dead yet!"

Silence…time to let the punch line sink in. Groans come from several of the students and Rick Coulder guffaws; the students grin and grimace and several of the more sensitive ones hold their heads in their hands whilst Ken Dotson looks like he has been hit by a London bus. Several of the boys snigger and I feel the performance has worked well in terms of characterization, location, plot and pace. Peggy seems to have frozen over and time stands still in the polar wastes of the rehearsal room. Then there is a smattering of applause from the other students and a fair number of grins on the faces of our audience. The iceberg that is Peggy Lewis finally cracks open and she slowly rises from her chair and beckons us to return to our places. She stands facing the group and I liken her stance to that of a particularly prim and fussy primary school teacher. After a few moments she speaks:

"This item, I believe, belongs to the category known as "sick" humour and it is not one that sits high within my own personal taste. I find the image to be distasteful and bordering on the amoral but nonetheless the group specifically followed my instructions and was skillful at establishing the "world "of the joke and for this I commend them. I do not commend them on their choice of material but then that is an individual's free choice...Well that's enough for this morning and I hope you now have at least a basic understanding of the problems of playing humour on the stage. That's it then, see you all next week."

With that she quickly gathers her papers, wraps herself in her cape and is gone and the class then noisily exits the room exchanging jokes that now suddenly surface from their collective memories. Sally, Miriam and I walk from the room together pleased with our effort but at the back of my mind I am sure that Peggy Lewis now marks the "new boy" as both troublesome and somewhat wayward and, for her, he is one to be carefully watched in the future.

Martin: First Week: Improvisation.

I stand in the car park outside of the main entrance, wrapped against the cold with my overcoat collar up and hidden beneath my long hair. I study the timetable and note that it quite clearly states: Friday 11.00am is Improvisation in the Theatre with Rita Scott. I glance at my watch and it is 10.50am but there is no sign of the rest of the group. Where the hell are they? They've had a term to learn the sodding timetable. I move towards the main window and peer into the students' refectory which is be-fogged with a combination of cigarette smoke, student body heat and an over active central heating system. I can just about make out the figures of Rick and Gordon hunched over cups of coffee with Rick idly flicking through last night's Evening Standard newspaper and Gordon slowly stirring his cup of coffee as if it were thick cloying mud. Well, I think to myself at least the reprobates are about... and this is duly confirmed as Christopher emerges from the Recording Studio, he waves to me and then strolls by smelling of sweet perfume and marijuana on his uneven passage to the theatre. He might be high as a kite but his almost biblical time-keeping is something to behold.

"Marty baby!"

I turn towards the call and along glides Anita Pendleton, clad in flowing robes and bangles, the Reigning Hippy Queen of Hampstead. She grins and gestures towards the theatre and then puts her face close to mine and murmurs:

"Time to improvise, Darling!"

Her long, wavy hair is sunset red and her perfume is exotic and powerful and I am unsure as to whether my glass is half full or half empty. In a second she is gone and is quickly followed by other members of the seminar group who emerge in a vociferous huddle from the college building. Julie Daverner, of the jet black hair and ruby red lips, slides her arm through mine and walks me groom-like down the path to the college theatre.

The double fire doors crash open as the unruly group plough through them and leave the cold January daylight far behind. My eyes take a few seconds to become accustomed to the dimmed lighting in the auditorium and the central pool of light on the stage area.

"Dahlings, my sweeties, that is not the way one should enter a theatre space, which for you, my dears, is a hallowed space!"

The voice comes from half a dozen rows back in the auditorium from behind a table on which is placed an anglepoise lamp. Slowly the darkened figure stands and there is the mini-skirted, middle-aged, attractive, alert and powerful figure of Mrs. Rita Scott, one of the driving forces behind this establishment of New College. She slowly takes off her spectacles and peers at all of us as we stand peppered around the aisles and seats.

"Coats on the chairs, dahlings and then find a space on the stage and face me!"

The student chatter has ceased and Rita's purred instructions are followed precisely; there is a short period of fumbling and stumbling as the individuals find their way to stand in the spotlight on the stage facing Rita Scott who looms spectre-like in the gloom of the auditorium. She sits and deftly flicks on the switch of the light on her desk. She is lit in a ghostly half-light as I strain to see her from my position on the stage.

She quickly has us carrying out our loosening up exercises as we "Rag-Doll" ourselves across the stage with creative student abandon and still those stubborn hidden magnets from this week's movement session enable Rick and Rob to cannon into one another like opponents in an ice hockey match.

"Raggedy Dolls Darlings!" She screeches from the shadows as Rick and Rob lollop in ever decreasing circles across the stage as the rest of us struggle to be doll-like in this phantasmagorical toy shop of Rita's imagination. Finally the cavorting of the dolls comes to an end as Rita orders us to: "Freeze on the spot!" The ensuing dramatic silence is broken only by Rob as he crashes most un-doll-like face down on the floor. My own doll-face cannot freeze as it is creased with a broad grin from deep within as I catch Maisie Tueart's twinkling eye as Rob's rear portion quivers in the toy shop between us.

Next we change our shapes and become the clanking iron men (don't ask me where the iron women have smelted to) and we crash about the stage in the iron furnace created by the theatrical industrialist that is Rita Scott. We are also instructed to belch out cries and sounds that reflect the nature of the creative iron foundry. I grunt and bellow my "iron sounds" and my molten vocabulary fairly flows along as I clunk around the stage with my girder-like gait. Our factory owner out there in the smouldering furnace of the auditorium directs us to a clanking halt and she leads with the following instructions as we all stand cross-girder broad on the stage: "From the fiery furnace the iron people have been cast…you are solid iron, heavy beyond reason and you clank and clash as you thrust your weighty limbs forward and you climb the steep path to the top of the cliff. You must get to the top, your iron neck must strain so that your iron eyes can view the ocean shimmering far below, you must stand erect on the cliff-top with the ocean's wind whirling about you"

There is a silence as Rita's words fade and then the brisk directive:

"Dahlings, you are the Iron Men on the brink…show me!"

Well "show me!" we do as we seethe and screech in our iron constructions and the second hand scrap iron merchants throughout London must have felt a shiver go down their backbones for those few metallic moments as we strained our iron muscles on the top of the cliff.

Suddenly Rita calls out "And relax and leave the impro!"

With a certain amount of relief I emerge from my iron cocoon and join the rest of the group as we sit in the front row of the auditorium to await the next part of the session. We are told that we are going to finish the session working on stage pictures in which units of three will present said pictures to the rest of the group who will be the audience. Miriam Ziegler whispers in my ear that this is all as clear as mud as we prepare for the exercise. I grimace and keep my head down not wishing to be thrown before these New College theatrical lions too soon.

We are quickly divided into "threes" and I am placed with the adorable and mature Pam Reason and the vivacious and shapely Jilly Bradcaster and we move off-stage left to await our call from Rita. There are several other groupings in front of us and it is soon clear how the session will pan out. On Rita's command the trio will walk on stage in a steady and professional manner and then Rita will bark a word and the group will immediately freeze in a picture to theatrically illustrate the command. Rita and the rest of the group will then discuss the picture as the trio freeze as best they can. Once the discussion has reached a satisfactory conclusion the trio can unfreeze and return to the seating.

"Martin, Jilly and Pamela, please" thus is Rita's summons and we stride purposefully towards centre stage and then Rita commands:

"Love!" (Cow! I think...) and whilst my mind judders between thoughts of love for one's fellow creatures and splendid pornography with Jilly, the ever dependable Pam takes control and makes Jilly lay on the floor as the dying parent with Pam and I as the bedside son and daughter sharing her last moments in a Renaissance image. As we concentrate on our pose I am aware of the discussion coming from the auditorium between Rita and the students and I'm afraid my dramatic concentration founders and my visions are still of lovely Jilly laid out before me. I am forcibly wrenched from my erotic reverie when Rita's voice expels my sexual fantasies to the dark side.

"That was lovely dahlings. So sensitive and thoughtful" (Little did she know what female image my piggish mind was actually embracing!).

I am just about to follow Jilly and Pam off stage when Rita says:

"Martin dahling, just stand there facing us with your hands on your hips, staring up at us, confronting us..!"

I duly stare and confront, to the best of my somewhat limited and surprised ability.

"Lovely dahling! You are my dear the look of 60s".., I shall be using you in our modern dress Shakespeare productions this summer."

Oh my God I'm the spirit of the bleeding 60s, (come back Terence Stamp all is forgiven) Now my time has come and Rita Scott will be Shakespearing me in the summer term... Needless to say, I am very wary of an Elizabethan farce coming my way with the force of an Atlantic storm!

Martin: The First Week. Literature.

It is Friday lunchtime and the group is indulging in a mass fish and chip feeding frenzy in the refectory; Winkie the cook must have a share in a potato farm because we all peer from behind our mountainous piles of steaming chips and for once no one attempts to dominate the conversation. The Theatre of the Absurd, Elizabethan Playhouses, Pirandello and Richard III all play a very poor second fiddle to Winkie's magnificent and masterful Fish and Chips and a generation of drama students succumbs to the delicious dish which is a precious recipe learnt long ago in the swirling salt mists of Winkie's sea-faring past. The current major social problem is that we are so full of food that a trip across the road to the Bull and Butcher pub is out of the question as we have not room for a thimble of beer let alone a foaming British pint.

Whilst a grinning and bountiful Mrs. Winkie clears the plates from the tables, we stumble downstairs to the Students' Union and collapse in untidy heaps on the various chairs and settees which cling to the dark, tobacco stained walls of this subterranean refuge. Rob informs me that this is where individuals can be found learning their lines, writing essays or just sleeping off hangovers; it is rumored that the several favoured students who have missed last buses or trains following shows have been allowed to bed down there in bohemian grandeur. It's at times like this that Mrs. Huckle's humble abode seems like the Ritz Hotel.

We have half an hour or so before we go to English Literature and Mrs. Diane Winter. I have been reading "Dr. Faustus", "Richard III" and "The Crucible" as these are the texts the students are studying and, as with the other subjects,

I have to catch up as best I can. I'm not sure Mrs. Winter will have a fully attentive group as most of them succumb to the after effects of that massive lunch. Apparently we're due a lecture on witchcraft this afternoon to give a social background to the texts and Ken Dotson calmly announces that Mrs. Winter will be flying in on her own broomstick to take the lecture. There is much giggling and laughter as the group picture Mrs. W. flying across Hampstead Heath and I appreciate that I'm soon to meet yet another of New College's teaching mavericks.

The time soon passes and we move to the lecture room adjacent to the library and seat ourselves in the desks and chairs. It is not long before the door bursts open and in bustles a black trouser suited Mrs. D. Winter who makes bee-line for the front desk and deposits her pile of books with a dusty thud. She quickly leafs through several copies and places colored pencils in the pages to which she will obviously refer. She is a small dark haired, square set middle-aged woman who, as this lecture is entitled European Witchcraft, I can imagine wrapped in damp, clinging cloaks prowling through the swirling mists of a long lost Celtic moorland. Her dark eyes flick across the faces of her fish fed fat tutees and on seeing me she gives a quick nod of recognition which I assume to be her form of personal greeting. I formally nod back and feel that I am now a bonafide member of the group in the eyes of Mrs. D. Winter. She is obviously a woman of few words and I await the beginning of the lecture with interest. Most of the students have already opened folders and have their pens at the ready and so I deduce that note-taking is going to be the order of the day. She walks to the front row of desks and then slowly turns her head to look at each of us in turn and then she begins her lecture:

"Well, D, let's now look at the pre-Christian religions in Europe whose ceremonies were untouched by the arrival of the Christian religion and their general fertility worship around the figure of a Horned God..."

Here we go again I think to myself, I am still in my first week but I have registered how the place seems to lurch to and from sex in one form or another for much of the time. Ah well, C'est la vie and When in Rome...

The rest of the group feverishly take notes to keep up with the very speedy and brittle dictation emanating from Mrs. W. I'm glad that our History Teacher at Grammar School taught me a form of short hand note taking which I am now finding invaluable as I write the witching and warlocking notes of the Middle Ages and Reformation according to the cultural historian that is Mrs. Diane Winter. I am pen deep in Horned Gods, Jesters and Fools when she introduces the concept of the Devil and asks a general question of the group concerning the plays we are studying: "Dr. Faustus", "Richard III" and "The Crucible". Ken Dotson, our erudite Scot proffers:

"Well Diane, wasn't the real idea behind 'The Crucible' one that had political associations and the whole religious allegory was merely the window-dressing, so to speak?" Diane's face drains of the small amount of colour it possesses and she leans against the black-board as if she has the cares of the universe on her shoulders. She slowly folds her arms and then snaps back at Ken:

"So to speak! So to speak! All the plays have political messages and 'Richard III' was Shakespeare's attempt at Tudor propaganda but all the plays have witchcraft and its associations sown within them…"

It is obvious to me on this cold Friday afternoon that Mrs. Diane Winter has definitely not gorged on Winkie's soporific Fish and Chips at lunch time and if we are looking for the devil incarnate, well he has taken urban Hampstead female form and is pontificating right here in front of the class. I feel sorry for Ken that she has turned on him in such a negative manner but he seems unperturbed by her outburst and the lecture continues as we explore the diabolical administrative methods of the various covens. I am now beginning to comprehend the earlier joke about her arriving for the lecture on her broomstick.

She continues to dictate her notes from the front of the class and we dutifully scratch them in our notebooks. We are well versed in Animal, Child and Godly Sacrifice when thankfully at around four o'clock Mrs. Diane Winter brings the lecture to a close. There is to be no escape from her clutches on that icy afternoon as she immediately sets an essay: "Discuss the relevance of the comic scenes in Dr. Faustus showing what they contribute to the play as a whole." So at least we can say we come away with some degree of comedy after a session with Mrs. D. Winter. We pack away our notebooks and the group begins to leave the room.

"Martin," Mrs. D. Winter beckons to me and so I walk over to her at the front of the class. She gives her imitation of a smile, "How are you catching up with things?"

"I think I'm catching up ok," I reply attempting to sound quite nonchalant.

"Well if you have any problems don't hesitate to contact me as I don't want you falling behind. I'm sure you'll manage;

you seem to have grasped what we're doing pretty well so far. Anyway any problems just get in touch."

And with that she gathers up her books and sweeps out of the room. Well that is all pretty confusing; one minute the Wise Woman of Hampstead is about to turn us all into literary toads and the next minute she is kindness personified supporting the new boy at school. Oh well, that's enough for me today, and I can honestly say that a week at New College is like an eternity on a strange planet!

Back to Mrs. Huckle's and a weekend of note copying and essay writing and, of course, the football match…

Martin: The Football Match.

The weather has slowly improved throughout my first week at New College and by the Saturday morning most of the snow has melted and Golders Green presents a damp, dank morning to the world. I hear Mrs. Huckle leave early in order to spend the weekend at her daughter's house in Rickmansworth and I spend several hours thereafter dutifully copying up notes from Maisie Tueart's Theatrical Representation notebook.

The team is supposed to rendezvous at midday by Golders Green bus station and then catch the 183 bus to Hendon Central. I spend half an hour packing my football kit into my sports bag and, at about a quarter to twelve, I leave Mrs. Huckle's flat and stroll towards the nearby bus station. As I turn the corner I can see a group of somewhat scruffy, long-haired individuals bunched by the café that stands at the entrance to the terminal. I note that most of the Rovers are there and I must say I am impressed by their punctuality (something not in evidence when the NCSD student body attends daily lectures.) I can clearly see that this outfit means business in the gladiatorial arena of the London University Colleges' Football League. If points could be given for turning up on time on a cold, wet January morning in Golders Green then the Rovers would be at the top of their league rather than their current position of somewhere near the foot of the division.

Several wave as I approach and I nod to my new team-mates: Kip Saunders, scowls under his large Zapata moustache and is obviously contemplating team tactics; Ted "Ramsay" Botterall, has his head deep in the Times Educational Supplement Magazine, as always never far from his beloved teaching profession even on such a red-hot derby day as this. Ted is a second year student who missed the training session last Wednesday as he was out on teaching practice. Ted is apparently a disciple of the Theatre in Education movement in British Education and wants to be one of the country's leading arts educationalists. He is a natural leader of men and our team regards him as great manager just like the England World Cup Winning Manager, Sir Alf Ramsay. Jack Chapson leans against the café wall and ostentatiously peruses the adverts for theatre work in The Stage and dear old Christopher Donaldson is perched on his bag like a sodden shaggy sea bird as he gradually floats back to the real world after a night on God knows what illegal substance in the rock music clubs of Camden Town. The two sixth formers, Mervyn and Ralph, from King Alfred's School are there happily grinning and laughing with the rest of the squad obviously content in the knowledge that this football team is the nearest they will ever come to the hippy-happy Hampstead world of the New College of Speech and Drama.

I speak briefly to William Cooper, who morbidly informs me that the Rovers have played the local Hendon College several times and have lost every game. This statistic does not give me any encouragement as I now face the rest of the season as the Rovers' new goalkeeper. There is sudden movement across the group as the 183 red double-decker Routemaster bus approaches and screeches to a halt in order for the assembled Rovers to board. The squad climbs to the top deck of the bus where they spread themselves amongst the empty seats. The diminutive uniformed bus conductor is soon up amongst us deftly taking the fares from the long haired Corinthian spirited drama students.

The rest of the journey to Hendon is uneventful with most of the Rovers lost in the enveloping clouds of cannabis smoke that roll across the upper deck of the bus. Finally the team float off the bus when it stops outside a large imposing red-bricked Victorian building which heralds the Hendon College campus with its adjoining sports pitches.

Ted reads instructions from the fixture letter and says that we are to follow the path that leads to the rear of the building where the Sports Complex and the changing rooms are located. The shambolic figures, bent-double in the cold Hendon wind, shuffle their way past the main building and slither on the icy path towards the sports hall.

Ted "Ramsay" Botterall, the Rovers' natural born leader, leads the team onwards and is as dapper as ever in his tweed-teacher jacket, ironed shirt and tie, creased grey flannel trousers and his polished brogue shoes. Ted "Ramsay" Boterall is always the gentleman teacher. He quickly disappears into the first building and the rest of the Rovers wait in a disorganized huddle on the path outside.

Suddenly a piercing female voice breaks the silence:

"Quick you lot, you're late and in the wrong place, you should be through here with the rest of them!"

A small long-haired girl wrapped in a huge overcoat and college scarf gesticulates wildly that we are to follow her and then turns abruptly on her heels and goes back up the path. With the masterful Ted no longer around to lead, the Rovers shuffle back along the path following the girl who probably knows exactly where the changing rooms are located. We turn the corner of the building and are welcomed on the front drive by a cacophony of noise as huge numbers of gaily dressed students line up as part of a huge procession. The girl quickly points to a gap in the line and we duly shuffle forward to take our place. We stand there for scarcely a minute when a discordant jazz band starts up and the procession moves forward with placards raised and banners waving and one cry breaks the air:

"Support the College Rag Week!"

I look around and can see bears, monkeys and Keystone Cops-I blink and believe that I am still high on the pre-match cannabis and then see a decadent gaggle of vicars and tarts, John Wayne, Marilyn Monroe, Henry the Eighth and Laurel and Hardy!!!

"Fuck me!" I think, "That bloody cannabis is strong!"

"New College! Back here, please!"

I turn to where the shout has come from and there stands a track-suited middle-aged figure who is obviously the Sports

Lecturer and, to a man, the Rovers turn and leave the Rag Procession behind and amble towards the portly gentleman in the orange tracksuit.

"Sorry about that chaps, but you seem to have got mixed up with the Rag Procession which is about to go into town collecting for charity. Can't see how you got muddled up with them as they're all in fancy dress!"

I look around at the Rovers' squad and, apart from the King Alfred Sixth Formers, there is an unholy dress code of long hair, beards and moustaches, brightly coloured flared jeans and shaggy sheepskin coats, beads, bangles, earrings and trilby hats; if this isn't a fancy dress student rag procession, then what is?

The PE lecturer takes us into the building where a somewhat bewildered Ted "Ramsay" Botterall is waiting and we all enter the changing rooms. These are grimly municipal and form a damp, brick backcloth to the Rovers metamorphosis from forlorn Lowry-esque winter wonderland figures to the power-primed Claret and Blue clad athletes honored to represent the New College of Speech and Drama in the deadly cut and thrust of the London University Colleges' Soccer League. Ted "Ramsay" Botterall leads the elite team out on to the sleet lashed mud of the Hendon playing fields and we find our soccer pitch. The grim-faced Polytechnic team, wearing grubby green and black shirts, stand scowling as their claret and blue clad, long haired thespian opponents saunter onto the playing field in a most jocular cavalier fashion. I squelch my way through the mud to the vacant goalmouth and field the sodden ball lobbed at me by my Rovers' team mates as we await the captains to toss the coin and finally arrange the kick off with the orange track-suited lecturer-come-referee. We are to stay where we are as the teams get ready for the kick off and here I stand, the latest incumbent as the last line of defence in the Rovers' rag tag team as it punches above its weight in the University league. I look at the players in front of me and question why Rita Scott is so concerned that her "Players Men" might limp across the New College stage with a football acquired injury as they Shakespeare their first year away. Kip Saunders and the errant Third Years I feel are now well and truly outside of Scott's universe and will continue to play football against her wishes until Hell itself freezes over.

The driving sleet has eased and the match kicks off with the Rovers' attempts to plough a champions' path through the thick and clinging Hendon mud. The Rovers are obviously a slick passing team as they soon have the lumbering Polytechnic players chasing dramatic shadows! When Hendon do have the ball the threatening and brutal presence of lecturer Frank Leer crunches into bone shaking and successful challenges! It is not long before the Rovers have established a two goal lead through the exciting and irrepressible twin strike force of Christopher Donaldson and William Cooper. I am most impressed with the Rovers' all round ability and I am glad to see that their talents do not just lay in front the New College Theatre footlights. I am hardly troubled in goal as the first half progresses and cut a somewhat lonely and rain-sodden figure in the muddy goalmouth. The half-time whistle blows and the Rovers huddle together on the veranda of the cricket pavilion in order to gain some shelter from the sleet and rain showers. The team talk is shared by Kip Saunders and Ted "Ramsay" Botterall and we are informed that we are by far the best team and will be able to score more goals as we have the prevailing storm-force wind behind us in the second half.

The drenched Rovers start the second half in a frenzy of attacking football and quickly score two more goals and the Neanderthal Polytechnic team simply slumps into oblivion and gives up the ghost. I am hardly troubled by two long shots which I manage to get well behind to stop the ball squirming over our goal line and I comfortably come and catch the soggy ball when it comes floating across from two corner kicks taken against the prevailing wind. This is fairly basic goalkeeping but I think it is enough to show the rest of the Rovers that their new goalkeeper does know what he is doing. Jack Chapson, who drifts a great deal in his midfield role, plays a long back pass to me and the ball does not bounce but sticks dangerously with a splash on the edge of the penalty area and the Hendon centre-forward is the first to the ball and with boots ploughing through the mud bears down on me in goal with breathtaking speed. I move forward to narrow the angle of his expected shot and do not take my eyes away from the muddy football. He strikes the ball hard and high to my right side and I immediately dive that way with my arms outstretched and the ball hits my gloves like a sticky Christmas pudding. I splash down full-length in the muddy goalmouth and hold onto the ball. I am pleased with that save but pay for it physically as I am totally covered in thick and squelching mud. Several of the Rovers call out to credit the save and I quickly kick the ball up field content that I have shown the team that I am pretty efficient between the posts. I see little more action as the game slips and slops through the last few minutes towards the wet and windy final whistle.

The Rovers' high spirits are soon to be dampened when we return to the changing rooms to find a boiler-suited caretaker carrying a bag of tools who informs us that the showers have just broken down and are now out of order. There is a great deal of cussing and cursing as the mud covered Rovers bewail their dripping and glutinous fate. The three wash basins are run with cold water to try to scrape the thick, stinking mud from the players' legs; these attempts are soon abandoned as the mud clogs the drains from the basins and the brown, stagnant water has nowhere to go. The grumbling continues as the victors scrape as much mud as possible from themselves and finally the grubby Rovers are ready for the return bus journey to Golders Green.

The jubilant Rovers have by now become used to their layers of dried mud and the team once more spread themselves across the seats on the top deck of the bus. There is much analysis of the game and the match becomes more theatrical in the drama students' collective memories as the bus edges towards Golders Green in the Saturday afternoon traffic. The match report is collectively written in glowing terms for the college magazine and it will be grudgingly included by the trendy art house editor alongside sycophantic theatre reviews and rambling student poetry. I smile as I look out of the bus window, content that my first public performance at New College was of a sufficiently high standard to ensure my place in the legendary Rovers football team for the next three years.

FROM: Rose-Mary
To: Martin
Subject: First Week
Date: January 3lst, 2012 3:32 pm
Hello Martin:

Your first week was captivating. I agree with including the football match and your abduction by the rag parade. I have to travel to Portland (5 hours away) to get a football fix with the Portland Timbers. When they score a goal (not very often as of late) but when they do, the mascot, a hairy, large lumberjack takes his chain saw to a felled tree and slices across the grain producing blue toxic smoke from the motor, the fans (The Timbers Army) go berserk. This is ironic as Portland, Oregon is known as the green, forward thinking eco city. Regarding Truro Football Club I think it is very sad when a football club folds. Is the cause of their demise financial? I am old school in that I believe we should revert to homegrown footballers so they have an affiliation and pride in their hometowns. Recently watched a documentary about Wembley FC with Terry Venables coaching as a guest manager, his line up and ideas are resisted by the current manager. Have you seen the show? My eldest son, Keir was forty recently and his wife, Maria bought him a trip across the pond to support Chelsea when they played Manchester United. I am not happy as the family team has always been United under my mother's rule and now the family has been betrayed by Keir. My grandson Bernard supports Manchester City, so for his fifteenth birthday I sent him a Manchester United shirt I have pleaded with his mother, my daughter, Alex to put a stop to this nonsense. I don't know where I went wrong to have offspring align themselves with teams other than Manchester United.

Back to the diary. Do you remember the date of the Helen Dunwell Prize? I do recall the utter embarrassment and ghastly experience I had with the director I was assigned to. Her choice of play and casting was a nightmare. The production still stings in my memory. Keep writing.

Love
Rose-Mary

FROM: Martin
To: Rose-Mary
Subject: Helen Dunwell
Date: February 2nd, 2012 4:39 am
Hi Rose-Mary

Do you have any documentary evidence of the time? See Helen Dunwell mentioned and do you have any list of our groups? I cannot remember our 3rd year director's name but I do the stage manager from that year but that's another story.....the director was definitely a freethinker - hence her choice of Rosmersholm!! Woeful memories of the whole farce....

Thanks
Look forward to hearing from you.
Love
Martin

Rosemary: Helen Dunwell Prize.

We are challenged in acting this term by the Helen Dunwell Prize. This is an in-house acting and directing exercise during which first years are randomly allocated to third year directors. The plays are chosen by the third years. First years are judged on their acting ability and techniques and the thirds years on their directorship skills. The Helen Dunwell is a showcase for first years, it allows the faculty get a glimpse of those students they are not familiar with and can determine future casting of productions.

I am assigned to a mousey, untidy female, Vicky. She has cropped bleached blond hair and skin, a negative personality and possibly half an iota of imagination. I should mention she has a three week old baby that she hauls around with her like a sack of potatoes. She leaves the infant unattended and squawking in dark corners of the common room while we rehearse. Her husband is a producer at the B.B.C. and she immediately informs her cast that she has a job lined up with Aunty Beeb. I don't know who I feel sorry for most the abandoned baby or Vicky whose play selection is abysmal.

She has chosen the 1940's period play, Ladies Of Leisure, without any thought to the four first year drama students she has in her charge, she has arbitrarily selected the parts for Kay, Duncan, Sandra and myself without meeting us. Kay is Elaine Clews described as "tall and striking" which Kay certainly is but the depiction continues "the perfect housekeeper of the period," her age is late forties. Sandra is cast as Lorna "a pretty young maid…she is rather a flighty type." Sandra is pretty despite her large black square rimmed glasses, but she is not fickle nor capricious. Duncan is Cyril Jones the housekeeper's criminal nephew the cast description is: "He is a little fellow of the type for which the term "cad" was coined." Poor Duncan who is a teddy bear of a man with a strong Birmingham accent also has to don a "touch of the cockney about him." I am cast as Sister John, "A fat, red-face jolly old nun with gleaming spectacles." Are you kidding me? We will have to dig into our inner Stanislavski if we have a hope in hell of assembling a stage worthy production.

Rehearsals are dire. Noel Niven is Vicky's mentor and he sits in on the rehearsals attempting but failing miserably to hurry the director along. Noel is a jolly, red-faced well intentioned, intense member of staff full of enthusiasm and encouragement. With our little troupe of disgruntled players he has his work cut out for him. Kay is intent on foraging for sub-text where there is none. She and our bleached, beached director spend hours minutely deciphering and decoding every word. Duncan, Sandra and I sit on the sidelines glum and collectively browned-off. To while away the time I have taken up knitting a scarf on jumbo two inch round needles which I pass to Sandra and Duncan the scarf is over six feet long and growing at every rehearsal. Parents and friends are invited to the performances. I don't tell my mother because I know she would not be impressed by this theatrical debacle.

During one rehearsal the third year Rosy comes looking for me. This is the senior who had given me the initial tour of the campus. She is still wearing her orange workman's boots from our previous encounter. I mistakenly believe I am going to be designated to another group for the Helen Dunwells. She takes me aside outside the rehearsal room and opens with;

"We have a problem."

"What is it?" I enquire.

"Well the staff have agreed that there are too many Rosemary's enrolled and this causes confusion amongst the staff. I have been instructed for you to select another name or another version of Rosemary.

"Really?" I ask incredulously.

"Yes, really." Rosy reflects momentarily and then offers, "My name is Rosemary but I shortened it to Rosy. One of the other Rosemary's in your year has taken Romi and another Ros."

"I don't want to change my name," I insist.

Rosy looks shocked that anyone would question the powers that be in the staff room.

"I am willing to change the spelling by adding a hyphen between the e and the m and capitalizing that letter."

Rosy pauses for a minute. "I think they will accept that."

So from there on in I spell my name Rose-Mary another agitation that I will not to disclose to my mother. Rosy, leaves as quickly as she appeared, her mission accomplished the glut of Rosemary's has been disintegrated.

Gerald, alias Prince Ivan the Ninny has been assigned to a loud, heavy set, sandy haired, third year female director. He has convinced her to produce an original movement piece that he has choreographed. For the performance his upper torso and face are smothered in gold paint and he wears white revealing tights. That as Micki declares:

"Shows off his lunch box."

I think he resembles Michelangelo's, David. His dance is breathtaking. After our performances Gerald insists I meet his parents who have travelled from their farm in Oxford to see the Helen Dunwell's. I am ushered before his parents in the garden of Ivy House. I am still clad in my nun's costume and I am confused when they collectively introduce themselves.

"How do you do Sister?"

They invite me to join them with Gerald for tea in Hampstead.

When we arrive Gerald has remnants of gold on his face. I have donned a mini dress, thigh high, light brown suede boots and a large floppy hat. I have dispelled their first impressions of me being cloistered. There are awkward silences as we wait for the tea. Gerald's parents don't mention his brilliant performance. They seem uptight about something. But they are putting on brave faces and his matronly mother shares that Gerald is the youngest of three boys. His brothers are lawyers. She doesn't enquire about my family. Thank god. After Earl Grey tea and Eccles cakes Gerald and I excuse ourselves. We walk back to New College hand in hand with not a word between us.

The culmination of the Helen Dunwell's is an open critique for all participants by a guest judge. At stake is the coveted Helen Dunwell Prize. This year the adjudicator for the Helen Dunwell's is a smug, balding man sitting in the centre of the auditorium, he gives his comments and critique aloud to all the students. He berates our director for choosing Ladies Of Leisure and I find a morsel of pity for her being demeaned in front of her peers. He makes the whole audience laugh when at the end of a slaughter of his review of our production he asks:

"Who let the nun in?"

Which although astute was hurtful. I did suddenly appear on stage without a sound or verbal cue. My ego is bruised for the thankless role of a nosey nun. I feel short changed as my creative and artistic abilities have been stifled by an imaginatively stunted director.

The winner of the Helen Dunwell Prize is The Lesson, the absurdist classic by Ionesco. Ronald Frobisher an ex-Naval officer and mature student at New College brings physical intensity and is exquisite as the professor, he is admirably supported by Jean Rogers as the student. The execution of The Lesson has been masterly directed by the smoldering, raven haired, swarthy Kip Saunders. I don't believe there is a first year student, either male or female who isn't a member of his admiration society.

Everyone in the audience was riveted by the performance. My mind remains with that production of The Lesson for I don't think there is one comparable.

At home my mother is in a funk. Her bank manager of thirty years has without her permission sold a portion of her stocks to pay my father's overdraft. She is shell shocked that she has been well and truly "swindled" by Mr. McMillan, her friend and confidante for over two decades. To make matters worse my father without consulting anyone has become a guarantor for a business acquaintance. The business has declared bankruptcy, my father is liable for the debt. My mother is on the brink, threatening to up and leave to live in America with her newly crowned prince, my unsuspecting elder half-brother, Terry.

She finagles an open-ended ticket to California. Before she departs she is determined for us to pay penance for our shortcomings. My mother buys herself a powder blue

Volkswagen. She returns to modeling for Norman Linton plus size dresses. She becomes a regular at the local King Harold Public House where she engorges herself on liquid sustenance and holds court with the regular patrons. My brother Tony has joined my father's glazing business. Tony is seen rarely. He comes home to take a bath and change before disappearing to dance the night away in clubs. My father arrives home from work later and later. He is hungry and diminished. I am expected to clean, make his dinner, and keep the house in order. My mother has abdicated from family life. For weeks I have been trying to keep up. I am in a strop this morning when I walk upstairs to the snoozing maternal head of the house. My mother usually sleeps until noon. I open the bedroom door, she is swaddled in blankets. I stand at the door and declare:

"You can't expect me to take on these household chores forever."

My inner voice warns me *What are you thinking?*" My mother catapults herself from under the covers and hurls herself towards me. She strikes me hard across the face.

"You will do what I tell you to do. You don't pay rent. You are sponger like your father. Now get out and let me get some sleep. Sleep is the only luxury I have left."

My face is stinging. I didn't have time to protect my cheek as she threw her punch.

"Bring me a glass of water for my pills," she orders.

I retreat obediently, holding the side of my face. I bring her the glass of water and place it on the bedside table, the drawer is open. I stop as I put the glass down astonished by the number of prescription pills stashed within the drawer. No wonder she is erratic and unhappy. From under the covers her voice whispers,

"Don't you have a bus to catch? Now leave me alone."

I shut the bedroom door and hastily leave. I don't know which is worse the pit in my stomach or the ballooning of my cheek with the tell-tale handprint.

During the first lecture, I keep my head down. Afterwards Kate grabs my hand and drags me into the more private upstairs loo.

"What's going on?"

She is looking directly at me.

"Nothing," I feebly reply.

She is relentless, she stares at the mark on my face.

"How did you get that?"

"I walked into a door."

"Right?" she smirks. "You don't have to tell me…except I hope your boyfriend didn't do this to you?"

With that she takes out a wad of Kleenex from her bag and runs them under the cold water tap.

"Here put this on you cheek."

"Does it notice a lot?" I ask.

Kate shakes her head unconvincingly.

"It wasn't my boyfriend. He's in Bath studying Maths and buxom blonds."

Kate giggles:

"Well that's good then."

Before we leave the loo I whisper:

"This is a family matter."

Kate turns, she places my hands in hers.

"Look Rose-Mary I want you to know, we are your family. Group C loves and adores you. We care about you and we are here for you. You can count on us. We are your family."

With that we head downstairs to the rehearsal room. We are greeted by the sound of the piano. Norway Martin is playing "Moon River". Group C is waiting on Elizabeth Leigh who is unusually late. When the Mancini score is finished, Martin makes eye contact with me, smiles and announces:

"This is for you Rose-Mary."

He commences playing and singing a la Dean Martin "I Wish You Love" I marvel at his perfect timing. I smile at him in appreciation. Kate is right. I look around the room and realize that I am part of the Group C family and I thank my lucky stars for each one of them.

From: Martin
To: Rose-Mary
Subject: Dunwell-done and dusted
Date: February 10th, 2012 9:35 am
Hi Rose-Mary
Attached Dunwell. It wasn't easy to recollect the Dunwells-what a strange time! Memories of love and anarchy. Are your familiar with the Cohen song?
All the very best
Love,
Martin

Martin: The Helen Dunwell Experience.
The term is progressing well on all fronts: I have caught up with most of the note taking and I feel confident about my

knowledge of the missed academic work. There is nothing to worry me about any of the practical drama work we have been undertaking. Rita is keen to rid me of my glottal stops (inherited from my East End background) so that I may be fully proficient in my Received Pronunciation or Central Southern English as it is known throughout the British Theatre and the British Broadcasting Corporation. A necessary evil I guess as I follow in the footsteps of other East End actors like the well-known Terence Stamp (an old boy from my Grammar School).

The social side of my New College life has also changed dramatically as I've left Mrs. Huckle's Victorian digs in Golders Green and I have moved into a shared house with other students in local Hampstead Garden Suburb. It is a splendid house and I'm sharing with a motley crew. There is Christopher Donaldson, a fellow first year and footballer, seldom on this planet due to a combination of drugs and general detachment from life. He is very attractive in a wild, Hippy-ish manner and his love-life is firmly scored on the walls of the house. He has a relationship of sorts with fellow tenant, Lynn Plant, a second year student equally happy thumbing a lift along the speeding expressway of drugs and rock and roll. She can be so far out but at the same time she is both cuddly and domestic in the style of an older sister. Judy Seymour is the second female of the house and she is a third year student and single mum and she seems to hold the place and tenants together with her wit and common sense. I like her a lot and she makes me laugh with her laconic observations about the fellow tenants and the daily social machinations at New College. Her little boy is David and he is looked after for most of the week by Eamon and Harriet O' Braden. Eamon is a benign psychology lecturer at the College who is adored by the students as he muddles his way through the daily crises of the College. And last but not least is Tony Tocci, a fellow first year student who in between bouts of Byron and LSD is attempting to create a new world in his own image. Tony has family roots in Mediterranean Europe and is gracious yet volatile in his College relationships. His love for his fellow creatures is tempered by his infatuation with both Christopher and LSD but not necessarily in that order. We go to College together on the 102 bus to Golders Green: me in my Levi jeans and jean jacket and Tony in his white robes and sandals and shoulder length black hair so that it would seem that I'm on a blind date bus ride with Jesus Christ! He is currently preoccupied with Christopher (as ever!) and his exploration of experimental "foot theatre" where he hopes to entertain and educate with a kind of puppetry of the feet... I have had to refuse his kind and considerate invitation to become a member of his "Foot Company" owing to my in-growing toe nails following an accident with a piano in the theatre. I will follow their progress with feigned enthusiasm as one does not like to upset dear old Tony and his manic theatrical ambitions. As we stroll up the hill towards college I'm turning John Donne's poem "Song" over in my mind. I first came across Donne and the Metaphysical Poets when I was studying at Avery Hill College last autumn and I immediately tuned in to his early love and erotic poems. This poem was also featured on Long Playing Record by folk singer, John Renbourn and now I have learnt the poem I can't wait for an opportunity to perform it at New College. I look forward to studying the Metaphysical Poets later in the academic year:

<u>Song : John Donne.</u>
Go and catch a falling star,
Get with child a mandrake root
Tell me where all past years are,
Or who cleft the devil's foot,

Tonight is the first rehearsal of the Helen Dunwells, which as I understand are a series of play extracts performed by the first year students and chosen, directed and stage –managed by the third years. I am cast in the Norwegian play "Rosmersholm" written by Henrik Ibsen in 1886. I seem to have drawn the short straw playing a Victorian former clergyman trapped in an age of social and political change and in love with an amoral free-thinking heroine. I'm somewhat concerned that all this has to be communicated to an adjudicator and an invited college audience in fifteen minutes. But, hey ho mine not to reason why?

During the busy day at college, I double-check the notice-boards for the details of the Dunwell rehearsals for this evening: "Rosmersholm" by Henrik Ibsen, Third Year Director is Alicia Paget with the third year Stage Manager, Shirley Helmes. Yours truly has been cast (in my absence) as Johannes Rosmer with fellow first years, Jilly Bradcaster as Rebecca West and Sally Shrewsbury as Mrs. Helseth, the housekeeper. Sally also has a major part in another Dunwell and is merely "helping-out" with her minor role. It is up to Jilly and I to engage and deliver what many critics see as Ibsen's masterpiece. We are performing (I use the term loosely) a few pages from the end of Act Four when the whole action is ratcheted up to cast doubts on late nineteenth century Christian ethics and contemporary morals and we see the couple leave the stage in a highly emotional suicide pact which is played out against the backdrop of a raging mountain torrent and the haunting vision of the family ghost, the White Horse of Rosmersholm. The third years have been away from college on teaching practice and the only ones I know are the players in the football team. The director and stage manager will have no idea about me as I wasn't even here the previous term when they were last in college.

I rendezvous with Jilly in the refectory before we venture down to the pre-fabricated buildings for our first rehearsal. Jilly is a charming and dramatic girl with an hour glass figure and is usually dressed in black. I have considered a possible relationship with her but I don't feel up to the trials and tribulations of the Camden druggy bed-sit world. Her magnificent breasts must be left firmly in the world of my imagination! We talk freely about our more or less total ignorance of Ibsen although Norwegian exile Martin Lordahl kindly did give me a fleeting seminar in the students' union common room the other afternoon. I gained some insight but learnt as much about the plumbing problems of his flat in Chelsea. But it was supportive of him to have a chat in the first place. Jilly and I are not looking forward to the two evenings per week when we have to rehearse before the Dunwells are performed later in the term. But we have been given the texts and both of us have attempted to learn the majority of the lines. I think at least the prompt corner will not be too busy during our Dunwell effort.

Jilly and I enter the rehearsal room at the allotted time and there waiting for us are the two third years (Sally is missing as she is rehearsing her other play) who have the responsibility for staging the last ten minutes of Ibsen's masterwork in a month's time.

Alicia Paget is the director and she is most earnest and particular about the play; she has obviously seen things in the work that I have been too lazy to explore. But good luck to her and I will do my best for her although I feel the Dunwells are rather like the Romans throwing the Christians to the Lions. There is a negative nervous energy in the college running through the Dunwell experience which strikes me as reflecting a kind of public school competiveness rather than possessing any intrinsic artistic value. I respond as best I can to both Alicia's explicit directions and officious matronly manner and can easily visualize her running the drama department at the Cheltenham Ladies College with both dynamic verve and tenacity. Jilly and I "block" our moves as directed using the table and chairs in the classroom and imagine the nineteenth century drawing room with the dominant French Windows leading to the bridge over the torrent at the bottom of the garden where our characters' suicide pact will take place. This will get them rocking in their seats in the college theatre if nothing else does.

Now the stage manager, Shirley Helmes, is a different proposition entirely; when the Dunwells were first cast Rob Dameron was standing with me and after glancing at the Rosmersholm production sheet said to me:

"Well this all might be shit but at least you've got "Julie Christie" in your group"

Now in the rehearsal room and looking at the seated and scribbling stage manager I can see what he meant. Shirley Helmes is a most beautiful girl truly cast in the mould of the famous actress, Julie Christie. She is tall and slender with a tan (apparently a winter ski-ing trip), long, luxurious shoulder-length blonde hair and even longer curvaceous legs. She apparently has the lead in the Third Year's final show in the summer term, the musical "The Match Girls", and from forecasts looks destined for a glittering stage career. But for now she is tied to the Dunwells and seemingly tries her best working with Alicia. Jilly and I wrestle with the smouldering relationship between Johannes Rosmer and Rebecca West which leads tragically to this Nordic suicide pact at the end of the play. We finish our first rehearsal and Alicia seems quite happy with our efforts; as we are packing up, a swarthy dark haired young man comes into the room and asks Shirley Helmes if she is ready to leave as he has a copy of "The Match Girls'" script. So this must be the third year student called Steve who is the College's "Warren Beatty" to Shirley Helmes' "Julie Christie". He totally ignores Jilly and I and we become invisible as he continues his conversation with Shirley. It does not take me long to realize what a piece of shit this bloke is and so I pitch in with a leading metaphorical left jab in my roughest Cockney accent:

"Oh not the Match Girls...my Nan always talks about them, and the 1889 Dock Strike and Jack the Ripper...all part of my world as I was born just round the corner and one of my grand-dads was a lighterman on the Thames until he drowned in an accident. I find the loss of the Princess Alice on the Thames in 1878 and the Silvertown Munitions Explosion in 1917 far more interesting. Now both of those, and the Siege of Sydney Street and the Battle of Cable Street would make really great musicals about The East End. I know the playwright Bill Owen is a socialist but he's not actually from East London. Perhaps Richard Wilkins will employ me as the

dialect coach and historical adviser for your production...?
See ya folks!"

I grin broadly as "Julie and Warren" stare open mouthed
as I collect my bags and saunter past them into the cold north
London night. The freezing night air takes my breath away as
I head down the hill towards Golders Green bus station and
before I know it I have launched aloud into Donne's "Song" for
the benefit of the neighbourhood:

"Teach me to hear mermaids singing,

Or to keep off envy's stinging,

And find

What wind

Serves to advance an honest mind."

The rehearsals continue for weeks in a similar pattern
and I begin to feel like the proverbial fish out of water as
this young student actor struggles to come to terms with the
character of the middle-aged Victorian landowner and former
clergyman. Why on earth had Alicia chosen such a vehicle to
place poor Jilly and myself in the theatrical stocks that will
be the bloody college performance? Member of staff, Sylvia
Gonzalez, who is Alicia's mentor on the production, pops
into rehearsals a few times. She is very positive and gives us
plenty of encouragement but I still feel like a condemned man
preparing for the scaffold! I feel that I am nowhere near Ibsen's
search to define "nobility of character, of mind and of will". In
fact, the theatrical cul-de-sac that this particular exercise has
left me in is emotionally nearer to Oliver Hardy than Henrik
Ibsen! We grind our way towards production date and trudge
through a despairing and depressing technical rehearsal in the
college theatre. Thankfully, Sally Shrewsbury has now joined

us and sweet Sally is a breath of fresh air. She provides us with plenty of support and good humour and assures us that the Dunwell play she is working on is a far greater disaster than Rosmersholm will ever be. I maintain a decent working relationship with the director although I think she largely inhabits another planet and Jilly, Sally and I follow the script with grace and humour. "Julie Christie" is as charming as ever and even laughs at some of my jokes, whilst "Warren Beatty" skulks around at the end of rehearsals and I nonchalantly ignore him for the dog turd shit face that he most surely is!

The costume fitting is a total farce and my Victorian suit has me trussed up like a Christmas turkey. Surly staff member, Beatrice Franky the Wardrobe Mistress, doesn't seem bothered with me and is obviously looking to dress other more favoured productions. I dislike her and am happy to re-create her as a Children's Theatre character: "Widow Twankie who lived far below the surface of the earth in the dank and insect infested Drobes." She is to suffer greatly in the future from my wicked satirical pen when I write for the alternative college magazine, "The Coil!"

The actual performance is acceptable and we perform in the college theatre in front of the nit-picking students who seem to be sucking up every mistake with relish and make me think what an appalling contribution this lot is going to make to the future world of drama and theatre. Fortunately we limp through with little going wrong (apart from the choice of play) and the adjudicator seems to think much the same and says we have tried our best shot but we are not convincing as Victorian gentlefolk on the brink of a suicide pact and both Jilly and I more or less agree with the adjudication. I just want to get out of the " turkey" suit and remove the "pantomime" make–up and put the whole thing down to bitter and bemused experience. We three cast soon settle into the bar of the Bull and Butcher Pub and gradually wash "Rosmersholm" out of our systems with copious amounts of white wine. As we graciously and rather drunkenly praise our gallant thespian efforts we are surprised to see Alicia and Shirley come into the bar and walk over to where we are sitting. They thank us for all our hard work (their words!) and then proceed to invite us to a third year "Dunwell Party" in the nearby suburb of Temple Fortune on Saturday night. They give us the address and as quickly as they have entered they are gone. I put the card in my pocket and the three of us soon sway back to college to spend the rest of the afternoon drunkenly dozing on the sofas in the student union common room. I am playing football for the Rovers on Saturday afternoon and have no other plans for the weekend and I therefore pencil in the Temple Fortune party to go to if nothing better offers itself to me.

Following a bruising and muddy football match on Hampstead Heath against the Southgate College opposition, I return to my home to find everyone, apart from Tony, away for the rest of the weekend. Christopher has left directly after the match to go to a South London Party with Lynn Plant. Judy is spending the weekend with her son, David, at the O'Braden's house. Tony is emotionally contemplating a solitary foray with his LSD supplies in the fridge and I warn him not to attempt to do so as he will soon be alone in the house. He looks at me like a chastised Labrador puppy and so I use my trump evasive card to inform him I am off to the third year party in Temple Fortune. The thought of a night in with the Christopher-less love-lorn Tony precipitates my social soiree and I am glad I have not thrown away the invitation card with the address. I keep out of Tony's way by washing my muddy football kit in the bath and I then hang it on the washing line in the garden in the hope that it will not freeze solid overnight. Tony and football do not mix at all and he gives me a wide berth as I scrub and swear in the bathroom and he reads soulfully aloud from Kahlil Gibran's "The Prophet" in the living room downstairs. When I finally emerge washed and party-perfumed Tony has departed leaving a note saying that he is going to the Arts Lab in Covent Garden for the evening. This usually means he will re-emerge next Tuesday or Wednesday having had all kinds of hippy experiences in the Wild West End of London.

I ride the 102 London Transport double decker bus to Temple Fortune (a medieval name that goes back to the knights of St John) which lies close to Hampstead and Golders Green and has one of the longest shopping parades in North London. I purchase two bottles of English Country Wine from the off-licence and I know from experience the content of these bottles is both armed and dangerous. It is approaching ten o'clock when I finally find the Edwardian block of apartments where the Dunwell party is being held. The door is ajar and I stroll in and the party is in full swing. Alicia sees me and greets me most theatrically with hugs and kisses which would make you think I was a long lost brother back from a far outpost of the Empire. She then takes my bottles and quickly gives me a full glass of white wine and disappears, robes flowing behind her, into the kitchen. I see Kip Saunders and we have a quick conversation about this afternoon's football match and agree that the Rovers were sadly off-form. He also tells me he's really pissed off with

New College and can't wait to leave and form his own theatre company. He feels frustrated with the curriculum and believes the whole place is out of joint with trends in contemporary theatre. He also admits he's got the part of the brutal foreman in "The Match Girls" and he's glad it's a relatively small part so he can keep out of the limelight and work with his own theatre group. He wants to run his own theatre company as soon as he leaves New College in the summer. The third year musical seems to be a major topic of conversation at the party and I leave Kip to his bottle of red wine as I can see Sally in the corner of the room with her boyfriend. They're a lovely couple (he's not from New College) and we chuckle about the horrors that were the Dunwells. There's no sign of Jilly-she's probably rocking the marijuana filled- night away in Camden Town and I wish her well. The smoke-filled living room is full of dancers and so I slip into the kitchen for another glass of wine and then find some space to myself in the hallway. I welcome the relative peace and quiet and lean against the wall with my eyes closed thinking of nothing much…

"Hello Martin"

I open my eyes and turn to the female voice and there stands "Julie Christie", a vision in a black mini-dress with her blond locks cascading around her bare shoulders.

"Hi Shirley, how's things?"

Her face breaks into the most beautiful smile and she asks how it is that I have come to arrive a term late at the College. I quickly regale her with my academic and theatrical autobiographical meanderings and I do not refuse when she asks if I want another drink. How can I refuse her? She takes my glass and glides into the kitchen. Well here I am being chatted up by "Julie Christie" and there's no sign of her dumb "Warren Beatty" Steve anywhere. She returns with two glasses of wine and an even more beauteous smile than before. No wonder most of the men in the college (apart from Tony) have a raging passion for her. I just feel that as the new kid on the block I come with no previous New College emotional baggage and "Julie Christie" is certainly not at all backward in coming forward as we stand close together in the hallway. I notice she has the bluest of eyes as we talk about the Dunwells. Apparently as she has been given the lead in the major forthcoming musical, "The Match Girls", she was not offered a directing role in the Dunwells but had to stage-manage instead. She tells me she is from Basingstoke (I won't hold that against her.) and she is hoping for a career as an actress. She has no desire for any teaching post and she is so pleased that their final teaching practice has now taken place. Shirley is very interested when I tell her about my year's post as an unqualified primary schoolteacher in the East End. She asks several questions about my background and I wonder whether she is carrying out some social research for her part in "The Match Girls". Shirley seems pleased that I am only a couple of months younger than her although I'm in the First Year and tells me that her stunning tan is the result of a recent twenty-first birthday present of a Swiss skiing trip from her parents.

"I thought you did really well in the part, Martin," she parts her luscious lips in a half smile. "It must have been one of the most difficult parts in all of the Dunwells. I enjoyed watching you in rehearsal; you worked really well with Lesley." She stops smiling and looks me straight in the eyes, "You're not involved with her …or anyone are you?"

I think for a second- well I'm involved with Tony, but that is basically trying to prevent him from blowing what's left of his brains away with his stash of LSD tabs!

I stare straight back at her ("Warren Beatty" watch your back)

"No, I'm not involved with her or anybody else at the moment. I simply haven't had the time or opportunity for relationships having to catch up on so much work since I joined in January. And Johannes fucking Rosmer and his love–life has kept me on the straight and narrow for the time being"

She laughs and throws her head back and then she looks towards the living room,

"Let's dance!" She gently but firmly takes my hand, "I really want to dance with you; you know…I've been wanting to for ages".

We smile and she leads me into the living-room where we join the dancing throng and dance to the Turtles' "Happy Together." She moves beautifully and seems to be concentrating on the music and I'm just happy to be here. We continue dancing through the Beatles' "All You Need is Love." Nobody appears to notice us together and frankly I don't give a damn as this is turning out to be a pretty good bloody party. Suddenly the mood changes with Procul Harum's "A Whiter Shade of Pale" and Shirley Helmes takes a step towards me and quickly puts her arms around me and pushes her firm body hard against mine. We hold each other tight as we dance very slowly to this song and I don't know about Tony's brains but I feel as though my head is exploding. I can honestly say I have never felt like this before. She looks up at me and we immediately kiss very slowly and deeply. Her eyes are closed and she presses herself against me and I feel the room spinning. Suddenly as Leonard Cohen is singing "Hey, That's No Way to Say Good-Bye" and the room is dark and full of the warmth of dancing couples, Shirley whispers in my ear:

"Quickly, this way!"

She leads me from the room and we climb the stairs to the next floor where she uses her key and opens the door of a small attic-style bedroom. The party is left far behind us as we enter the room…

"If thou be'st born to strange sights,

Things invisible to see,

Ride ten thousand days and nights,

Till age snow white hairs on thee,"

The room is warm and a candle burns on the window ledge sending flickering shadows across the walls. She kisses me and then moves to the small bed in the corner of the room and slips out of her dress. The candle light caresses her nakedness before she climbs into the bed. I'm all fingers and thumbs and shirtsleeves and socks before I'm naked with her in the heat of the bed…

"Thou, when thou return'st, will tell me,

All strange wonders that befell thee,

And swear,

No where

Lives a woman true and fair."

Our limbs are entwined in erotic knots of love and we crave each other's kisses both deep and holy. Our strangers' bodies are excited by the prospect of splendid exploration and we fall locked together in love's everlasting embrace. Our mutual cries of justification are soon becalmed with the softness of lovers' kisses…

"If thou find'st one, let me know,
Such a pilgrimage were sweet;
Yet do not, I would not go,
Though at next door we might meet,"

I hold Shirley Helmes in my arms until dawn. Her long, blonde hair is spread across the pillows and I press my lips to the nape of her neck. Now I know that I am no angel but I have never felt like this about a woman before. It has all rather taken me, Mr. Cool, by surprise. I quickly and quietly dress and leave my telephone number on a card beside the pillow. I silently leave the room and walk down the stairs through the mess of beer cans and empty wine bottles left by the revelers from such a short time ago. I carefully unlatch the front door and close it quietly behind me as I head for the street and, in the early morning spring sunshine, stroll back to Hampstead ...

14 Martin age 19

"Though she were true, when you met her,
  And last, till you write your letter,
  Yet she
  Will be
  False, ere I come, to two, or three."

From: Rose-Mary
To: Martin
Subject: Helen Dunwell Prize
Date: February 11th, 2012 3:36 pm
Hi Martin:

Solid, splendid piece on the Dunwell. I am familiar with the Cohen song. I saw him perform at a tiny folk club in Harrow before he became celebrated. I was taken by his Canadian accent, and laid back demeanor. Next I will include a mention of teaching practice which was before the summer production. I will follow this with the details of the 1968 spring break because as it happens I was an extra in Oh What A Lovely War filming in Brighton directed by (Richard Attenborough) and the drama on and off the set was worth including. Hope you can add your teaching practicum and I can only guess what you were up to during spring break after reading your recent passages describing your personal life, they make for compelling, impressive reading.

  Keep going
  Love
  Rose-Mary

From: Martin
To: Rose-Mary
Subject: Dunwell done and dusted.
Date: February 11th, 2012 4:19 pm

Hi Rose-Mary

Thanks for your splendid support. I found that Dunwell period really difficult to put in perspective. I'll of course write about Teaching Practice---Noodle and I were subjected to geographic and cultural isolation in a Catholic Infant/Primary school run by nuns (students of Rita's!!!! in far off Hemel Hempstead. We traveled daily from Euston with the odd foray back, squeezed into Rita's sports car! Some amusing recollections will be put to paper. Puff the Magic Dragon, Noodle and me and the nuns....you won't believe it!

Spring break was working in a huge chemical factory in Plaistow....some amusing anecdotes there however as the money was tremendous and the work dangerous.

An old friend of mine, Malcolm McFee, had a decent part in Oh What A Lovely War-please let me see what you write about it as I was still in touch with him then for good or ill. He died about ten years ago from liver cancer and I went to his funeral but there were precious few showbiz people there apart from Ian Lavender and some of the Please Sir crew. He kept in touch with me over the years and always wanted to work on something together but I always felt he had not learned anything from our teenage drama workshop years. He did produce a rather pedestrian version of Under Milk Wood at the Theatre Royal in the early 70s. He survived as a jobbing actor when his youthful looks (as seen on tv in Please Sir) faded and ended up directing pantomimes. He is allegedly the subject of the Morrissey song, Little Man, What Now?

Will get back to scribbling asap.

Look forward to hearing from you.

Love

Martin

Rose-Mary: A Chance Meeting in the Lunch Queue.

Every day at noon those of us who are brave enough to sample Winkie's menu line up in front of the porthole door that leads to the refectory. Lunch is scheduled for noon but more often than not we are salivating in line until Winkie deems he is ready for the onslaught. Waiting invites us to interact with other first years who we only see in passing. I find myself alongside the fabulous flaxen haired Martin from Group D.

"What do you think wacky Winkie prepared today?" he enquires smiling.

"Smells like curry," I reply.

"He's mastered that not too spicy. What group are you in?" he asks.

"C, I'm Rose-Mary." I answer trying not to blush.

"Pleased to meet you. I'm Martin. Group C that is the one group according to Kees that hasn't gelled."

"I have heard that remark before but I disagree. We all get along, there are strong personalities but that shouldn't indicate non compatibility."

"Are you one of those?" He questions.

"What?"

"Strong personality?"

"I don't think so."

Suddenly I feel brazen. I look into his azure eyes.

"Surely, you need to make that judgment?"

He laughs. "Is that an invitation?"

My inner voice whispers *could he possibly be interested in me?* I look up at him coyly.

"You can take it how you like it."

The porthole door is flung open and we file along the counter. Winkie dishing up delicious Greek flavored curry whilst admiring the exposed legs of the mini-skirts on display before him. The long suffering Mrs. Winkie, his wife of many years smiles as she is the cashier at the end of the line. Martin begins to join me in line daily. I am trying to relax in his company. I enjoy his sardonic wit. He likes to challenge authority. He joins us at the long table in the middle of the refectory he and Micki hold court and decry the nonsense that happens within the confines of Ivy House.

We are also joined by my tongue twirling conspirator Doug, with his wiry Einstein hair. He makes no bones about how he fancies me, which is disconcerting for I have done nothing to deserve his adulation. Rumor has it that he some kind of incurable joint disease but he never mentions being debilitated. He seeks me out in the refectory sitting opposite with large woeful, puppy eyes attempting to make small talk. Doug is a Renaissance man, a lost poet. His ardent pursuit is a little disquieting. He continually asks me out. I don't want to hurt his feelings or shatter his illusion of me but currently my heart leans towards a lunch time anarchist.

Doug attempts to join in the lunch daily diatribes with Micki and Martin but he is no match for the militant socialists. During their comic denunciations Martin will sneak a look and smile at me across the table. I can't tell if this is his way of chatting me up. He is congenial and funny with everyone. But I sense he is attracted to me and his attraction and humor are endearing. He has nicknames for the staff and he is particularly critical of the moody wardrobe mistress Beatrice Franky whom he renames Widow Twankey. When I confide in him about my enforced name change because "There are just too many Rosemary's for the staff to remember." He is openly outraged.

"You should have changed your name to Rita or Peggy or Diane and seen how they handled that."

He is genuinely seething on my behalf. I think he might be a knight in shining armor or some such rubbish.

"That is tosh Rosemary. Have they all gone mad? Too many Rosemary's." He announces to the lunch queue. "There is only one in my mind," he winks and whispers in my ear.

Duncan, Sandra and I sought refuge in the catacombs of Ivy House known collectively as the common room during the endless mindless rehearsals for Ladies Of Leisure. We read, caught up on assignments and took turns knitting a scarf with my giant needles. We have maintained this routine after the Dunwells so when we have a free period, we congregate in the bowels of the building along with most of Group C. Duncan has found his passion in the Alexander method and is plugged into books about the intercostal muscles and diaphragm. Sandra is absorbed with diagramming lighting plots, she is obsessed with becoming a stage manager.

Across from where we sit there is an office. Within the flimsy walls the sound of typewriter keys can be heard for this is where the New College magazine, The Ring is produced. The editor-in-chief is our very own Clive still sporting his black cloak and now a black beret, rattles and writes poetry on the Olivetti like an unstoppable chatterbox. There is only one door to the inner sanctum of The Ring office and few are invited or encouraged to cross the threshold unless they can prove lineage to T.S. Elliot, Ted Hughes or memorize every poem from the pen of Yevtushenko. The writers of this rag are earnest fellows "Sighing like furnace, with a woeful ballad made to his mistresses eyebrow."

The sighing this day was urgent and audible from within the interior office walls of The Ring, followed by a voice urgently whispering "hush." At that moment the door inadvertently swings open and to my utter shock there is Martin with his back to me. My Arthurian legend locked in an amorous embrace with Shirley, a third year Marianne Faithful, look alike complete with magnificent blond hair that falls to her shoulders and pouting lips. I am aghast. I drop a stitch from my knitting. Shirley, with her free hand manipulates the door knob and closes the door. She remains in a passionate kiss with Martin who is enraptured and unaware that his lovemaking is playing to an audience of three students of Group C. Duncan clears his throat and raises his eyebrows slightly.

Sandra whispers "That's some sonnet they are writing."

I hand her the knitting.

"I'm going to take a breather," I announce.

I ascend from the bowels of the common room into the garden. The cold afternoon air bites against my arms. I walk towards the statue of Anna Pavlova in the pond. I can't blame Shirley, she has a sweet disposition and is one of the only third years who acknowledges first years. She always smiles and says hello. I don't blame Martin either. He is a virile hunk. He can have his pick of lovelies. I feel foolish in that I was beginning to have real feelings for him. I don't want to be a conquest. Shagging is fine. I need a lover that I can communicate with. I want more than a carnal relationship. I need a partner who I can share ideas, inspirations and disappointments. So there you have it. I stand at the edge of the pond next to the statue of the greatest ballerina that ever lived. I proclaim to Pavlova

"I will never go out, date nor marry that narcissistic species of homo-sapien known as actor."

15 The statue of Anna Pavlova in the pond at Ivy House.

From: Martin
To: Rose-Mary
Subject: Teaching Practice
Date: February 12th, 2012 8:07 pm
Hi Rose-Mary
Received your teaching practice. It was an excellent piece....don't know so much about the "flaxen haired yoof" I remember I was always attracted to you but 2 and 2 never made 4 if you know what I mean! I am currently sandwiched between Noodle and Dominican nuns but hope to have my Teaching Practice with you asap.

Take care
Love
Martinx

From: Rose-Mary
To: Martin
Subject: Mathematics
Date: February 13th, 2012 10:23 am
Hi Martin
Thanks for bolstering my confidence. However I always thought 2 and 2 always made 4 or are you referring to a new algorithm or quadratic equation?

Looking forward to receiving your Teaching Practice.
Love,
Rose-Mary x

From: Martin
To: Rose-Mary
Subject: Update
Date: February 19th, 2012 9:22 pm

Hello Rose-Mary

Several updates------have produced copious notes regarding Teaching Practice with Noodle at convent school in Hemel Hempstead-stranger than fiction!

Plans lined up for Easter holidays and Merchant of Venice. Hope to conclude asap.

BUT

Have just been reminded by consultant that my long silent cancer needs some more attention and they are sticking me on hormone therapy next week to try to stabilize things (It is 13 years since my initial diagnosis- so the innings is still pretty good!). This could be for several months or perhaps a year-I'm seeing the consultant next week for details. I've undergone similar for 3.5 years before and this is another burst to settle things down. Never had any symptoms or pain-only from medical/surgical interventions!!! Real bugger is I've got to trim some of the Brecht shows coming up as the first few months of treatment can make you feel most unlike touring and performing. Keeping positive and will keep you informed. Any ideas on the final presentation?

Very best
Love
Martin

From: Rose-Mary
To: Martin
Subject: Health
Date: February 19th, 2012 11:59 am
Dear Martin:

Please do not feel any pressure of time constraints on our joint venture. Your health is your priority. Only participate as you see fit and are able to. In another life time politicians may decide that finding a cure and prevention for cancer takes priority over endless medieval turf wars. Keep rested, positive and know I believe our collaboration will continue. Whenever you are ready send me your Catholic comments, chemical factory internship and summer Shakespeare shambles. I look forward to reading your next installments. But again there is no hurry. Please let me know how you are doing during your treatments. My good thoughts are with you. By the way you will owe me a pint of lager next time I cross the pond.

Keep well
Love,
Rose-Mary

From: Martin
To: Rose-Mary
Subject: Update
Date: February 27th, 2012 5:18 am
Hi Rose-Mary

Went to the consultant on Monday and relatively good news which made me feel much better and back in the land of the living. He said my prostate tumor (like a little brother) was low grade and subject to slow growth. It did not surprise him that it had stopped in adjacent lymph node and I would simply return to the hormone tablets I was on ten years ago when recovering from radiotherapy. I had little or no side effects for 4.5 years and he is putting me on twice a week tomoxifan as well to prevent any breast growth. Although some testosterone is blocked there is still libido (not that I shall be hanging around Cheltenham Ladies' College) and whilst not being Robert Redford I do not want to be like Mr. Pastry! The drug will cause the tumor to shrink and even possibly "commit suicide". Once my relatively low blood tests are back to normal I should then have a few years off the drug until blood tests merit a return-it's called intermittent therapy. He did not think it would be the cause of my demise and thought with me one should be concerned with the quality of life as opposed to just quantity. He did not think I was under any real threat but needed to keep my "little brother" as quiet as possible. He said there were several new drugs in the pipeline and these would benefit me in the long term. I will need to see him again in 3 months. I should continue to keep fit at the gym (he said I was a "young man"). Keep working creatively, brush aside any side effects and follow a dairy free diet with no red or processed meat.

So I will shortly return to New College project and well get copy asap now that this blip is behind us.

Love,
Martin

From: Rose-Mary
To: Martin
Subject: Update
Date: February 27th, 2012 12:22 am
·Dear Martin:

Great report card. What a relief for you. Be jubilant, continue the never ending story. Robert Redford is overrated. I think Mr. Pastry is human not a product.

Love

Rose-Mary.

Rose-Mary: Teaching Practice.

Teaching Practice begins next week. Sadie and I have been appointed to St. Joseph's Infant and Junior School in Garston, Hertfordshire. Sad has returned to living at home in Bushey having been discarded by darling Judy for more wonderful upwardly mobile flat mates. On our initial tour the headmistress, Sister Alphonse makes us feel welcome. She is a Dominican nun, young and upbeat. Sad has chosen the kindergarten and I have selected a class of thirty-three eight year olds. We have been well prepared by Rita with a simple lesson plan formula unlike her over the top model tutorial complete with horse and capuchin monkey. I am confident and excited. Soon all first years will vacate Ivy House for over a month. Following our final lecture on Milton's Paradise Lost Gerald asks me to remain behind in the upstairs lecture room. He has been withdrawn of late, as if he is just going through the motions. He stands staring out of the window, he takes my hand in his, he avoids making eye contact.

"I'm going to leave." he murmurs.

He then glances downward as if he is ashamed. I am in disbelief

"Why?" I ask.

There is a long pause.

"I can't see myself as a teacher. I want to dance. I don't want to waste any more time."

I look at the anguish in his troubled blue eyes.

"Are you sure about this?"

"Yes, I've already informed the registrar and Kees. This is my last day."

I stand holding his hand, I don't know what to say.

Gerald continues:

"I wanted you to know, I can't face the others. By the time teaching practice is over I will be long gone and forgotten."

"Of course you won't. I will always remember you."

There is a hint of a smile about to cross his lips as he lets go of my hand. He bends down and kisses me on the cheek.

"Goodbye Rose-Mary with a hyphen."

With that he leaves the lecture hall. I turn and face the window. A tear trickles from the corner of my eye.

Surprisingly I embrace teaching. The students are receptive. I have come to the conclusion that there are a great many similarities between teaching and acting. In order to peak the pupil's interest you must investigate the subject thoroughly taking the topic down to the bare bones. This is what is required when you take on a character in a play you peel away the layers. Another aspect of education that is apparent is that you must enjoy what you are doing. The students will detect deception. I have learnt to quiet the class with a strong stance accompanied by a vaudevillian stare down. I am sailing along enjoying the differences of the students, preparing lessons that not only capture their imagination but have academic components that will improve their reading and writing. I honestly can't wait to stride into the classroom and look at the sea of shining eager faces. My actual teaching of drama is limited due to the teacher's inflexibility to stray from the dictated English curriculum, she is a firm believer in children conforming by sitting upright in their desks. When I am fortunate enough to be allotted the gymnasium without her eagle eye supervision I have the students respond to Korsakov's Flight of the Bumble Bee and thematic music that encourages them to move and use their creativity. We are able to strive towards improvisations of animals and pirates and interpret the poem by Leah Bodine Drake 'Fantasy In A Forest' in all of its jungle glory. The students are like sponges. Their execution and imagination is amazing. Though, I think I noticed Sister Alphonse, the principal frown in the doorway of her office as we passed her on our way back to the classroom as howler monkeys, stalking tigers and shy gazelles. Sadie on the other hand is flailing. Once when I visited her in the kindergarten she was bent over tying an errant shoe lace of a freckle faced five-year-old girl as a tousled haired scamp of a boy placed conkers on her bum. On seeing me Sad stood up and the conkers ran on the floor. As Sad collected the errant horse chestnuts she rolled her eyes and said:

"Yes, it is always like this."

Then she whispered to me,

"I'm in hell."

Our adviser from New College is Sylvia Gonzalez the voice coach. She reviews our apprenticeships in the staff room. Sylvia gushes over my teaching ability in front of a visibly uncomfortable Sadie. When Sylvia leaves I apologize for her insensitivity. Sad is insistent:

"Look if you are good at teaching you should be chuffed. I know I'm a tosser in the classroom. I want to work in the theatre. I would take a job at any theatre selling ice cream cornets in the aisles at intermission if it would give me a foot in the door."

Sad is unconcerned about the consequences of her lack of teaching ability. She is non-chalant about her teaching grade and getting kicked out of New College. The faculty know that Sad is an unabashed artist, she is extremely capable and lauded in the less popular character roles which she undertakes with flourish.

I empathize with Sad's inaptitude for teaching. I enjoy being in the classroom but only as a fall back option. I still secretly yearn for a life treading the boards but I draw the line at hawking chocolates, ice cream cones and confections during the interval.

There is another student teacher at St. Joseph's she is from Brick Hall, of all places. Her name is Maureen, she is from the Midlands and she is lonely. Originally she was standoffish and aloof but since she senses Sad's ineptitude she has become pleasant and friendly. She always makes Sad a cup of tea between classes to keep Sad's spirits up. We invite her to accompany us to the Regal Theatre for the production of Joe Orton's Loot. I am there not only to attend the play but to see Pearce Sullivan parade his latest female conquest. During the interval I find him staring at me in the bar, he smiles and raises his glass to me across the room. Sometimes he is so irritating.

From: Martin
To: Rose-Mary
Subject: Re: New College diary
DATE: March 19th, 2012 9:17 am
Hi Rose-Mary

Good news is that I'm now back writing and tucked into the teaching practice which saw the two Martins banished to the wilds of Hemel Hempstead where they were confronted by the Dominican Sisters of St. Catherine's Catholic School whilst at the same time being sensually supported by merciless Rita Scott in heat!! It was a truly absurd interlude which reflected the madness that was New College in the first year. We were all beyond salvation!!!

Feeling much better after cancer blip and don't seem to be suffering too much with the tablets.....fingers crossed.

All the very best
Love Martin

From: Rose-Mary
To: Martin
Subject: New College Diary
Date: March 22nd, 2012 10:40 pm
Hello Martin

So glad to hear you are back in the saddle. I too was paired with the Dominican Order at St. Joseph's a small primary school in Garston, Hertfordshire. I thoroughly embraced teaching and loved every minute of the experience. I always have been able to relate to children and enjoy their company. I think that is why I have five unique specimens of my own and believe me I wanted more, but time ran out.

Keep feeling better and keep taking those horse pills. I am including my next segment for your approval. I am on R and R for a week but will return to writing with a vengeance upon return. I will send you a postcard. I am ready for some time with the fish (you will understand later)

Hope you are taking care of yourself.

Rose-Mary

From: Martin
To: Rose-Mary
Subject: Teaching Practice
Date: March 25th, 2012 7:05 am
Hi Rose-Mary

Teaching Practice attached as promised. It's amazing how much comes back when you turn your mind to it. It was the most bizarre month and I really only scratched the surface as I wanted to keep it to a reasonable length. It was really as anarchic as portrayed and whenever Noodle and I meet the conversation still gets round to that teaching practice. Now to Easter break.

Love,
Martin

Martin: Teaching Practice.

A large group of animated first year students gather around the main notice board in the foyer of Ivy House. There is an indecent amount of thespian screaming, shoving and pushing as ruddy-faced excitable students discover with varying amounts of pleasure, pain and discomfort the primary schools to which they are allocated to spend the month before the Easter Holidays locked into the existential struggle known as teaching practice.

I am not that bothered by the prospect as I spent the whole of the last academic year undertaking unqualified primary teaching in the East End of London, working for the Borough of Newham. I was well paid and comfortably handled both a class of seven-year-olds and a class of ten-year-olds in two different schools that were critically short of teaching staff. I was basically supported by the teaching staff and the head teachers but had to sink or swim in the roughest educational seas that the East End could throw at me. I am, therefore, not that concerned about my teaching practice fate that has just been allocated by the staff of the New College of Speech and Drama. As the screeching theatrical figures slip from foyer to the refectory to digest their geographical and educational repast, I am left alone by the notice board. I peer at the lengthy list of names and immediately notice that I am not at the top of the list as my surname demands but I am tucked away at the bottom of the list, almost as an afterthought, with my fellow late arriver, Martin Lordahl.

The two Martins are not to be shackled by any old London school but we are to be located way out of the city well on the way to Birmingham in the new town of Hemel Hempstead. This is in the county of Hertfordshire which is nearly thirty miles away from north London. It is not only the distance that is intriguing but it appears that we are to grace the corridors and classrooms of a Roman Catholic School staffed by Dominican

Sisters from a nearby Convent. This is going to be an interesting challenge with aristocratic Norwegian, Martin Lordahl, and the East End grammar school boy, Martin Banks, both worldly wise and opinionated, and who are about to be thrown into the welcoming arms of the Dominican Sisters of St. Catherine's Catholic School. Our staff supervisors are Rita Scott and Noel Niven and we are shortly due to meet with both of them before our teaching practice begins.

Martin and I sit in the College theatre awaiting Rita and Noel to discuss our Catholic–bound Teaching Practice pilgrimage. I must say Martin seems quite distant from the proceedings and is only concerned that we both rendezvous at Euston before our train carries us to the promised-land which is Hemel Hempstead. I put all this down to his aristocratic upbringing and I'm not sure he even knows what a seven-year-old school child looks like.

"Well let's hope there's a damn good pub nearby because I might need a stiff drink if I'm surrounded by bloody nuns all day!" From Martin's comment I guess he is from a strong Protestant background in Scandinavia and he is not going to let a gaggle of nuns stand between him and a good British pint of beer.

The door of the theatre crashes open and Rita Scott sweeps into the auditorium followed by a puffing and perspiring Noel Niven. She sits down between us and gives us both some sheets of paper containing details of the journey, school and lesson plans. Noel hands out copies of a teaching timetable which we are to complete once we have agreed our hours with the Headmistress. Noel insists that the completed forms are returned directly to him once the timetable has been agreed with the school.

"Now Dahlings," Rita purrs through thick make-up and crosses her long legs in the shortest of mini-skirts. "You're going to absolutely love this school. The Head is an absolute sweetie......she's totally beside herself that she's got two gorgeous fellows coming to work for her. You're the first students she's taken as the school has only recently been opened and it's staffed by the Dominican Sisters from the convent across the road. They'll simply LOVE you, Dahlings!"

I notice Noel Niven gets more uncomfortable as Rita's gushing introduction continues unabated.

"Sister Margaret, she's the Head, she just loves Speech and Drama and she wants to see it taught throughout her school. I've already given her plenty of ideas!"

My heart sinks and Martin smiles weakly at Rita.

"Noel and I will try to get to you for a couple of visits but it is a long way away and so we can't commit ourselves at present."

Your're telling me! I say to myself.

"The Head wants you to get the 9.05am from Euston on Monday and will give you all the details you'll need when you meet her. Oh Dahlings you'll have such a lovely, lovely time and you'll soon both have those dear Sisters eating out of your gorgeous hands!"

I have never considered my hands "gorgeous" but with Rita in full flow anything is deemed possible and I can foresee Martin and I sandwiched between the succoring Sisters and the curriculum devouring Warrior Queen that is Rita Scott. This was our teaching practice planned as far as Rita and poor Noel Niven are concerned and as quickly as they have arrived like a morning mist they are gone. Martin and I amble down the hill towards Golders Green and arrange to meet at Euston Station the next Monday at 8.45am in order to catch the 9.05 train to Hemel Hempstead.

Sure enough there is Martin by the Birmingham line platform at 8.45am the following Monday morning and as organized as ever, we have both purchased our necessary train tickets and we are eager to meet our fates at the St. Catherine's Catholic School in Hemel Hempstead. The train journey takes thirty odd minutes and our two vacant faces stare out of the carriage windows as we hurtle towards Hemel Hempstead. Exactly on time the two drama students are deposited at the station and the express train speeds on to the Midlands. We walk purposefully from the station, across the main road roundabout and then up Union Road over the canal bridge and past the Fisherman Pub on our way to the Catholic Primary School. We enter the grounds of the primary school and we head directly for the school office.

It is a very new school having only opened last year and after we announce ourselves to the doorway intercom we are admitted by a plump and very jolly middle-aged school secretary. The thing that strikes me immediately is the complete lack of noise and I wonder whether we have actually arrived in the middle of a school holiday. Mrs. Lloyd advises us that the Headmistress, Sister Margaret, will be with us shortly and graciously provides coffee and biscuits as we sit and wait in the office. I think we are being splendidly treated considering we have only just walked through the door on the first morning of our month's teaching practice.

"Ah, there you are Gentlemen!"

I turn to the voice and there coming towards us along the corridor at a brisk pace is the white habited figure of Sister Margaret, the headmistress. Although it is difficult to decipher because of the veil, scapular and habit I guess that she is in her early thirties and so must be something of a convent "Whizz-kid" to have been given the top job in this new school. Martin and I rise and greet her with firm handshakes and she smiles kindly and leads us into her office.

The office is tidy and well-equipped and she seats herself behind the large modern desk and gestures that we sit in the two chairs which had been pre-arranged for us facing her. She then describes the background of the new school and the Dominican convent which provides the teachers. I gather that it had only been open just over a year and that the school is far from full with no top age class expected until next year. The School Motto is "Truth" and I hope that the truth will not be that we are both up the education creek without the proverbial paddle. I nod sagely as Sister Margaret continues her introduction and Martin is gracious and positive in his comments about the school and its environs. He is certainly a charmer and no wonder he is so popular in the pubs near to his Chelsea home. Still, I think we are giving a good impression which is all we can do for now before the enormity of our task finally dawns upon us. We learn that there are five other Sisters teaching at the school and that they are attempting to carry the four theoretical pillars of the Dominican Order into the daily life of the school. These erstwhile pillars are: community life; common prayer; study and service. Sister Margaret then calmly states that the Sisters aim to create a happy, stimulating, lively and disciplined environment in which to assist each child to develop spiritually, intellectually, physically, socially and emotionally and to thereby attain high levels of achievement in all areas of the curriculum. She beams ecstatically at us and I almost feel as though I should leap to my feet and shout "Hallelujah!" But we both sit there and nod in agreement as the values of the school cascade over us as if directed from a spiritual waterfall on high. Sister Margaret then says how pleased she is to have two drama specialists "onboard" for the next month as she strives to provide high energy, fun, musical theatre, dance, drama and singing for the four to nine-year-olds of St. Catherine's. She wants to see the performing arts boost confidence and expression as well as provide a stimulating fun-filled environment. I cannot help but be swept along by her ardent fervor and eagerly take the sheet of paper on which she has typed the daily expectations of all those in the school. They are as follows: We show respect for everyone; We call each other by our Christian name; We are kind, caring and loving; We are always friends with everyone; We listen to each other; We always take turns; We share our games and toys; We always walk indoors and We never run; We welcome everyone and We are always polite; We always say sorry and We easily make friends.

I don't know about St. Catherine's but I feel this could be placed above the main entrance to the New College of Speech and Drama as it wouldn't hurt most of those inmates to consider some, if not all, of these guidelines. But then again I bet none of them would even think to share their games and toys!

Sister Margaret wants Martin and I to team-teach much of the time with mostly half class size groups as apparently there is a new timetable to accommodate the two "specialists" for the month. We are based in the hall and the groups will be brought to us on a kind of nun inspired child conveyor belt! Our first class will be at 10:00am (we left Euston on the 9:05 train) and we will have lunch in our own staff room and would finish at 3:15pm in order to catch the fast 3:51pm train back to Euston. Sister Margaret also informs us that she is often at Ivy House as she is part of an adult group which studies part-time for the Licentiate Diploma of The Royal College of Music in Speech and Drama (L.R.A.M.) with Rita Scott.

Ah! I think all has been revealed. And it is therefore no surprise that Rita is the main staff tutor for this educational expedition into the ecclesiastical unknown.

We look at our planned classes and Martin immediately claims the grand piano (he is a fine pianist) whilst I rapidly re-arrange the percussion instruments so that I become the Ginger Baker of primary school drumming. We are Brothers in Arms as we literally blow the curriculum apart and St. Catherine's School is the unknowing recipient of drama in education courtesy of both London's East End and the gentrified suburbs of Oslo. The whole thing is one crazy, anarchic merry-go-round and the Sisters of St. Catherine's believe our appearance to be the most important thing to have happened in Hemel Hempstead since the arrival of sliced bread!

Sister Monica's class of seven and eight-year-olds has just started the jazz version of "Joshua Fought the Battle of Jericho" and whilst Sister Monica somehow makes them learn the ten verses and five choruses, Martin and I are responsible for the music and movement that accompanies the singing. We surely need divine intervention or a few creative extended lunch hours in the nearby Fisherman Pub. We seem to feverishly rehearse forever with the large group of children but they are great troopers always willing to fight battles, become inanimate objects, and gallop around the hall on their charging Persian horses or, quite simply, rise from the dead. We could never be blessed with such a receptive theatrical company at New College! Nonetheless the rest of the school are finally invited to watch Joshua fight the Battle of Jericho and the two arty Marties are to choreograph, conduct and score the piece which will be recorded in the annals of the great stage shows of primary education. The whole hall rocks and rolls as the manic Viking strikes crescendo after crescendo on the grand piano and the demented Cockney delivers screeching recorder solos and clamoring tambour beats to accompany the storming of Jericho and the collapse of the walls. A seven-year-old skinny ginger mite smites with his sword and spear as his sparrow legs carry him onto the central staging for him to blow his ram's horn as the walls (ten children balanced on each other's shoulders) come tumbling down. The damage to the walls includes two cut knees and one grazed elbow! If there is a God, He surely does indeed know that Joshua fights the Battle of Jericho this Wednesday afternoon in Hemel Hempstead, Hertfordshire. The Sisters rise to their feet as one and give us rapturous applause. Joshua, his army and the walls indulge in too many thespian curtain calls and consequently a jubilant Gilbert and Sullivan have to dash like Keystone Cops to catch our train back to Euston and the world of adult sanity.

Rita Scott visits one day when we are up to our necks with: Magic Dragons; Slimy Creatures from the Oceans Deep;

Moon-Monsters; Nightmare Hounds and Those Dreadful Things that Go Bump in the Night. Rita sits perched on a high chair in the corner of the hall whilst Martin tinkles on the ivories and I act the various fantastic creatures as the children of the Catholic School of St. Catherine's stare open mouthed and wide-eyed at my theatrics and then willingly mime, move and roar as dreadful child-eating monsters whilst Martin smashes the keyboard into submission like a deranged Jerry Lee Lewis! Rita is beside herself and is positively orgasmic in her response to the Martins' primary school extravaganza on magical creatures. She rushes in to see Sister Margaret and then whisks us both away to the Fisherman Pub for a lunch. We sit in the corner like naughty schoolboys as she purchases our pies and pints:

"Dahlings! Dahlings! That was one of THE most exciting primary school classes I have ever SEEN!! You were BOTH superb and had the little darlings in the palm of YOUR hands. THEY loved you, they ADORED you, they BELIEVED in you!"

We both smile inanely as Rita continues with the accolades. It gets worse: Noel Niven has flu and will not be coming at all (lucky man!) and after her meeting with Sister Margaret this afternoon Rita will drive us back to Barnet Tube Station in her MG Midget Sports Car (unlucky men!).

Two wasted and emotionally drained drama students are finally deposited by Rita "Fangio" Scott at Barnet Station and our first NCSD Teaching Practice is soon complete. Martin and I have survived both our time at the dear Dominican Sisters' Primary School and Rita Scott's overpoweringly theatrical supervisory sessions. He was to spend the Easter break in Oslo whilst I was to return to the East End of London for further heavy chemical duties at Shaws Sanitary Compounds.

From: Rose-Mary
To: Martin
Subject: A Papal Teaching Practice
Date: March 26th, 2012 12:43 pm
Dear Martin
We both experienced an ecumenical teaching practice. I was impressed at your recall. My drama teaching experiences on that first outing were limited. The teacher I was mentored by was strictly conservative she did not like to stray from the conformity of the curriculum and the children bound to their desks. I would have done anything to be a fly on the wall during Rita's effusive babbling. I loved your conveyor belt analogy. I loved the whole piece. Take a pause and enjoy another divine event. Easter.
Love,
Rose-Mary

Rose-Mary: Easter Holidays.

Teaching practice is over and I am genuinely sorry to leave the classroom. The Easter holidays loom and I am broke. I am able to convince myself that since I am on break from college, I am not strictly under the jurisdiction of Ivy House. Therefore I call my agent Desmond who has provided plenty of extra, voice over and walk on parts in the past.

"Des. This is Rosemary, remember me?"

"I remember you" he sings into the 'phone a la Frank Ifield "I need a job."

"So you came crawling back to old Des?" he laughs.

"I'm not crawling, I'm in drama school, I told you."

He hesitates, "Something about not being allowed to work in films or television as I remember."

"Please Des," I beg.

"Well as it happens you are in luck. I have a job at the seaside, starts Monday should last a week. Are you interested?"

"Of course I am. Where is the location?"

"Brighton," he answers.

"Brighton that's far enough away, I'll never get caught down there."

"Good, report at 7 a.m. Monday morning to the Royal Albion Hotel. By the way, the name of the movie is Oh What A Lovely War."

"Thank you so much Des."

"I always come through for you Rosemary." He returns to his Frank Ifield impression singing, "I'm the one who made your dreams come true."

Subsequently he hangs up. Now all I have to do is organize transportation and lodging.

My mother's mood has improved and she is counting the days until she can jet off to visit Terry in California. She is actually washing up in the kitchen with the door open, eavesdropping on my conversation with Des.

"Brighton?" she asks.

"I have a job as an extra on Monday."

"That's a long way to go?"

"I know. I will have to take British Rail at the crack of dawn on Monday morning if I am to be in Brighton by 7 a.m."

"Why don't I call Aunty Margaret, you can stay with her in Broadwater and take the local train that would be much easier."

Aunty Margaret, is the spinster sister of my mother's first husband Saint Rick. She was a staff nurse who contracted polio in the 1950's, she wears iron braces on both her legs to assist in walking. She is the local Girl Guide leader and quite intimidating with a stern voice and severe manner.

The arrangements are made and I am glad that I do not have to take the post train which stops at every station, leaving from Victoria at 4 a.m. as it chugs southwards. Aunty Margaret's house is only nine miles from Brighton, even if she does insist lights out at 8 p.m.

The first day on set I am kitted out in a 1912's sage green full length skirt and ruffled jacket accessorized with a large straw hat. My hair is swept in a tidy bun, my shoes are dainty lace and pointed. I am instructed to meet with Jules the assistant director on the pier. I am familiar with Jules from another film "Caressing The Tiger." He is known to be fair and competent. The Brighton Pier is decked out in Victorian finery and filigree. Jules points 20 feet down the stony beach and indicates that I should join

"The bevy of beauties down there by the breakwater."

He points to two young women huddled together in the brisk cold morning air, one is dressed in light blue and the other in navy blue. I maneuver the uneven pebbles, shivering as the sun is absent and the wind is wicked. As I approach the two newly clad Victorian ladies nestled together, the one in dark blue with a shawl across her shoulders begins to beam at me. She looks familiar but I can't place her.

"I'm supposed to stand with you," I utter shivering.

The petite girl in dark blue laughs, gathering her shawl tighter for warmth.

"Rosemary it is you?"

"Yes, that's my name," I respond perplexed.

"It's me Marilyn from Italia Conti."

Immediately I recognize her voice and smile for she is Marilyn Dern, the potential Pavlova of Piccadilly and Clapham North.

"You haven't changed a bit," she says.

She introduces me to her companion, a tall striking girl with dark hair pulled tight off her face in a knotted coil. Her name is Hope Coleman and she is a Lucy Clayton model. She is stunning but seems unaware of her beauty and is very self-deprecating which is refreshing. We snuggle together, teeth chattering, exchanging our history, awaiting Jules to shout action over the loudspeaker, which is our cue to walk along the freezing strand of beach acting as if it was a sweltering August afternoon. Hope in jest announces:

"Anyone for a swim?"

All along the beach are groups of extras shifting from foot to foot to keep warm. I recognize some of the females from other films. Gina, from Chelsea, Meg from the Slade School of Art and her best friend Laura from Oxford and chatty Beth from Whitechapel. We have been thrown together many times over the years assigned as screaming teenagers at pop concerts, background in historical dramas, Hitler youth and hippies.

We look out for each other. Being within a group is safer than being prey to our male counterparts, crew or actors and extras who seem to possess the collective crazy notion that we are moonlighting call girls as they are forever propositioning us, fair and attractive young ladies. Gina is a friend of Jules and after the many takes she joins our threesome to give us the scoop. Richard Attenborough is the director and this is his inaugural film. His nickname for some reason is Sticky Dicky. He is an agreeable man because he is still in the process of learning film making. Gina informs us that if we are given any trouble by anyone we are to report to her and she will enlighten Jules and he will sort the offenders out. She teases that Jules calls us his "seven virgins." We laugh at his folly. Beth has been for years the mistress of an actor who portrays Sherlock Holmes on television. Meg is being pursued by one of the musicians of the Small Faces. We are content to allow Jules his fantasy of innocence. Gina warns us of a local girl named Daphne, she looks like Patti Boyd and wears an army jacket. She plays cards all day, never sets foot on the set and is known for wearing her knickers on her head. She is a hard scrubber who likes to recruit unsuspecting females for drinks or a game of cards and then attempts to convince them to engage in sexual intercourse with all and sundry making a pile of money and being assured of never having to stand on a chilly beach out of camera.

Gina and Beth have secured digs at the Station Hotel and they invite me to share their room. We are in Brighton for the week and when we are not prancing along the promenade or on the pier, we read, play gin rummy and gossip.

On the last day I am paired with a shy good looking male with sapphire blue eyes and black curly hair. His name is

John and he is a student at Sussex University whose thesis is to document the making of Oh What A Lovely War. We are directed by Jules to stroll arm in arm beside the sea wall. Between takes I espy a man in a lavish tan sheepskin coat out of shot, he is intently observing the shooting. He is talking animatedly to the second assistants and gaffers. On his arm is a willowy blonde wearing a darker shade of sheepskin coat. I instantly recognize this dreamboat with his shock of thick dark hair graying at the temples. When the word cut is shouted he strolls towards me beaming.

He shakes my hand formally which is out of character for he usually gives me a bear hug. He introduces me to the striking woman hanging on his arm.

"This is Rosy," he says.

Rosy he has never called me Rosy before. I say to myself.

He continues gushing.

"Rosy and I go way back, Rosy is an old friend of mine."

Then he winks at me. My jaw drops. In my head I am thinking. *What is he talking about old friend?* Without pausing he continues introducing his lady friend.

"This is Lily."

I reluctantly shake Lily's outstretched hand. Lily with bleached blond hair, long legs, sheepskin coat draped on my "Uncle" Galen's arm. He turns and heads towards the camera crew. He is the Equity shop steward and he has come I presume to check on the proceedings.

I am numb. "Rosy, a friend?" This coming from the man, my father's cousin and best friend, who along with my father took me to my first day at nursery school and returned home with me fifteen minutes later because I cried that I didn't want to go. The man that had faced my mother's wrath.

"Two grown men let a four-year-old little girl manipulate them!"

The man that is married to gorgeous, generous "Aunty" Matilda. How could he call me Rosy? How could he be so blatantly disrespectful as to introduce me to his "friend" Lily. I feel like a traitor for shaking her hand. This is the last day of filming I will be glad to get home and forget this awkward episode. Late in the afternoon Jules sidles up to me and whispers.

"Everyone else is cut but I need you to stay on for another week for continuity." "Uncle" Galen had fixed this turn of events to ensure my silence. Little does he know I will never mention his indiscretion as I respect my Aunty Matilda too much. I am left alone in a huge room at the Station Hotel.

Gina and the others feel sorry that I am on my own and warn me to keep away from the predator Daphne. During the next few days I catch on reading assignments. I am still matched with the bashful John, the student from Sussex University. Jules informs us that we are cast as newlyweds on our honeymoon and there is to be a close-up of us to be shot on Wednesday at the entrance to the pier.

On the day there are hundreds of onlookers. My beau John and I are smack dab in the foreground. Front row and centre. We actually have a small cameo as we enter laughing and hugging each other on our fictional honeymoon excursion to the pier. During a break from shooting I hear my name being shouted from a voice in the crowd.

"Hey Rose-Mary, Rose-Mary Harrington, over here."

I scan the faces. I trace the voice to a petite dark haired girl standing on tiptoe three rows back. She is wearing her tell-tale cravat. Oh hell, it is Miriam Ziegler the broadcaster of rumor from New College. Now the cat is out of the bag.

From: Martin
To: Rose-Mary
Subject: New College
Date: March 27th, 2012 4:34 pm
Hi Rose-Mary

Plans for Easter hols well under way with East End chemical factory, the Shaws Fluid brigade and the first East End pub with drag queen performers (after loosening of Homosexual Laws in 1968) one of whom was my "buddy" as we became the Sanitex Twins! I was the only "straight" allowed into his/her dressing room. And from that slice of sterling showbiz I was thrown into Rita's mind numbing madness that was the Merchant of Venice!

Think we have achieved a great amount from very humble beginnings (on my part)

Over to you
Take care
Love
Martin.

From: Rose-Mary
To: Martin
Subject: New College Diary
Date: March 28th 2012, 2:34 pm
Hi Martin:

I believe our collaboration has documented our experience honestly. I am having difficulty when I attempt to make the text double spaced, all the paragraphs run together and computer refuses to adhere to the demands of indentation. My daughter/secretary, Irene has returned to help her big brother and his family with babysitting in Arizona until May.

She is my go to girl where computer literacy is concerned. Amazing that she is learning disabled but mechanically gifted. I certainly miss her and her expertise as my computer ability is so poor.

I am looking forward to your Easter holidays at the chemical factory. Just typing the word Shaws Fluid makes my nostrils flare at the pungent recollection of the toxic smell the toilet cleaning product would emit.

Did you receive my postcard from Hawaii?

Hope you are taking care of yourself.

Rose-Mary

From: Martin
To: Rose-Mary
Subject: New College Diary
Date: April 4th 2012, 9:27 am
Hi Rose-Mary

No postcard as yet. Feeling fine but look tired. West Ham have Olympic Stadium! Truro have been relegated to Southern League but at least the club is still solvent.

All the best
Love
Martinxx

From: Rose-Mary
To: Martin
Subject: Lost post card and football
Date: April 5th 2012, 12:28 pm
Hi Martin:

So no post card? I went to the big island of Hawaii, so many topographies, volcanic, desert, rain forest and best of all ocean. Encountered a giant sea turtle when snorkeling off a sparkling white sandy beach. I don't know who was more surprised me or him?

How many spectators does the Olympic Stadium hold? Does this mean the end of the Green Street Hooligans? My home team Watford won yesterday. I am rooting for them to be promoted. Go Hornets.

I played soccer in the 1980's. Two mums and I concluded that sitting in our cars when our sons were at practice was redundant so we formed a soccer team. Now there are over 200 teams in that league. My mother on one her visits stateside observed one game and afterwards declared for all to hear "Ladies don't play football." I continued being a wing until 1988 when Brendan was born. My team mates were my support group during my prolonged, ugly divorce in 1984. They will always be ladies in my eyes.

Love
Rose-Mary

From: Martin
To: Rose-Mary
Subject: Football
Date: April 6th, 2012 5:18 pm
Hi Rose-Mary

West Ham Olympic Stadium will hold 60,000----No more Green Street. Glad to see you were a footie left winger, it was always my second favourite position to that of goalkeeper. Right wingers always dribbled head down into the corner whereas left wingers could put in lovely crosses to the centre forward's head.

I bet you were skilled on the dash to the bye-line and then the accurate curled cross! But beware the sliding tackle from the frustrated full-back...

Am locked into Easter and hope to finish soon.

All the best.

Love
Martinx

From: Martin
To: Rose-Mary
Subject: Easter
Date: April 9th, 2012 10:01 am
Hi Rose-Mary

Easter now finished. Hope I capture the lunacy of those times. I am sending picture of the Duke of Fife pub as it is now- closed and an Irish bookies. Will start Shakespeare ASAP.

All the very best love
Martin

Martin: Easter Vacation.

Shaw's Sanitary Compounds Ltd Factory in West Ham is for all local students a welcome source of holiday finance if you are prepared to work in the dingy Victorian buildings amidst the stifling fumes of chemical cleaners in production. I am more fortunate than most as my Uncle Sid is a foreman at Shaw's and so when I require work I simply phone him and he is happy to employ me on the next shift. Uncle Sid is a typical "Ealing Studios" London Cockney character and the only time he left his roots in the East End was during the Second World War when he became a POW in Italy. Unfortunately for the family war history he was imprisoned by the Allies for selling army blankets, overcoats and tins of anything and everything to Italian civilians whilst on active service. This amounts to Uncle Sid's somewhat dishonorable war record but he always speaks with humor about his days as a POW during the Second World War and it is rumored in the family that he was also bravely involved in heavy fighting on the front line. He often appears with various "goods" for sale at my parents' place and there are quite simply bargains galore to be had via Uncle Sid. He is married to Auntie Violet, a glamorous woman who worked in local factories during the war and always had the latest clothes and cigarettes from her "friends" amongst the American forces from the nearby bases. Auntie Violet always had surplus stock of most things to sell in large quantities on the black market whilst poor Uncle Sid languished for several months in the British Military Prison well behind Allied lines during the latter stages of the conflict.

Shaw's is a large factory producing Shaw's Fluid, Washing Up Liquid, Toilet Rolls and the particularly potent Sanitex Disinfectant Powder. Jobs are varied and include: repetitive packing duties on the conveyor belts; the making of Shaw's Fluid in the huge iron vats and then running the pumps which fill the tanker lorries to the brim; driving the fork-lift trucks in the vast store-yards; feeding and shredding paper in the paper store and working for double danger money in the dusty, acrid Sanitex production sheds. I always look forward to my sojourns at Shaw's as the work force is friendly and sociable and there are always plenty of old student friends there from colleges and universities throughout the country. The money is good and there are always opportunities for overtime in all areas of the factory. Beggars cannot be choosers and when you sign on for overtime you can be detailed to any section in the factory which could mean a Saturday morning scrubbing clean the Sanitex vats or a Thursday night shift filling the tanker lorries with Shaw's Fluid. At the end of a holiday shift at the factory I always buy a new pair of industrial boots as a few weeks amongst the chemicals causes the soles to peel away from the uppers in a manner more suited to the boots of Charlie Chaplin's famous tramp.

This Easter holiday I start my work in the Shaw's Fluid and washing up liquid sheds where huge vats of boiling chemicals are produced by a team of boiler-suited hard-helmeted souls who spent their time filling the huge vats, adjusting temperature controls and dodging the scalding steam that spurts from the lead pipes that rattle incessantly as the pressures fluctuate madly throughout the Victorian industrial plumbing system. The factory is to be closed in a couple of years as the whole company is to relocate to a new plant in Essex and so the company is getting the last foul fractious usage from the ancient steaming equipment. I report to George, the elderly foreman who is a kindly soul and has spent all his working life in the factory and he is due to retire when the place is closed down. I work with him on our vats of Shaw's Fluid and when we think we have boiled the chemical to its exact constituents, I take a sample jar over to the chemists in the main administrative block who test the boiling, dark, brown tar–smelling liquid to see if it has achieved the legendary status of Shaw's Fluid. It is an unholy mix of tar acids and an array of chemicals that make it one of the most powerful disinfectants ever produced.

"Ok Martin boy," George announces through a cloud of foul smelling vapor.

"Take this lot over to the labs there's a good boy."

"Boy" is a term of affection in the East End and I am pleased that George values my presence in the team that works in, between, and around the boiling vats that rumble continuously as the steaming concoction is produced. I must lower a long handled ladle into the boiling liquid and then pour the sample into a plastic jug which I will take to the laboratories. I put on large, rubber protective gloves and carry the bubbling sample across the factory yard until the administrative block and the laboratories are reached. There the sample is handed in and at this point in the proceedings a break is required which means sitting in the waste paper stores for twenty minutes or so and then wandering back to the Shaw's Fluid plant to continue my work. Other employment in the factory is to be found on the conveyor belt packing the boxes and in the paper store manufacturing the toilet rolls: this latter option is pretty good value, as following liquid lunches in the pub across the road, we can sleep off the alcohol in the huge paper shafts stuffed full of toilet paper. We just have to make sure we vacate the shafts before the paper is funneled onto the large container lorries which take the paper to the new factory in Essex. Unfortunately one drunken student did not regain consciousness and was subsequently transported to Essex and he awoke on the forecourt of the rural factory some six hours later! An episode that is now highly ranked in the student folklore annals of the factory.

There is extra money to be made if you join the team making Sanitex powder in the stinking bowels of the factory. This product is made from a formulation of hydrochloric and phosphoric acids plus the most diabolical of chemicals and is a highly dangerous activity. The Sanitex team sits together in splendid isolation in the works canteen wearing white boiler suits and they are all red-eyed, bald zombie men with pasty white complexions and no teeth and few fingernails. They take home extra money but at what price and none of us fun loving students can be enticed into that brotherhood of Sanitex sprites.

"Halloooo boys!! Hands off cocks Chrissie's not wearing frocks!"

This cry comes from the packing rooms and is from Jimmy who would rather be Chrissie and is a legendary character who features in the everyday life of the factory. Jimmy is a Glaswegian and former merchant seaman who had washed up one day in the East End via the Royal Docks and he has ultimately relocated working at Shaw's. Jimmy is in his late twenties, small and dark and of a stocky build but with his permed back combed jet-black hair and sweet dulcet tones he looks and sounds like a woman. He is always happy and loves the company of the young male students in the factory and when he discovers I am a drama student he is beside himself with admiration and tells me how he "longs" for a life in show-business. For this is, of course, only his "day job" as Jimmy spends the weekends starring as Drag Queen, "Chrissie" at the nearby public house, the Duke of Fife.

16 Duke of Fife Public House

This Victorian pub is grade 2 listed and is an architectural gem towering over the rows of tiny terraced houses in the backstreets of Forest Gate. The pub has a huge interior with wood and brass decoration and several large bars which support a small stage area where the various acts take place. During Mondays to Thursdays week nights and on Sunday lunchtimes the Fife is packed with male customers as the female strippers ply their trade amidst the smoke filled and beer stained atmosphere. Alcohol and lust are rampant amongst the audience as the strippers perform their erotic acts across the stage and on, under, and around the grand piano but, in spite of the rapturous roaring male applause following their naked finale the girls' heavily made-up faces always look so sad and terminally bored.

However on Friday, Saturday and Sunday nights the Fife becomes a carnival palace of raucous Drag Queens with packed audiences of locals, gangsters, tourists, homosexuals and, of course, the student contingent from Shaw's who are the youth wing of the unofficial Chrissie fan club. The Drag Queens are mainly London based although there are often "Steam Queens" performing and these are merchant seamen from foreign ships unloading in the docks who arrive fully costumed by taxi and quite outrageously are looking for local "Lurve!" before, during and after their performances. The whole 1960s Drag Queen phenomena is in full swing following the theatrical and TV success of Danny La Rue and, of course, the liberalization of homosexual activity following the 1967 Sexual Offences Act.

We always go to see the Cabaret on Friday nights and Chrissie, who is the compere as well as Top of the Bill, always reserves a large table for us adjacent to the stage. This gives us the best view in the pub plus easy access to the throbbing scrum of the bar; it also means, however, that the long-haired young men are "fair game" for any audience participation. This normally requires someone to go up on the stage to help unhook basques during stripteases or provide laps to be sat on as the Queens spread their sequined selves amongst us. Chrissie has arranged with the bar manager that we get drinks at a greatly reduced rate and so we feel that we should support the Queens as they rock and roll on the tiny stage and shimmy amongst the baying and bawdy audience.

Chrissie's act consists of sets of pretty rude but often hilarious jokes interspersed with a period of audience banter followed by mimed singing routines and a sultry striptease. She's a nervous bundle of energy on stage and you can only help admire her confidence in strutting her stuff in front of such an animated, drunk and potentially hostile audience. She hits the stage running:

"Well my lucky lovelies, it's Friday tonight, which in the Fife means Cocktails followed by Cocktales!"

She grins defiantly at her audience, winks to us in the front row and continues with the jokes which form part of the introduction to her act. Chrissie stands centre stage and waves her arms in her tight satin gown:

"A Drag Queen with very hairy armpits goes into a pub and there's a drunk standing at the bar. He looks at the Queen and then instructs the barman to buy this lovely ballerina a drink. He keeps referring to her as the lovely ballerina and buys her quite a few drinks as the evening progresses. At last the barman enquires why he should think that the Queen is a ballerina. The drunk replies: "Anyone who can lift their leg up that high must be a ballerina!"

There is a roar of raucous laughter from the audience and Chrissie is once more well on the way to another successful evening with the pub cabaret. She often spends the interval moving amongst the audience where she has many admirers, if not friends, and quite often sits with us on the "students" table. She tells me how she just loves the life onstage and in the pub and ultimately wants to turn professional and join the mainstream Drag Queen circuit a la Danny la Rue. As I talk with her I feel as though I'm on another planet as regards popular urban entertainment and the watery cultural pap we are currently fed at New College. Perhaps I should try to get Chrissie some lecturing work on the Drag and Steam Queens of the East End and she could perform her act to the Ivy House inmates who could then mumble incessantly about the dumbing down of culture in the contemporary popular arts. I would also love to be a fly on the wall as a glowering Widow Twankie attempts to dress the ebullient Chrissie in her glittering ball gown. The mind boggles!

The evening's entertainment is finally complete, the Queens are backstage preening and proud and the pub is closed and the audience pours out onto the pavements and surrounding streets as drunken people wander somewhat forlornly homewards. I depart quickly as I know I'm cleaning out the rancid factory vats at eight o'clock tomorrow morning and as I walk along the narrow streets I cannot help but wonder whether Jimmy and Chrissie will ever gain the fulfilling happiness that their presence on this earth deserves…

17 **Jimmy Carrol**

From: Rose-Mary
To: Martin
Subject: Easter
Date: April 10th, 2012 2:34 pm

Hi Martin

Your Easter piece is touching and amusing. I have to wonder about the long term effects of working with venomous chemicals? I believe Jimmy deserves a knighthood for coming out in 1967. My son, Brendan is now living in England with my brother. He went to see Watford play yesterday his comment was that the game was uninspired and lackluster. My daughter, Erin's

French boyfriend skyped me today from France to ask permission to marry her. I did give my consent. I think the nuptials will be in France.

Love

Rose-Mary

Rose-Mary: Summer Term 1968.

Returning to New College from Easter break I am approached by fair weather students as to how one becomes a film extra. I try to be as helpful as possible but I am apprehensive that I will be called before Kees who had made it clear at my interview that as a student at New College "working in film or television was not an option." The fuss dies down as all first and second year students are preoccupied with the second year productions.

These plays are part of the Practical Test in Drama for the University of London Diploma in Dramatic Art, along with lengthy written examinations of history of theatrical representation, history of drama, voice training, English, poetry and education for after all our goal is to become qualified drama teachers.

Originally I am consigned to the costume department along with two of my Group C peers Micki and Elsie. Elsie is a free spirit with an aptitude for all technical aspects of theatre. Her acting ability however is negligible. she is hindered by a strong flat Geordie accent. Elsie is popular with students because she hosts wild parties. She attempted to befriend me earlier in the term by asking me around for afternoon tea at her digs. Instead of Typhoo in china cups, Jimi Hendrix reverberated off the walls from a shabby record player and an assortment of drugs were offered freely on a gold lacquered tray by Elsie and her stoned room-mates. Along with frequent disappearances into bedrooms for quick shagging sessions. I made a lame excuse of needing to catch the train homeward I made a hasty retreat with Purple Haze and the sweet smell of marijuana following me down the street.

Unfortunately Micki was more than willing to fall under Elsie's spell Micki and Elsie become fast bacchanalian chums. The result of their revels is Micki is placed on academic probation. She becomes belligerent with the staff. She refuses to turn in assignments and is chronically absent due to hangovers. Kate has tried to counsel her but she gets defensive and refuses to listen. Her final infringement is when the academic scholar Michael Meyer from Oxford is invited to give a lecture on Milton's Paradise Lost. Elsie and Micki stumble into the upstairs hall tardy, carrying balloons tied with string. They cause a commotion as they make their way to the back of the lecture room and sit on the windowsill. They are intoxicated and high. Every time the learned scholar mentions the serpent they hiss and giggle. Their misbehavior does not go unnoticed and they are reprimanded by the faculty. Micki is given a second warning of pulling up her socks or being sent down.

"Fuck them." Micki retorts with contention.

For Micki paradise might be lost.

"O Sun! to tell thee how I hate thy beams
That bring to my remembrance, from what state
I fell. How glorious once above thy sphere;
Till pride and worse ambition threw me down."

In the catacombs of the wardrobe shop Micki, Elsie and I are led by an often time irritable Beatrice Franky who has no patience for a seamstress who doesn't know how to sew on a button, let alone a doublet or ruffled collar. Beatrice Franky sports a severe short bob that falls around her upturned nose and cross face. But it is her lack of dress sense that is amazing. Beatrice wears bunches of pleated skirts, thick knee high socks, brogues and ratty cardigans in various shades of slush. She is enshrined in an aura of humorless grey. She is known for her rants and tantrums at any minor infraction within the wardrobe shop. Her only light is her dog Feste, who matches his mistress with a snarl and wiry fur in off shades of brown. Frustrated with my futile attempts at needle-work Beatrice willingly swaps my services to Rita as she requires a prompter and errand runner for her undertaking of Shaw's Major Barbara.

The second year cast laugh heartily when Rita blithely announces at rehearsal:

" Darlings, Rose-Mary is our call girl."

My job description includes moving from backstage, to the dressing and green rooms alerting the actors of the time before their cues.

The lead roles in Major Barbara are doubled. One Barbara is played by Pooh Harrington whose real name is Priscilla. She is an eye catching waif with perfect shoulder length blonde hair that flips up at the ends. Priscilla possesses an endearing disposition which shines through in her performance giving the character of Major Barbara vulnerability. Lucy Letts is her counterpart, she is composed and reserved. She portrays

Major Barbara as strong as tempered steel. Thomas Cain plays Andrew Undershaft the wealthy munitions dealer. Thomas has the "Capacious chest" that Shaw describes in his stage directions as well as a capacious talent that he brings to the role. Paul Howard with his tousled dark curly hair, cheeky smile, Roman face and charm, corrals the complexities of the role of Adolph Cusins, the fiancé of Major Barbara.

We assemble in the afternoons in the rehearsal room. The sun streams in through the floor to ceiling windows. The play is three long acts driven by discussion; words abound and I have to be on my game to follow along in case an actor calls for a prompt. During the next few weeks the production begins to take shape. My main task as the "call girl" is to scurry around Ivy House giving the actors the half, the quarter, and ten minute warning before their entrances. Rita is pedantic and draws out the best from the cast. She is always rational and approachable despite the rumors of her terrorism. The play was a success. My only complaint would be the enormous amount of wind that was passed in the Green Room by the male leads who seemed to compete in smelly explosions just before they were to make an entrance.

Following Rita's mammoth production of Major Barbara and continuing as we have been with course work, we are allocated to a member of staff to direct our final first year production which will be a Shakespeare play. This end of year production will act as a showcase for us. The faculty invite directors, actors, and agents. We are encouraged to invite family and friends. We are to be assigned a grade in acting followed by final exams that determine if you will return the next September. The threat of expulsion was brought home at the beginning of the year by a red, swanky sports car with the license plate ACT 1 parked in the courtyard of Ivy House. The owner had been ousted the previous year for failing in acting and finals. He was protesting his eviction and obviously had difficulty breaking the bond and returning to the real world. After a week he and the spiffy spitfire vanished. His dismissal serves as a warning that no-one is guaranteed a place as a second or third year student at New College.

Group C is again paired with the congenial Elizabeth Leigh as our director, for the end of year production, the play is Cymbeline. Because we have so few males we are double cast, swap genders and in some cases we are quadrupled cast. At the opening of the play I am a hairy non-speaking Celt, wearing a false beard and caveman like wig. My stage direction is to squat by a cauldron, gnawing a chicken leg and grunting alongside Sad and Elsie, the husky voiced Geordie with a gorgeous curvaceous figure but little acting ability combined with a flat intonation in her voice. Sad and Elsie have been instructed to bind their breasts to disguise their femininity and recite the lines of Guiderius and Arviragus, the kidnapped grown sons of Cymbeline. Sad and Elsie speak their lines keeping in male character, simultaneously wrangling a rambunctious golden retriever who has a nose for chicken legs. This is for authenticity, Elizabeth Leigh insists. She has cleverly transposed this scene to the front of the play to allow for a comprehensible exposition of the plot and characters. I am joined at the cauldron, by a fellow unwashed early Britain in the guise of Nora, clad in fur, moustache and beard. Elizabeth Leigh has designed the action to take place on a dimly lit stage and I believe the audience is unaware of the enforced cross dressers spouting iambic pentameter before them. Though they may be curious over Sad's high pitched voice that sounds like a castrati.

Kate and Kay share the role of Imogen. Kate brings sensitivity and empathy to the princess. Kay on the other hand struggles. Her Imogen is intense verging on neurotic. Clive plays the smooth tongued Iachimo and is enjoying every minute of trying to seduce his Imogens. He is delighted to receive a promotion as a lover. Danny is Posthumous, Imogen's banished husband. Micki is cast as the villainous queen. Bringing up the rear are our Nordic Martin as Cloten and Duncan as the title character, Cymbeline. Poor Duncan is miscast, he tries his best but can't find the core of the character. Consequently when he is informed of the queen's death, he throws away the line without an ounce of remorse "She was naught," comes off with a strong Birmingham brogue as if he was paying the milkman. During the dress rehearsal with the second and third years in attendance there is a titter as he nonchalantly says this line. Nora and I are paired together in a number of scenes. After portraying hairy Britons we change hurriedly into our Roman ladies togas. We once again serve as background for Posthumous and Iachimo as we lounge on the steps of a villa veranda eating grapes. Micki is also a Roman lady and she has devised a game in which she gives a grape to any Roman just before they are to speak a line so that they have to garble through with half chewed fruit. She sarcastically calls this "being authentic" much to the dismay of her victims. At the same dress rehearsal for our peers, Nora and I have managed to change into our Roman dress seamlessly. Nora is stage left to my stage right decadently reclining on the steps, when the lights go up to my horror I see she is gracefully recumbent on the silk pillows, wearing her saffron toga but sporting the beard and moustache from her previous hairy Briton incarnation. She is smiling and has no idea. Our peers in the audience begin to hoot and holler at the unsuspecting bearded lady. Nora is chagrined but there isn't any time to dwell on her facial hair as we run to change our costumes into Roman soldiers. We grab helmets and breastplates from the prop room and both sprint on stage to repeat our lines announcing the Roman army is approaching. Now the second and third year audience is roaring. They begin chanting:

"Fire, fire, start the engines, London's burning."

Jill and I have no idea what has set them off. After I announce:

"The legions garrison'd in Gailia
After your will, have cross'd the sea attending
You here at Milford-Haven with your ships."
They are in readiness."

We make a hasty departure upstage right to be met backstage by an irritated stage manager.

"Are you two idiots?'

Nora and I look at each other perplexed.

"Are you trying to sabotage this production? Those are bloody firemen helmets. I had placed the Roman helmets for your convenience on the prop table."

"Thanks" we both say sheepishly.

I don't have time to dawdle as I am Imogen's serving woman and have to don a long white chemise and unravel my hair to become a female again. The performances are critiqued and graded by the staff. I am amazed that Noel Niven is as generous in his assessment of my performance. He felt that I gave every scene energy and lifted the scenes I was in. I am grateful for his confidence in me. As many of my cast mates were castigated.

Elizabeth Leigh has arranged to take the production to the George Inn which the bard himself frequented. We are to be paid in beer and jam tarts. The Inn dates back to 1542 and has an authentic Shakespearean stage. The George Inn is favored by American tourists, who are about to witness a Shakespearean production like no other they have seen.

Sad and I have cemented our friendship. She is living at home in Bushey full time and we travel to and from New College together. Sad is an avid reader on our daily journey. I am content to gaze out at the world and wonder what mood my mother will be in upon my return.

My mother seems happier because of the prospect of the great American adventure. She plans to be absent for at least ten weeks. She isn't indulging herself in her gin soaked nights, reserving the booze up for Saturdays when she and my Uncle Anthony nearly come to blows over religion and politics in the lounge. Last weekend I happened to see my uncle storm out by way of treading across the sofa cushions and sprinting over the arm of the sofa shouting:

"Bloody Catholicism is a human myth, woman."

"That's rich for someone who trained to be a priest and is now the father of six offspring," my mother yelled back.

Uncle Anthony slammed the front door. He is sheepishly followed by my Aunt Vanessa a sweet, passive woman caught between the weekly eruptions of Krakatoa and Etna. My mother relishes these confrontations and enjoys them immensely, this is her Saturday night entertainment, driving Uncle Anthony to distraction.

"Why do you have to get him going Gwen?" my father implores, shaking his head.

Elsie Gwendoline is economizing on her liquor intake in order to pay for the sojourn across the Atlantic. She is budgeting on petrol and doesn't take her white Jaguar or blue Volkswagen out to the shops but insists on walking and socializing with the villagers of Bushey Heath. There is a quasi calm at the house. She is intent on attending the performance of Cymbeline at New College. I haven't mentioned the production to be staged at the George Inn. My mother arrives at New College in grand style; swathed in a fur stole completely ignoring the fact that it is the middle of June. After the performance she announces loudly:

"Not quite up to the standard of R.A.D.A."

At least twice a week after college Sad and I traipse up to Covent Garden to take dance classes at The Dance Centre. We begin with ballet where we are joined by another New College first year student, Sheila Bruce, who is an accomplished ballerina. She tends to boast about her aptitude which doesn't win her friends. Even her posture and body language suggest superiority and condescension. She has perfect swept back hair in a bun, perfect leotard and leg warmers together with perfect disdain of other dancers. Sheila Bruce is intolerable and Sad and I avoid her and her leg warmers as much as possible. We feel we need to improve our modern dance skills. We enroll in a Jazz class taught by Gillian Lynne. Gillian always tries to stretch the capabilities of her students. One minute we are executing a pirouette and the next a cartwheel. To my amazement Sad attempts every movement in the routines. Sad is fearless and surprising in that she can catapult herself clockwise, keep the tempo simultaneously maneuvering her lofty frame through the air with ease. I am in awe at her bravado. I am a total coward opting to never attempt the gymnastics and still awkwardly trying to keep time and pace with the music.

In addition to the production of Cymbeline, attending lectures and seminars, all first year students are preparing for end of year exams that will determine our fate. If a student fails the academics they are immediately terminated without reprieve. On top of all of this course work we are required to crew a first year production. We are assigned to Much Ado About Nothing. Sad, Micki, Elsie and I are gaffers and will man the lighting booth during the performances. Duncan runs the sound system squeezed like a chipolata sausage into the corner of the booth with a tape recorder. The stage manager is Kate.

Prior to performance we have to attach the lights to the fly system. The cues for lighting are indicated on the lighting board by a red and green light controlled by the stage manager offstage. Each of us has four dimmers on the panel which control the voltage to the lamps. Micki has had an altercation with Sheila Bruce during the installation of the lights. During performances of Much Ado About Nothing Sheila Bruce tends to upstage her fellow actors and stand in their light. Micki is peeved and executes her retaliation by eclipsing her on stage. Micki slowly takes down any light within the vicinity of Sheila who recites her part totally unaware of her increasingly shadowy status. This goes on for performance after performance. Micki finds a willing accomplice in Duncan after Sheila admonishes him in front of the entire cast at rehearsal. Duncan takes his revenge by intentionally producing Sheila's sound cues late. Duncan is such a kind, lovable soul he certainly did not deserve a public reprimanded by the self-important Sheila Bruce.

On opening night Val O'Brian's father has come to see his daughter play the messenger in Much Ado. He is a distinguished gentleman, with a trimmed moustache sporting a Burberry mackintosh along with a black umbrella. Val has secured him a front row seat. He removes his mac and places it on the back of the seat, his black brolly he nonchalantly puts on the table a few feet in front of him. The opening scene reveals the sun-soaked Italian town of Messina with the addition of a large black umbrella front stage and centre on the set piece table downstage. The actors obviously espy the intruding prop and know they will have to improvise around the umbrella. To our cumulative surprise it is none other than Sheila Bruce who takes up the challenge. Her line as Beatrice is:

"And a good soldier to a lady: but what is a lord?"

Sheila snatches the intruding umbrella from the table manipulating it as a sword pointed at the messenger, the congenial Val O'Brian. Val recites her line:

"A lord to a lord, a man to a man; stuffed with all honorable virtues."

Sheila Bruce takes the point of the umbrella and slowly moves it from Val's chin to her nether regions while saying:

"It is so, indeed; he is no less a stuffed man: but for stuffing, ----
Sheila pokes Val in the crotch, then continues with:

"Well, we are all mortal!"

With that she tosses a wide-eyed Val, the messenger, the offending brolly which miraculously Val catches. We in the lighting booth are dumbfounded by Sheila's ingenuity, from there on out Micki never places Sheila Bruce in the gloom during a performance.

For the production of Cymbeline at the George Inn we travel by tube, again lugging costumes and props in a cumbersome hamper. Upon arrival we discover that no-one has thought to bring an iron. Imogen's attire, especially her flowing crisp, white nightgown has been reduced to a crinkled, crumpled shift. This gives our leading lady a forlorn, destitute, neglected appearance. The doublets for the men have been compressed and creased. We take a positive approach to our ironing mishap, by telling ourselves that our disheveled clothes are adding authenticity to our otherwise unconventional Shakespearean production.

The theatre at the George is a copy of the sixteenth century DeWitt drawing of the Black Swan. The stage is immense and juts out into the audience on three sides. Recessed at the back, upstage, is the inner stage, this area serves as Imogen's bed chamber for the seduction scene. We are undertaking a hurried technical rehearsal when we are interrupted by American tourists, with cameras slung over the shoulders, standing in awe at this Shakespearean shrine. Many have pints of warm beer as they make their way to their seats. In the wings Kate is visibly upset at her wrinkled appearance but tries to put on her "the show must go on face" as Act One begins.

The hairy Britons are now sans one large drooling Labrador retriever as Elizabeth Leigh our director realizes that controlling the canine from absconding with the three week old chicken legs during the scene was becoming nye impossible for Sad and Elsie. They both manage their scene much better without having to handle their slobbering companion.

The Roman decadent scene goes off without a hitch, except our togas are a tad cockled and crinkled as if we had been wearing them for an equinox. I change into my Roman soldier gear which has escaped without a wrinkle. I sprint on stage from the wings treading on an errant jam tart as I go and it now adheres to my barefoot. My arm is outstretched in the form of a salute ready to announce:

"That the Roman legions are hence."

However Imogen and Cymbeline skip over my cue. There I am in full view, centre stage, my arm extended and a jam tart hanging precariously from the sole of my foot. The scene continues for six minutes. I remain like Eros without his bow hoping that the two actors will improvise so I can recite my greeting. The scene concludes and I exit with the king and princess, having never uttered a syllable and my arm outstretched in salutation.

I am thoroughly fed up and annoyed, despite the apologies from Duncan and Kate. I run into Sad backstage and explain the debacle that has taken place. When I show her the sticky jam tart on the sole of my foot she laughs.

"It's not funny," I insist.

But of course it is. Sad then lowers her voice to a whisper:

"I was combing my hair backstage and I needed a hair pin from my bag. I was looking in my compact mirror, combing my hair as I crossed backstage when to my horror I realized that I was actually traversing the inner stage during the seduction scene between Imogen and Iachimo. I was in full view of the audience, Rose-Mary" she confides.

"What did you do?"

"I kept on walking, hoping that no-one would notice," she giggles.

"Oh my god!" I exclaim.

"That will give those American groundlings something to think about," she adds laughing.

To everyone's astonishment the play receives a standing ovation.

18. The George Inn where Cymbeline and The Merchant of Venice were performed.

The end of term is fast approaching. It is now time to hunker down and study. My mother has buggered off to America without a return date. My father's life consists of work, work and work. He has lost his appetite for Gordon's gin and barely eats anything I cook. Perhaps his fast is due to my inexperience in all things culinary. We sit down for dinner in the evening. He mulls over his plate, moving the morsels around with his fork occasionally taking a sample bite. He thanks me for dinner, then he is up to bed, to sleep, until the cycle repeats in the morning. My mother sends air mail letters by the dozen, describing in minute detail the wonderful time she is having and how warm, generous and welcoming the transatlantic cousins are. She certainly doesn't miss the humdrum life of Bushey Heath in comparison to camping in Yosemite Park, the beaches of Santa Barbara and the attention of the yanks who she says "love her accent." She is in her element, front stage and center. She never mentions missing her family in her overly long descriptive missives.

I too am tasked with writing. Essays are the format for the end of year finals, which are taken in the silence of the library upstairs in Ivy House.

In Psychology I am faced with explaining the contention that recent psychological insights have tended both to liberate and enslave us? Now I know why Eamon O'Braden spends so much time looking at the floor. He is concocting convoluted test questions.

That scoundrel Frank Leer's exam paper asks what reasons account for the scarcity of great dramatic literature in the period 1741-1860 even though the theatre was increasing in popular appeal at the time? If only Frank had spent more time on concrete facts and less on the sexual libido of the eighteenth century I might be able to present a reasonable answer. Instead my head is full of "may prick nor purse never fail you" and "merry" being a euphemism for "sex," which happens to be

Frank's favourite word He has also informed us that "sex" didn't arrive in the Oxford English Dictionary until 1799, followed by sexual function in 1803, "sexual organs" in 1828, and "sexual instinct" in 1836. I remember all the frolicking sexual details of Mother Clap's molly house. I am going to have to dig deep to salvage an answer that is based in dramatic literature.

The congenial Elizabeth Leigh, our insightful Shakespearean director keeps her exam on point by asking what constitutes a masque? What elements do we find in the theatre of the 1660's that owe their existence to the court masques of the 1640's? Thank the drama gods for Elizabeth. During her seminars we have been baptized in Restoration theatre and drama. We discussed at length the influence of Inigo Jones on the court masques. We have held staged readings of plays by of Etherege and Wycherley. If I can't justify an expanded intelligent answer, I don't deserve to be enrolled.

I wade knee deep through the exams. I am both frazzled and challenged. I amaze myself at the answers I write. I have learned so much over the last few months. The price of failure is high - expulsion from New College, followed by exile.

I am heartened when Elizabeth Leigh catches me in the foyer and informs me I made some good points regarding the masque question. When I received the marked paper she had written: "For a short answer it goes quite a long way."

In contrast on my paper based on a production of Elizabethan text on a thrust stage, Diane Winter has scribed in ink: "This is rather padded out, essential points of open stage production are few. You repeat many to make points out of quotes instead of the other way round." We had to time our answers for Diane

Winter and I had taken 3 hours. She had scribbled boldly in the margin, "How could it possibly take so long?"

My inner voice shouts in response: *Because I am trying to convince you Diane, I belong here at New College. I am not a usurper. I love Ivy House, the zany curriculum, my peers, even my teachers. This is my refuge from the insanity that I know as home. I am trying Diane Winter to make you my ally but to no avail. And as Micki, my outrageous comrade in arms would ask. What the fuck do you want from me Diane?*

During the last weeks at New College before summer vacation the campus is abuzz with the third year final production. A musical, The Matchgirls penned by the actor Bill Owen who is espied on the grounds, in the refectory and in the Phoenix theatre. Bill Owen is a well-known character actor who first came to fame as the London army corporal, in the Carry On Sergeant film. The musical is about the strike of 1888 by the young women exploited in a match factory in Bow, London. The leading lady is Martin's bed fellow Shirley but she is upstaged by the incredibly gifted Emma Warner. Emma transforms herself into Kate the leader of the factory workers. The male lead, Joe is played intensely by Craig a slender, angular faced fellow with tawny hair and an engaging stage disposition. The production is a showcase for the immeasurable talents of Emma Warner. Emma has a round face and reddish brown hair that she pulls tight in a high pony tail. She is unremarkable in features but on stage all eyes are on her as she transforms into a nineteenth century cockney sparrow.

Emma proved her versatility earlier in the year when she played Snow White in the Christmas pantomime for the student body. Emma played the title role mimicking Rita

Scott. The seven dwarfs were depicted as other recognizable staff members complete with all their short comings. Grumpy was a portrayal of Diane Winter, Sleepy was Kees, and Bashful of course was a caricature of Eamon O'Braden. Emma's portrayal of Rita was a carbon copy. The student audience was thoroughly entertained by the send up. The staff was not. The pantomime was performed in good fun and was not malicious. However, I will never forget seeing Emma Warner red eyed and tearful at the foot of the oak carved staircase in the foyer of Ivy House following the show, after being chastised by the Rita. I am glad to see she has not been deterred as her performance in Matchgirls is incredible. I am in awe of her talent. The finale song is "Waiting Life of Mine." Emma Warner brings the house down and the audience of her peers to their feet shouting "Bravo."

During the rehearsals for The Matchgirls the third years have been joining us lowly first years in the refectory for lunch. The second years are away on a six week teaching practice. I seem to have caught the attention of Craig the leading man in The Matchgirls. He likes to hold court at an adjacent lunch table when I notice him eyeing me up. I am somewhat surprised when I am collecting my belongings from my upstairs locker to be accosted by Shamus O' Braden a congenial third year, the son of Eamon O' Braden our downcast psychology professor.

"Excuse me," he utters nervously.

"Would you mind accompanying me to the music room?"

"Okay, if you will give me a minute," I respond.

I am in the process of loading my homemade, floral plastic bag with texts and exercise books. I have to stuff my giant knitting needles and yarn in the top. I can't help thinking that

Shamus O' Braden has been sent on behalf of the staff who want me to change my name again, or to align my jaw so that I don't have a sibilant 's' or worse still the discovery that I have been employed in the film industry during the Easter break. I follow Shamus downstairs deciphering these notions and seeking viable excuses. He as a gentleman opens the door of the music room.

"Wait here," Shamus instructs.

Across the room by the piano in deep confabulation is Craig with Kip Saunders. Craig has a rope across his neck, his wrists and ankles are bound. He is in rehearsal for what looks like Waiting for Godot. He looks up and bunny hops towards me still shackled. His eyes are brown and intense.

"Do you want to go for a drink on Friday night?"

So this is what I was sequestered for. I am not before an inquisition of the faculty. I am being asked out. I smile with relief.

"Okay."

Craig looks at the cluster of students passing us in the corridor on their way to the adjacent rehearsal room.

"Not around here, too much gossip. The Old Rat and Parrot Pub in Belsize Park.

Eight o'clock then?"

With that he turns and bounces back to the piano and the discussion with Kip Saunders. He doesn't look back.

During the days leading up to Friday I reprimand myself. *What about the pledge to Pavlova that I would never date, love nor marry an actor.* I argue with myself. *That I didn't mention going for a drink. What can be the harm in that?* Subconsciously I have to acknowledge that my motivation is that Martin, my knight in shining armor is having a fling with Shirley, Craig's leading lady. I surely can have a drink with Craig. He's not my type, too intense. He probably has a girlfriend as all the males at New College get nabbed by the females because there are so few of them. Craig hasn't been at Ivy House without being claimed.

On Friday I don't have time to slog all the way back to Bushey Heath. So I bring a change of clothes with me. I wear thigh high light brown suede boots, a blue floral dress that I bought at a jumble sale and altered into a mini and a large brown floppy, velvet hat. At Belsize Park station I ask the ticket collector the whereabouts of the Rat and Parrot, his directions are:

"Turn right when you come out of the station love, and keep walking up Haverstock Hill." Then he cheekily enquires "Meeting someone?"

I smile and go on my way. I find the pub and enter the saloon. I am the only female.

Craig is sitting in a wooden booth at the bay window. He stands when he sees me, asking:

"What would you like to drink?"

"A bitter lemon, please," I reply

"A bitter lemon it is."

He strides confidently to the bar, returning with a bitter lemon in a wine glass. There follows and awkward silence after I say:

"Thank you."

Craig is half looking out of the window.

"Have you had a chance to see The Matchgirls?" he nonchalantly asks.

"I did," I respond as he anxiously awaits for more of an answer. "I thought the production was excellent."

That seems to tick his box as he smiles and sips his beer.

"Yes."

He is bathing in his expectant glory when I add.

"Emma Warner is fabulous."

"Fabulous," He repeats somewhat dejectedly.

"I thought you gave a thoughtful outstanding performance."

"You did?"

Craig is now coming out of his self- imposed ego doldrums.

"Have you seen any more of my work?" he enquires.

"Yes, I caught you in American Dream at the beginning of the year. The use of Dave Brubeck's Unsquare Dance was a very good idea."

"And the production?" he asks.

Again I detect he is forlorn.

"Very good."

Now he appears despondent again.

"You were very good," I add.

Immediately his ego is stroked and he feels gratified. He questions again.

"You thought I was very good?"

He is looking pleased with himself. He has not asked me one question about myself.

"Last year I was in Rhinoceros by Inescoe. The play was remarkable."

He takes out his wallet, he pulls out a photograph:

"This is the director. She was amazing her name is Carol. She graduated last year. I have her composite proofs. I'm helping her choose one for Spotlight."

He removes a large envelope from his bag. The contents contain headshots, fashion shots and character shots of Carol.

"Isn't she beautiful?" Clive declares.

I nearly spit my bitter lemon all over the table. For there spread upon its surface was this ill-favored, plain woman. I put my glass down. I pause trying to think of something positive to say

"She has a lovely smile," I respond. "She looks like a lovely person."

Craig begins to gather up the proofs.

"Oh she is." He enthusiastically offers up. "We've been going out for over a year."

My inner voice smirks *I knew he was claimed.*

"Carol thinks I'm one of a kind."

My inner voice is laughing *Oh you are one of a kind Craig. I've never been out with a fellow who has a serious girlfriend and totes her photographs to show other females on a date.*

Craig continues:

"Carol believes I have a stellar future. She believes I'm fabulous."

What do I say to his bravado? Then I blurt out:

"Well it is always nice to have someone believe in you."

"Yes it is."

He swigs his beer.

"Another drink?" he asks.

"No thanks, actually I've got to dash. Long way home."

"Sure you don't want to come back to my place?"

"No."

I stand up.

"Please yourself," he offers a little sarcastically, as he finishes his brown ale.

"Oh let me assure you. I do please myself, thanks for the drink," I respond.

And with that I exit. Why did I break my promise to Pavlova? Never again, not even a drink with a bloody actor.

The results of the exams are in. I squeeze by. The last assembly in the Phoenix Theatre also serves as the graduation ceremony for the third year students. Relatives and friends are not invited. The audience of peers applaud and stand as the matriculated receive their New College of Speech and Drama Teacher Diplomas. How many will actually venture into the halls of education remains to be seen. They form a processional to the rehearsal room and garden where they will partake in a strawberry cream tea with the faculty. This is their rite of passage.

19 Ivy House garden

Leaving the ceremony as I cross the forecourt I pass my former shining knight in armor, Martin Banks, he smiles saying

"Have a great summer."

"You too." I reply

Martin laughs.

"I don't know about that. I'm working in a chemical factory in the East End."

I turn around to see if he is joking. But he has disappeared into Ivy house. His visits to the lunch queue have dwindled as his attention to the third year Shirley have become more transparent.

Group C is about to disperse. Clive has secured a gig as a puppeteer with a Punch and Judy stand at the seaside in Weymouth. He is insistent that the characters and routines are based in Comedia del 'arte. When he is not hidden behind the striped tent, between shows of strangling and bludgeoning Judy, his puppet wife. He intends to sit on the beach in his black beret and cloak with his newly trimmed goatee taking inspiration from the ocean to write an epic poem of love. He is indeed a true Renaissance man. Nora returns to her previous summer job. She wears a strapless leotard, satin ears and a fluffy white tail together with fishnet tights paired with high patent black heels, she is a Playboy Bunny. Nora has acquired a posh place to live, next to Hampstead Heath as the trophy live-in girlfriend of a balding, smarmy older man she met at the club. Jolly hockey sticks Fran is the daughter of an admiral and is returning to the family estate in Gloucestershire to ride her beloved horses. Rumor has it she was recently the date of a certain Cambridge student who may one day be king of England. Kate and Sandra have gained summer employment in a show travelling to the Edinburgh Festival. Kate is in the chorus and Sandra is a stage-hand. Duncan through Rita's recommendation is furthering his studies in the Alexander Technique at a clinic in London. Pat with her long lank locks parted in the middle has changed her hairstyle into a short Twiggy cut. This evidently has boosted her confidence as she is engaged to a Spanish concert pianist whom she met through her landlady and she is going to accompany him on a tour of Europe as she plans her wedding. Joann is having an operation to have her voluptuous breasts reduced followed by fun and frolicking in Ibiza. The inseparable Liverpudlians, Kay and Lynn are remaining in London pretending to be models. Really they are working as fetching serving wenches at a Bavarian themed restaurant in Kensington, where they wear hot pants posing as lederhosen along with tight bodices as they lead patrons swinging steins and singing beer songs. Afterward they hope to dance the nights away in the clubs along the Kings Road. Nordic Martin is headed home to the fjords of his fatherland and the welcoming arms of his doting mother. Danny has a job as dogsbody with a children's theatre in the Midlands. Elsie has forsaken Micki and is raking in a cache of money posing nude and manacled for "Gentleman's" magazines. Sad has acquired full-time employment at the nursing home where my grandmother lives. Sad has been volunteering there at the week-ends. She enjoys the elderly and relishes their stories and histories. Her eyes swell with tears when she tells of how some depart this world with only her hand to hold. Sad has an amazing gift of empathy and kindness. Our number is to be tragically reduced by one. Micki did not show up to sit the final exams. She has been expelled. She does attend the graduation assembly to make a tearful farewell to Group C in the refectory. She is distraught. She is pregnant.

"I've been a fucking fool. But now I have to think about my baby. I'll probably end up behind the counter of my dad's fucking sweet shop." She chuckles between sobs.

Micki so earnestly needed to be liked by everyone. She has such talent and intelligence. I am sickened and saddened by her departure. Micki puts on brave face before exiting, she addresses us, as she passes through the porthole door.

"I'm counting on all of you to fucking graduate in 1970."

Upstairs I empty out my locker. The scarf I had begun knitting during the Helen Dunwell dire rehearsals is now over seventeen feet long. All members of Group C have taken turns to knit rows during the year. I like to think that each one contributed a foot of yarn. We have certainly grown mentally, physically and spiritually this our first year. We began the year with fifteen members, after Christmas we were seventeen and now we are back to fifteen. We were a group of strangers who have woven friendships and acceptance of each other despite our quirks and faults. We are family.

I am heartened to know I will be returning in September. I've made it through the first year. I am more determined and resolute to complete my second and third years and if Thespis is listening to my prayers I aspire to become a jobbing theatre actor upon graduation. In the meantime I have my forsaken father to look after. Kevin my so called boyfriend is returning from university. I will have to find ways to avoid him. I need to make money so I call my agent. Kees didn't say I couldn't work in the holidays and he never mentioned Oh What A Lovely War and he must have been aware because the college was a whirr with the news. Desmond, my agent answers:

"Des here."

Sheepishly I reply to his greeting:

"Hello, it's me your favorite Rose-Mary."

"So they haven't kicked you out of drama school?" he laughs.

"No, not yet."

From: Martin
To: Rose-Mary
Subject: Update
Date: May 5th, 2012 8:32 am

Hi Rose-Mary

I have almost finished the Shakespeare and I'm writing about the performances at the George, Southwark. Do you know what the other plays were? I think our Merchant of Venice was sharing the bill but can't remember the play so I've basically not mentioned it but I don't want to contradict anything that you might write about those Shakespearean "farces."

Have heard from Noodle- he is due in London this summer but is thinking of selling his London flat. We hope to meet when he is here.

Look forward to hearing from you

Love

Martinx

From: Rose-Mary
To: Martin
Subject: George Inn
Date: May 5th, 2012 5:48 pm
Hello Martin:

Cymbeline was the play I wrote about at the George Inn. I don't think we shared the bill with anyone. Elizabeth Leigh was the director and originally the production had included a large dog that Elsie and Sad had to control as they were cast as the two sons of King Cymbeline. Both had to bind their upper torsos for as you know too well there was a shortage of men at Ivy House. The canine did not make the George Inn. American tourists swigging tepid beer, awe struck by what they perceived to be an authentic Shakespearean tragedy. One that Elizabeth Leigh had re-written, cut and chopped to accommodate her limited cast. I admired her tenacity and refusal to direct the play in a straight line. She was a wonderful influence on me.

Sorry to hear Nordic Martin is selling his London flat. He mentioned this in his Christmas card that arrived in March. You are lucky to have him as a friend. I treasure my ongoing fellowship with Sad. New College threw the most unlikely people into compatibility and life-long relationships.

Keep going,
Love
Rose-Mary

From: Martin
To: Rose-Mary
Subject: Over to You
Date: May 6ᵗʰ, 2012 6:55 am
Hi Rose-Mary
And now you have my Shakespeare.......
We are blessed with some spring weather here in Cornwall as I look towards Newfoundland.
Love
Martinxx

Martin: Summer Shakespeare 1968.

The summer term Shakespeare casts are chosen by the staff and are not open to free audition which seems to be a practice that indicates a tendency towards typecasting as opposed to any imaginative initiatives on behalf of the drama students. I mull over this theatrical trait for a while and come to the conclusion that this approach simply reflects the thespian immorality of New College as a whole.

I am in Rita Scott's version of "The Merchant of Venice". She had already forewarned me that I was to work for her (never with) and she has been busy editing and re-writing the play so that it lasts for an hour and a quarter. I have a feeling that her bowdlerized version will provide several months of creative anarchy and cultural bewilderment whilst at the same time become a Shakespearean time warp of epic proportions.

A group of Scott-selected and silent students sit in the College Theatre and await the operatic flourish of a Rita entry and we are soon not to be disappointed. There is a crashing at the rear of the stage as the Green Room door bursts open and striding downstage comes Rita ferrying a pile of scripts that are ultimately destined to wear down our spirits over the next six weeks.

"Welcome Dahlings! Venetians one and all!"

Rita beams at us through her heavily made up face and quickly hurls the scripts to us in the auditorium with the style and accuracy of an Olympic discus thrower. She perches on a chair centre stage and without a pause for breath launches into her introduction and appraisal of the production:

"Dahlings! Dahlings! Shakespeare's Venice is now our Swinging London of the 60s. We will fill the stage with fashion, style and colour. You will be the most fabulous young things to observe and hear. Your acting will be both delicate and grand; you will play with the audience like a cat with a mouse…"

My heart sinks. I clutch the script. I want to be anywhere but here…

"Our play will speak of our times, our loves and hatreds, greed and intolerance, its backbone will be several scenes of great drama laced with finely drawn characters and notable speeches. Our stage will be a riot of colour, character and sexuality…"

Oh, oh, it didn't take long for the "S "word to rear its well-worn New College head again. She's definitely on theatrical heat and this play is going to propel her through the long, hot summer.

"We will delight in the loves of Bassanio and Portia, Lorenzo and Jessica and Gratiano and Nerissa. We will explore the ambiguous and possible homosexual relationship of Antonio and Bassanio…"

Oh my God! Please no! I feel myself slipping into this theatrical bucket of emotional molasses with no-one to pull me out.

"And of course we must not forget the greatest loan shark of them all; the play's most prominent and famous character, the rich Jew and moneylender, Shylock himself."

Rita beams and then quips :"We could even have a sell-out here in Golders Green"

We all smile weakly and Miriam Ziegler looks embarrassed. I wink at her and she rolls her eyes skyward…I am not alone in my misgivings about this Venetian theatrical romp in contemporary London.

I sit singing the lyrics of "Hey Mr. Tambourine Man" to myself as Rita runs through the parts with the other students. Ken Dotson, our dour, uncomfortable and humorless Scot, will play Antonio, The Merchant of Venice. Gordon Holmes, our good mate and Stanislavski groupie will peel back his proverbial onion skins as he penetrates the mind, soul, skin and bones of the rich Jewish moneylender, Shylock. My other mate, Rick Coulder will play Gratiano, the likeable young gallant who is often flippant, overtly talkative and tactless. Or should I say Gratiano will play Rick Coulder! Rob Dameron, a pleasant but depressed student will play Lorenzo in love with Miriam Ziegler's Jessica, the daughter of Shylock. Poor Miriam hates the play and her "Jewish" part in it even before the rehearsals commence. Pam Reason will play Nerissa who is in love with Gratiano and dear honourable Pam will do her honest best to make the unworkable work. Friendly, funny and attractive Sally Shrewsbury is to play opposite me as Portia and I feel somewhat grateful to have her around in my hour of need.

"Martin dahling! You will be our dear Bassanio who is in love with Portia. You are so much a Bassanio of our age..."

I feel physically sick and smile sweetly at Rita.

"You are young, trendy, handsome, physically gorgeous, in love, impulsive and romantic..."

Jesus Christ, get me out of here!

"You are not a powerful hero but you are certainly a most sympathetic one and the audience will just LOVE you to bits. You are full of dash and daring; you fearlessly show immediate, uncalculated generosity and honest love. And as an actor Dahling you have some of the most memorable verse in the play. But we'll have to work on those glottal stops of yours"

Ouch - this means more one-to-one diction sessions alone with Rita in the Voice Room...Ouch again!

A rehearsal schedule for June is distributed followed by performance dates in both the College Theatre and the George Inn, Southwark. The George is an Elizabethan pub with a courtyard theatre where Elizabethan and Jacobean plays are performed in the summer mainly for the tourist market. The month starts badly with Bobbie Kennedy's assassination on the fifth and I am suitably depressed to take little interest in our Venetians swinging through Sixties' London, I dutifully attend rehearsals, learn my lines and move about the stage where Rita places me – a melancholy lonely piece on the crazy theatrical chess- board that is Rita Scott's Venice in London! The cast struggle through rehearsals and Gordon emotes in splendid isolation as he immerses himself within Shylock's painful character. Rita huffs and puffs and blows the Venetian house down many times during the manic rehearsal process. Ken and I do not feel we need to immerse ourselves in the possible homosexual liaison between Antonio and Bassanio and keep our distance from each other and a joint low profile in front of Rita. Unlike our Stanislavskian chum Gordon we do not feel inclined to peel back the onions on that particular relationship. Gordon carries his Holy Bible, "The Actor Prepares", with him all of the time and is certainly living the part of the sly, old Shylock.

I spend a break in the College Library and idly flick through some Stanislavski texts feeling that I should attempt to at least try to understand what is causing the apparent psychotic malfunctions of disciple Gordon, I come upon a diary entry which in no time alienates me from the wealthy Stanislavski then and there:

"Young actors, beware of your female admirers! Make love to them if it amuses you, but do not discuss art with them. Learn in time to listen to, to understand and love the bitter truths about yourselves. And get to know those who can tell it to you. It is then you should discuss art."

This is certainly not the way I have been introduced to theatre via Joan Littlewood and my radical school teachers and I have no inclination to wander down this particular Stanislavskian highway. I am happier with Littlewood and Brecht who, then again, might just as well be aliens from another planet as far as the culture of Ivy House is concerned. Rehearsals come and go and we all, apart from Gordon who is maniacally "inside out and outside in" as his Master would have termed it, work amiably together philosophically realizing that the sooner we perform the bloody thing then the sooner the nightmare will be over. I have lost all intellectual sense of my character Bassanio and I feel that I simply need to strut about the stage like a Kings Road, London fashion freak fresh out of public school for Rita to gush:

"That's it Dahling, you're so so sixties you sexy boy!"

I feel nothing, I am numb and I am beyond salvation. The girls play their parts with passion and humour, Rob and Rick bellow and bluster about the stage, Ken, the sorrowful Scot, is ushered further along his road of personal anguish by his anaemic Antonio and Gordon's Shylock seems to me to be a composite of a pantomime Sheriff of Nottingham and a lisping, grubby Fagin from Lionel Bart's musical "Oliver." I am sure that Shakespeare is spinning in his grave as this meaningless, lunatic romp gathers momentum.

Rehearsals continue to occupy our time and I feel most uncomfortable with the whole charade especially as Rita seems to allow Gordon to indulge himself totally with his Method Madness. I rehearse with him and feel that I am working with a black hole into which my lines disappear and his lines are spat back to me as though I was an extra in a "Carry On Shylock Film."

<u>Shylock:</u> "…Are you answered?"

He peers at me and grimaces in what I suppose to be his understanding of the look on Shylock's peevish face. I continue with the scene:

<u>Bassanio:</u> "This is no answer, thou unfeeling man,
To excuse the current of thy cruelty."
To which he responds:

Shylock: "I am not bound to please thee with my answer"
*No you certainly don't chum…*I think to myself. We continue:
Bassanio: "Do all men kill the things they do not love?"
Shylock: "Hates any man the thing he would not kill?"
Or kill off what little life there is left in this farce. I reply:
Bassanio: "Every offence is not a hate at first."
Shylock: "What, wouldst thou not have a serpent sting thee twice?"

I shuffle downstage as Antonio takes over with our pantomime villain and Rita fusses with Antonio's stilted movement. Poor Ken totters centre stage like an dying parrot on a slippery perch and I know he longs to be anywhere but in this rehearsal alongside a cynically imprisoned Bassanio and self-absorbed Method actor who appears to have taken on the eternal, legendary mantle of The Wandering Jew.

Another hot afternoon finds us all in the gardens of Ivy House for our costume parade. The show is in modern dress and Rita has requested that we each bring our entire wardrobe for her and Beatrice "Widow Twankey" Frankey, the costume lecturer, to be able to costume the beautiful young "Dahlings" who inhabit the lunatic world of Scott's Venice.

Widow Twankey is dour, sullen and shabbily dressed in various shades of grey. I am amazed that as a Costume Lecturer / Wardrobe Mistress she seems to take no care in her own appearance and seems to be permanently cast as a female tramp in some obscure absurdist drama. She sits with Rita making copious notes as each of us sullenly parades in front of them in our fashionable clothes and a long afternoon is finally completed with us dressed to suit Rita's view of Elizabethan Venice parading in Swinging London. I wear tight white flared jeans, a pink shirt, a long blue neckerchief, a brightly striped summer blazer and high heeled brown leather boots. Widow Twankey grimaces in my direction and I grimace back; the mean spirited woman is in my opinion as nutty as a fruitcake!

We discuss make-up and the girls have their faces painted like Soho prostitutes and Shylock's bedraggled locks are powdered grey and his face wrinkled with putty and cream whilst he glues a fleshy proboscis to his face which makes him look more like Mr. Punch than Mr. Shylock. I despair as the farce continues its merry way towards two evening and two matinee performances in the College's Phoenix Theatre. I feel there is little hope for a Phoenix to rise from these particular ashes and I resign myself to the theatrical abyss that awaits me. I sit soulless and vacant in my Sixties costume in the Green Room with my fellow performers who prepare themselves as best as they can. Our Method Madman has been wandering the college gardens searching for his character and has just returned to sit Shylock-bound in his chair. He is well and truly locked into his character and as far as I'm concerned is frequenting another planet. Ken runs through Antonio's opening lines which I think aptly sum up our collective predicament:

"In sooth I know not why I am so sad.

It wearies me, you say it wearies you..."

I think of my own opening lines later in the scene:

"Good signors both, when shall we laugh? Say, when?

You grow exceeding strange. Must it be so?"

I couldn't sum the whole thing up any better really. But as it is so and we have to get on with the bloody thing I bite my particular bullet and plough on with the performance. I move about the stage speaking my lines as if in a trance and in my dealings with Shylock feel that our black costumed and storm clouded Method Man is now metamorphosing into Shakespeare's Richard III's, "bunch-backed toad." The only real highlight of our play as far as I'm concerned is Sally's portrayal of Portia and her beautiful delivery of the "Mercy Speech" in Act 4 Scene 1:

"The quality of mercy is not strained,
It droppeth as the gentle rain from heaven
Upon the place beneath it is twice blest:
It blesseth him that gives and him that takes…"

Her rendition is well worth the entrance fee alone. Sally Shrewsbury is a fine performer and a lovely person. I wish Rita had spent more time working with her towards some theatrical truth as opposed to me in my tight, white flared trousers and the Prince of Method's Pantomime Villain.

Thankfully we take our curtain call and the show is finished at the Phoenix but I coldly contemplate that the next performance looms at the George Inn in Southwark just like the ice-berg awaiting the Titanic.

Rita has arranged for Shakespeare at the George Inn over the next few weekends with the New College Shakespeare teams. These performances have been widely advertised throughout London. The George at Southwark is an authentic London inn where Shakespeare is supposed to have both played and socialized. It has an Elizabethan courtyard where the stage has been erected for the open air performances. It is the last remaining galleried pub in London and it has always been popular with the tourists … whether it will ever be again after the New College Shakespeare Festival is open to conjecture.

We arrange to meet at the George after lunch and we will be performing in the early evening on the open air stage in the cobbled courtyard. It is a hot summer's afternoon and the courtyard gives us welcome shade. I have visions, however, of Shylock's encrusted make-up and proboscis melting in the heat leaving him emoting on the stage as the incredible "melting man," who is a lost and tortured soul staggering in from the amazing world of 1950s science fiction movies! (The classical SF movie. The Incredible Shrinking Man", has long been a favorite of mine). We have a small backstage room for our Green Room and we prepare ourselves zombie-fashion for yet another nightmare in Rita's contemporary Venice. There is quite a large audience filling the courtyard and I consider them to be somewhat like the original Elizabethan audience as they are standing packed closely together, drinking profusely, talking and swearing and, as it is the twentieth century, wildly waving cameras in the air. The front row is full of grinning Japanese tourists with cameras bigger than themselves. There are also American accents amongst the crowd. What on earth they will make of the forthcoming hour and a quarter God alone only knows.

We cast our pre-show nerves to the wind and soon have the rude boys in the audience clamoring for a taste of Rita's swinging London-Venice extravaganza; I'm sure most of them are too drunk to really have any idea as to what is going on up on the swaying platform stage but they nonetheless play to perfection the Elizabethan audience's role in the proceedings... Our Method Man draws boos and hisses from the audience and I'm so glad that he has successfully emoted enough to become the pantomime villain of the show. Shylock scowls and spits his lines at the audience but receives rapturous and raucous laughter in return from the Southwark crowd and I laugh my way through my performance and become the beautiful youth who can grace the velvet pavements of London's King's Road. We cavort through the piece artistically quite content that only the drunks in the audience can make sense of what we are playing on this balmy summer's evening in Shakespeare's old tavern...

We take our curtain calls in front of the baying mob that the audience has now become and return to the Green Room exhausted but, gloriously happy that the run is over. Rita cackles amongst us like a mother hen and extols our efforts as though we were experienced and worthy professionals. Rick and Gordon present her with a large bouquet of roses on behalf of the cast and crew. We are all her "Dahlings!" and she informs us that we are a credit to the New College of Speech and Drama. I smile at her, glad that I have survived the emotional theatrical rollercoaster that has been Rita Scott's "The Merchant of Venice". The cast move to the bar of the George and begin an earnest post-mortem discussion of the production which I require like a hole in the head... I go to the public telephone in the oak-paneled corridor and ring my parents telling them that I will be home later tonight and to leave the front door unlocked. They are not surprised as I often appear back in the East End relatively unannounced. I slip away from the gaggle of New College thespians and stroll to London Bridge Underground Station where I take a train eastwards. I arrive at Plaistow Station, alight and make my way through the warm and dusty streets to the historic Black Lion pub where I know old friends will be drinking on this summer's

Saturday night. The pub is packed with drinkers and I push my way to the crowded bar where I see some familiar faces.

"Hey it's Mart…!"

"What brings you back?"

"Get him a pint."

I smile and I am content to be once more back in the real world:

"Well you'll never believe what I've been up to…"

From: Rose-Mary
To: Martin
Subject: Shakespeare
Date: May 10th, 2012 2:03 pm
Hello Martin:
Great Shakespearean piece. Were you aware that Rita arranged a meeting for Gordon aka Shylock with "Darling Larry", Laurence Olivier after the production of The Merchant of Venice to discuss Gordon's future in the theatre? When we were all supposedly training to become drama teachers.

Love
Rose-Mary

From: Martin
To: Rose-Mary
Subject: Diary
Date: May 16th, 2012 7:32 am

Hi Rose-Mary

Trust all is well. Loved your Shakespeare and summer term---full of humour and vivid contemporary details and memories of some of the characters. Sheila Bruce...dare I say it but I had to literally fight her off sometimes as she almost became my stalker! She was attractive but mad as a hatter. When we undertook the theatre directing project I involved some dancers from the Laban School (I met them at a party) in my production. Shelia went ape shit with jealousy and envy particularly when they came regularly to the Bull...did she ever complete the course, utterly crazy? Then there was Elsie...bound for adult magazine glory in the outside world. I loved her attitude! Craig was a fool although I gave him the benefit of doubt as he played football. He was always sucking up to Kip Saunders although Kip told me he couldn't stand him. Can't remember too much else in that term- The Merchant blew what was left of my brain and my body was pre-occupied with Shirley.

Love,
Martin

From: Martin
To: Rose-Mary
Subject: Update
Date: May 24th, 2012 5:13 pm
Hi Rose-Mary:

Have seen some good stuff recently at Hall for Cornwall, Truro.....The Misanthrope a new version by Roger McGough, Birdsong based on the novel. The Moscow State Symphony Orchestra and yesterday the 60th anniversary touring production of The Mousetrap and no I won't tell you who did it!

Look forward to hearing from you.

Martin

From: Rose-Mary
To: Martin
Subject: Murder Mystery.
Date: May 27th, 2012 12:45 pm
Hello Martin.

I saw the Mousetrap when I was eleven and I can't recall the villain.

Have a great bank holiday.

Love,

Rose-Mary.

From: Martin
To: Rose-Mary
Subject: Diary
Date: June 14th 2012, 10: 06 pm

Hi Rose-Mary

Have read in the Guardian and the Observer newspapers a critical article about mumbling British actors.....come back Rita all is forgiven.

It's scorching over here at the moment but the ocean breeze is pretty good in Cornwall Off to Truro this evening to see Priscilla, Queen of the Desert which is the West End hit musical currently touring the UK and back next week to see the National Theatre's Pitmen Painters. An ex-student of mine has been directing at the RSC at Stratford and is keen that I go and see his latest play.

Let me know how the diary progresses - I'm missing the daily pounding of the keyboards!

Take care

Love

Martin x

From: Rose-Mary
To: Martin
Subject: Productions
Date: July 16th, 2012 1:38 pm

How impressive having a former student a director at the RSC. My dream was to join the Royal Shakespeare Company. I applied when I was all of ten years old. Did your ex-student show exceptional aptitude in college?

My play Many Miles is to be produced in July by Theatre Southwest in Houston, Texas. This nonsense play is out of my realm, it is a comedy centred on Miles the cat that we inherited from my daughter, Erin when she was living in a studio apartment in L.A. Miles is now going on 17 and has lived more than nine lives. He wears a tuxedo, is de-clawed and (Erin's doing) meows like a soprano. He is a ferocious feline with a penchant for taco chips and salsa. He can't wait to relocate to South Carolina and have a yard and even an alligator to altercate with. I can't wait to relocate though I am scared of the proliferation of those large reptiles.

I will keep you posted.

Love

Rose-Mary

From: Martin
To: Rose-Mary
Subject: Inanity
Date: July 26th, 2012 8:35 am

Hi Rose-Mary

My student at the RSC was always a favourite and he literally absorbed everything I had to say about anything. It's a wonder he's not in a lunatic asylum!!!! Great bloke and very talented - good working class stock.

Saw the Pitmen Painters this week in Truro with the National Theatre on tour. Great show with strong socialist content and profound views on working class attitudes to the arts. If only our staff had told us about the Pitmen Painters of NE England we could have developed such a show....more relevant than Dark Side of the Bloody Moon!

Keep in touch

Best wishes

Love

Martin.

From: Rose-Mary

To: Martin

Subject: A reprimand

Dare July 29th, 2012 1:38 pm

Hi Martin:

Don't knock Dark of the Moon I think the play is theatrically viable and valuable. I am ardent and enthusiastic about the production we were cast in during our third year.

Love,

Rose-Mary

From: Martin

To: Rose-Mary

Subject: Shakespeare and Stanley (RIP)

Date: August 9th, 2012 8:26 am

Hi Rose-Mary

Lost Stanley, my cat (see photo) today aged 17 due to kidney failure. Vet tried to save him but he finally hit the buffers! Dehydrated, anaemic and miserable but not in pain...at least I had the option of E!

Been tearful most of the day and now must turn attention to brother cat Oliver who is in relatively fine fettle for an 84-year-old!

Love,

Martinx

20 Martin's beloved cat Stanley

From: Rose-Mary
To: Martin
Subject: Stanley
Date: August 10th, 2012 1:07 pm
Hi Martin

Sorry to hear about Stanley. From his photo he looked like a well contented feline. If only we could use euthanasia on terminal patients to lessen their suffering. Over here the prognosis is governed by the dollars the hospitals and insurance companies can rake in at the expense of the ailing.

Love,

Rose-Mary

From: Martin
To: Rose-Mary
Subject: Ideas
Date: August 11th, 2012 1: 39 am

Hello Rose-Mary

Have ideas fermenting re the cover for the book..... perhaps a view of Ivy House as well....what about a composite background of events in 1968: student demos, Vietnam, underground theatre, Covent Garden Arts Lab, Pavlova and Ivy House?

Off to Truro theatre for professional production of Mansfield Park which I studied at A level....Mansfield Park and Medieval History at the East End Grammar.... no wonder I ended up at New College!

Love,

Martin

From: Rose-Mary
To: Martin
Subject: Ideas.
Date: August 12th, 2012 2:52 pm

Hi Martin:

With regard to your last thought. "No wonder I ended up at New College!"

I beg to differ. We should thank Thespis and our lucky stars we commenced at New College of Speech and Drama.

All the graphic details will fall into place. What is important is that we have made the writing finish line for the first year.

Bravo.

Rose-Mary

Made in the USA
Columbia, SC
16 March 2018